MW00744775

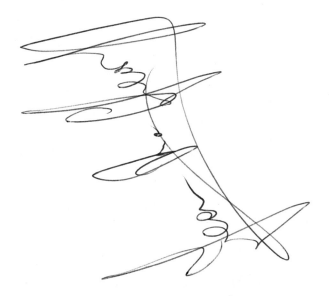

LOSS OF VISION OF THE MODERN WORLD

Jean Ricardy Georges

Copyright ©2007 Jean Ricardy Georges
All rights reserved.
www.cbhbooks.com

Managing Editors: Cliff Clark and Samuel Pearson
Cover Design: Alisha Anderson

Published in the United States by CBH Books.
CBH Books is a division of Cambridge BrickHouse, Inc.

Cambridge BrickHouse, Inc.
60 Island Street
Lawrence, MA 01840 U.S.A.

Library of Congress Catalog No. 2007011712
ISBN 978-1-59835-041-8
First Edition

Printed in Canada
10 9 8 7 6 5 4 3 2 1

*For all of the genuine people in the entire world,
especially my lovely mother Gracieuse Romain, my
courageous heroes, heroines, philosophers, and
educators such as Jean Jacques Dessalines, Toussaint
Louveture, Capois Lamoire, John F. Kennedy, Henry
Christophe, Catherine Flon, Carter G. Woodson, W.E.B.
Dubois, Frederick Douglass, Nelson Mandela, and others
who have led, inspired, taught, and educated me so well
to write this great book for the people.*

CONTENTS

Acknowledgments

I want to thank my favorite law professors Steven D. Murray, Joseph H. Parys, Daniel J. Donavan, Louis Procaccini, Christine Barkett, and Pamela A. Downey for educating and enlightening me.

I want to especially thank my dear mother Gracieuse Romain and my father Fritz Jacques Georges for their great love and support.

I want to thank my colleagues Robert Shaw, Bill Blackington, Peter Geradi, Sarah Brenneman, Dennis Whelmena, Fred Kamynin, Leonarda Hernández, Xiomara Álvarez, Sean Mitchell, Amado Amezquita, Joseph Soares, Dale Gaulin, Stacey Theroux, Bryan Gottlieb, Shane Poole, Alan Weisberg, Sean Henry, Warrick Monahan, Valerio Álvarez, Junior Laverdure, and my Hope High School principal, Harry Potter, for their great encouragement to write this book.

Finally I want to thank my brothers, sisters, and loved ones Evens Romain, Fabre Fedener, Jude Cyrius, Alabie Daniel, Agoro Fasawazat, Kettelyse Compere, Guenaude Delva, Marie-Andree Moise, Cindy Francois, Jean-Pierre Schneider, Jean Baptiste Richardson, Francois Duracinier, Henry Duracinier, Adrienne Ciceron, Richnardy Quetant, Adrianne Henderson, St Louis Noailles, Jacques, Yvon, Bernard, Mirlene, Robinson, David, and Joshua and Nicholson Patrick Georges for believing, supporting, and encouraging me to write such great books.

Loss of Vision of the Modern World: Part I

To really understand how this great country and the rest of this great world ended up in such undesirable conditions, everything must be viewed in the world's historic setting. The situation today has been determined by what many selfish and self-centered people have done since ancient times. Through a careful study of world history, we can see more clearly how to make the world a pleasant place for future generations. We can better understand what our role has been and how to improve it, for this country's interest and that of the rest of the world.

The idea of leading the world well is largely a result of philosophical beliefs. Well-educated and clever people have the attitude of misleading and mis-educating students just to oppress and exploit them, instead of properly teaching them how to develop themselves, this country, and the rest of the world sufficiently for the people. The institutional leaders of the world have continued to follow the same old biased, inadequate, and egotistical teaching methods that were created only to benefit certain countries, races, genders, and social classes; and to dismiss the rest as people of little consequence or nonentities. The leading institutions in this world have continued to refuse to develop modern courses and programs to better the world. Most of the courses and programs the leading schools have offered teach students that the elite white males are superior, and segregate Asians, average white males, females, blacks, gays, lesbians, Jews and others, so as to convince them of their incapability and inferiorities. Many professors still drill the thought of inferiority into the students' minds by

9

using the same biased books or following the same ancient method that was written by mostly biased and incompetent writers. Therefore, by the time these students become adults, they end up resenting and disliking homosexuals, females, Hispanics, blacks, Asians, Jews, and others. As a result of this educational system, practically all of the successful people in this country mostly lack a formal education on how to uplift, respect, and tolerate one another, to develop the world for the children of the future. Many professors and experts in the best universities are all but worthless. They have not developed modern teaching methods for the students and the rest of the world to truly unite, love, respect, and admire. They still do what their predecessors did, and are selfish and self-centered, they dislike and oppress each other, and they exploit the weak instead of developing the world for the modern era. Like most of the professors before, the present ones never become a constructive force in the development of the weak people. In fact, many of the professors continue to handicap the world by teaching their students to resent and oppress underprivileged people and feeble countries, instead of preparing them to assist others in their struggle. By following the same inadequate teaching methods, the majority of people have their dreams and hopes shattered. Therefore, these disadvantaged people doom their countries to higher poverty, illiteracy, crime, disease, and huge deficits. Instead of bringing a new light to uplift, they are continuing to teach their students to make the situation worse. This system of teaching is crushing us, because hatred, discrimination, oppression, exploitation, resentment, sexism, bias, and racism among people would be much less prevalent if it were not first taught in the classroom.

To be more explicit, most of our best experts who can better the world have no time to deal with such matters. They mostly focus on misleading their students to resent and exploit different races, ethnicities, classes, groups, sexual orientations, countries, and continents. Most of the methods of those so-called experts in leading institutions have let the rich get richer and have allowed certain groups, races, or countries to remain in power, instead of developing a method for the country to move forward. Since their attitude towards education and intelligence has been borrowed from Greece (Socrates and Aristotle), the same teaching methods used two millennia ago still exists in modern times. As a result of following and imitating dead people, worn-out theories, and false traditions (and not creating modern teaching methods of their own) the same problems from the past are still occurring or getting worse. For example, the countries that were poor are getting poorer, the races that were considered inferior or incompetent are still perceived the same way, and the immigration and war problems of the past still exist. All of this results in people never seeing the light they have been looking for since beginning of time.

They do this instead of developing modern literature and philosophy theory courses to teach each of their students to value one another; to teach them that the philosophy of certain countries, genders and religions was inaccurate, because each race and gender possesses the same gift in their own way, possesses the same brain and intelligence. They should develop a system to teach children to help one another, to teach young boys that girls possess the same brains and rights as them; to teach white children that the world doesn't belong to them, or to any other race, that it belongs to the citizens of the world; and that this country doesn't belong to them either, it belongs to the people, regardless of their ethnicity, race, economic status, religion or sexual orientation. They should create modern courses so heterosexual, slim, tall children can love, care, and respect bisexuals, the overweight, and short children, because God created all of us equally. Under the modern constitution of this country, everybody is created equal, regardless of what the authors had stated and written; therefore, they are entitled to the same rights, unlike in the past. Let the world experts develop new modern world leadership programs, so that before any world leader is elected, they have to learn about their countries, their citizens, world interests, and global peace; that war is not a good way to solve problems, because war equals death and destruction; and to respect and admire one another and put aside their differences to serve the people.

Most professors have been educated by those who used knowledge as a way to oppress and exploit certain human races, countries, genders, sexual orientations, and religions, but did not educate them to develop their countries for future generations. And by deriving their sense of right from many self-centered philosophers, the imitators of such philosophers can have no better message or hopes to improve their countries. In fact, most professors are not even imitating great leaders such as John F. Kennedy, Mahatma Gandhi, and Martin Luther King, who were unbiased and interested only in the common good. These so-called experts or distinguished professors fail to realize that in order for their graduates to be at peace with one another and become great leaders, they must do their part first by teaching and preparing them properly.

For instance, these world business experts could create a modern business method of their own, but they use centuries-old methods instead. The leading business, economy, and finance schools could educate and train business experts worldwide. They still follow the same biased and inadequate business system as before, teaching and training students exclusively in the psychology and economics of upper-class white males, Wall Street, Europe, and some Asian economies. None of the world's business and economy experts recognize that in order to boost the world economy, they have to do their part first, by educating and training business experts for each country, not just for Wall Street or others. If they established great business experts in every country, and had them come every year to Harvard, MIT, Penn State, Yale, and other leading schools to update their business and economy skills and programs, this great country and the world would never be at such a deficit and have such immigration, poverty, and other social problems as they have at present.

But these so-called world business experts would rather follow self-centered and biased teaching methods to corrupt students' minds by teaching them to oppress and exploit the poor communities and countries for cheap labor. They teach students to take advantage of business opportunities in their communities and countries so that certain groups of people or certain countries can grow richer rather than enriching the entire world. They never recognize the huge mistake they are making, because the white males' upper class cannot grow richer, nor can we Americans grow any richer, since we are already the richest and the most powerful country in the world. We simply need better business leaders and management for our national economies. The world's business experts do not realize that in order for Americans to keep our status as world leaders, we have to learn to modernize the teaching of business, economic, and financial theories, methods, and programs, in order to help other countries get back on their feet economically, because we are their leaders. And by helping and assisting them in their economic and social struggles, we would get them to respect and admire our leadership, instead of labeling us as greedy and selfish Americans. As leaders of the world we cannot be selfish, self-centered, and egotistic; if any leader is selfish, it is not a leader, it is an exploiter and oppressor. By developing modern business methods to help the rest of the world to flourish economically, they would respect and admire this country rather than calling us greedy, selfish and want to exterminate us. They would love and respect our leadership, not because this country is the richest and most powerful country in the world or because we are Americans, but because our great leadership would result in less resentment and hatred towards us and this great country, and more respect and cooperation for us as Americans. This, in turn, would mean less hatred and war on our soil. And even if a country ends up disagreeing with us for any reason, they would be more willing to talk it out in a peaceful manner. However, if they decided to attack us on our soil, other countries would stand at our side. Even that country's leaders would oppose it; they would be willing to fight with us or assist us in our battles, again, not because we are Americans or the wealthiest country, or for a certain interest, but for our great leadership to them and to the rest of the world. Such a method would mean less fear, fewer terrorist attacks, and less interest in war; additionally, the rest of the world's citizens would be happy and grow rich as well. Illegal immigrants would not have to come here for employment, and the American people would be happy because they would not have to worry about people coming here to take their jobs away from them or have their jobs go overseas. As a result, the immigration problems and the other social and economic conflict between countries would diminish drastically rather than increase on a daily basis.

The main reason these bright students turn out to be so biased and selfish with their fellow Americans and toward their fellow overseas citizens, thus handicapping the world, is because most of their professors who are in charge of the school system are choosing to follow the philosophy of those who had little or no training at all in working for their countries and the interest of the world. By imitating them, they would always lead us to believe that it is impossible to see a better light and fix the world's social and economic problems. Teaching these students to follow this kind of leadership will always result in a huge failure. The world's university teaching method is not in the world's best interest; such biased and selfish teaching methods have caused many well-educated men and women, who could have been great business leaders, to end up corrupt, under investigation, or in prison. These bright men and women were not taught to develop this country or the rest of the world; they were trained exclusively in the psychology of exploiting the weak, their countries, and the rest of the world, regardless of the consequences or the outcome. These bright men and women were learning the inaccurate psychology and philosophy of business methods from those so-called Ivy League experts, in order to make millions, not to make economical products. As a result of their selfish and self-centered business training, the MBAs or Ph. Ds merely equips these students to serve a certain group or race rather than this country, the average American, or the rest of the world. Most of the business theories or methods are designed to exploit the weak for the benefit of a certain people or country, not the exploited country or the rest of the world. These experts teach their students that they deserve millions while the hardest-working men and women work sixty hours a week at close to minimum wage, cannot even get medical insurance, cannot pay their rent or mortgage, cannot care for their families, cannot even afford gas for their cars or oil for their houses; in other words, can hardly get by. These

15

professors, just as the ones before, are more concerned with their status and high tuition rather than confronting or solving the social and economic problems that the world have faced. They spend their time writing and teaching their students to exploit and control the weak for their own selfish purposes, rather than managing the general welfare. These professors could modernize their business methods to teach the harmony among world financial experts, and teach each country's business leaders the proper way to invest in natural resources, raw materials, and oil, and to use them for the benefit of every country in the world rather than fighting over them. They teach their students, who are about to become world leaders, the exact opposite: to control these resources for selfish purposes by any means necessary. Instead of creating new methods to reconstruct the world economically, these great and distinguished experts keep following the same inefficient system. In fact, they do not realize that if the rest of the world is doing poorly economically it will continue causing social and economic problems such as immigration, both here and abroad. These so-called experts fail to realize that the cause of immigration, resentment, and hatred towards this country and other countries, is chiefly the people that these bright students are made to imitate and duplicate. The oppression and exploitation are not altogether the fault of these so-called businessmen and women; the fault lies at the feet of their business professors and school officials. Again, such a mess would never propagate if they did not start it in the classroom.

These professors and school officials could develop a new program on their own to confront the immigration problems; instead they blame the poor immigrants. They teach and train their graduates to oppress and exploit countries for cheap labor and selfish purposes instead of developing and expanding the resources for the common good. Since these professors fail to properly study the psychology and philosophy of business, they teach their students to go oppress and exploit the lowly races, gender, social classes, communities, countries and the rest of the world. By teaching and preparing their students in such a way, nothing good can result: more tension, damage, and hatred in this country and overseas. Business is one of the most important keys to build or to cripple a community, race, country, and the world; so far, it only cripples this country, because most of the people who want to go to college or technical school cannot even afford it due the lack of jobs and opportunities. Restricting people from getting an education will cripple the world more for the future unborn. Without a quality education, millions will have no choice but to become liabilities, as the majority of us are in the modern world, instead of assets to the world. The government will have to support them and their families financially instead of them providing for their families and paying taxes as they do now. They will have to turn to immigrating to this country and to others, breaking the law instead of rebuilding the world. Their home states would have to pay their medical bills and provide welfare, instead of the immigrants paying more taxes for schools to reopen and for real teachers to get better salaries. The business professors and leaders have to drill this into their minds: better quality business methods means prosperity and wealth for this country and for the rest of the world.

Many who label themselves business and economy experts are, as a matter of fact, not true business experts; the majority of them never created gigantic businesses and corporations of their own. If they could do this, they certainly would not work for others, because who wants to work for other people or be told what to do? In fact, most of them are just workers like the average Americans; they may have a Ph. D or MBA, but it does not make them real business experts. These degrees just show that they have learned and studied some business education and know some business theories, but they are not experts. If they were experts as they claim, why have so many major businesses led by these Ivy League graduates filed for bankruptcy in the last five years? If they call themselves experts, then the young kid who makes French fries at McDonald's is an expert as well. If those so-called business experts were so confident about their expertise, they would build their own businesses or develop the third world economies. In fact, many of them work in Boston or other major cities; most major cities are overcrowded with menial workers, uneducated whites, blacks, Hispanics, Asians and more. So, why do not they go and teach these disadvantaged people how to take business opportunities in their communities to grow rich, so this country and the world can grow richer? Business experts are people who develop their own knowledge and methods to open closed doors and become dominant and well-known businessmen, people who love and appreciate their customers, their communities, their country, the world and their employers, instead of looking for any loophole to exploit them economically.

GRE scores and high grade point averages have little to nothing to do with success; if people had good intentions, they would charge creative business leaders with the economic development of black, Asian and Hispanic communities and countries. Besides, people who emerge as business experts do not even label themselves as such: e.g. Bill Gates, Martha Stewart, Jay-Z, Oprah Winfrey, 50 Cent, Donald Trump, Tyra Banks, Wyclef Jean. Business experts are self-made men and women, not workers, imitators, or beneficiaries. Many who claim the title of expert probably only have the expertise to mislead these bright students to go exploit and oppress the average American and other lowly natives. They train their bright students to go exploit and oppress the weak, and afterwards they blame these disadvantaged people for wanting to immigrate. Real business experts would utilize their expertise for the common good of the society and the rest of the world, not to justify their misguided business methods to the economic debasement of the black, Hispanic, homosexual, or low- and middle-class white communities to the point where many face starvation, lack access to medical care, and lack college education. Real experts would remedy the impossible economic hope.

The majority of the graduates who are in charge of the world's economies are sincere and considerate people; in fact, many of them think that they are doing the poor races, communities, and countries a great favor by offering their businesses opportunities, or exploiting them for cheap labor and for others. They truly believe that they will develop their communities and countries economically, but they fail to realize that they are a part of the social and economic problem. Sadly indeed, these professors do not even realize that they are turning great students from heroes and heroines into exploiters and oppressors. Many major corporations have CEOs from Ivy League schools who were trained exclusively to make millions by any means necessary. Instead of learning the right business philosophy to develop the world economically, they are taught that they have to make millions of dollars a year. Therefore, when the graduates cannot make the kind of money that they were told to make by their professor despite coming from a certain school, they usually opt to take raises or small bonuses away from the hardworking citizens who are doing the best they can to extricate themselves from their uncomfortable predicament, or they embezzle money

19

from the company and corporation or commit tax fraud. Unfortunately, most either end up in jail or prison, are smeared in the media for a couple thousand dollars, or end up corrupt, while many of them are worth millions or billions. Most of their professors teach them to go to exploit and oppress as if the world owed them something, instead of developing modern business philosophy methods to teach them that they do not have to do this because they are already rich and powerful. It is sad indeed; in the last ten years more-high level business men and women have resigned or been convicted of embezzlement or other illegal activities than have been helping their fellow Americans and their fellow citizens overseas with their economic crises.

Due to this inadequate method of teaching, this great country, which is leader of the world, has preferred allies. This is a huge mistake for us as world leader, because as a world leader we cannot be biased, and we certainly should not have allies. By having certain countries as allies, we would have to pick sides before looking out for the world's interests. In other words, we must be leaders first, because that is what we are, and what the title and the position require. A CEO cannot take a senior manager's side when they conflict; he or she has to be unbiased and impartial in order to best serve the company. If sides were taken, it would eventually result in a problem for the company, because the other party would feel mistreated and neglected, become unhappy, and eventually feel hatred, resentful, and vengeful. The same method should apply for a world leader: we have to be unselfish, and to take advantage of all resources so every country may benefit from them. By teaching these bright students to be selfish and protect their own interests instead of developing the world, they continue to make other countries call us greedy, selfish, and self-centered, as they have for many generations. Since many of these countries are too small to confront us directly, they devise other ways of hurting us: terrorist attacks, acting alone, or World War III, with allies. When a country feels mistreated, abused, neglected, it will eventually explode. Just as a wife would leave a man who repeatedly ignores her and their children, a mistreated, abused people or country will also react eventually. It could take years or decades, but unless the conflict is resolved, it is inevitable. Those that have grudges against this great country must have them for a reason; if we have problems with them, it must be for a reason as well. They are not going to stop retaliating and hating us, because they think they are right; we as Americans are not going to stop, because we believe we are right as well. As a result, we are going to spend more money on weapons and security, and they are going to develop modern methods to better train and equip those so-called terrorists. The next generation is surely doomed to have the same problems. If the professors were doing their jobs right, developing better and world leadership methods to benefit and develop the world, and to make better use of resources for the greater good, then countries would respect each other more economically and socially, regardless of size. They would all look out for the world's best interests and bring all countries' leaders and citizens into harmony. The crisis would die out and many lives would be saved.

This great country is like a loving mother who has three children. One was savagely killed and the mother felt so much pain that she became handicapped mentally and physically. But she still must recover and be strong for the rest of her family. Everybody knows that 9/11 was a tragedy and a catastrophe for this great country; much innocent blood was shed, and many innocent children and people were killed. Even today we are still losing large numbers of soldiers on a daily basis in Iraq and other combat zones. Sad to say, many children are still wondering at this moment if they ever are going to see their fathers or mothers again, many wives are still losing husbands, and many husband are still losing wives. Even we hurt as citizens in this country. We have to develop modern methods to rebuild our relationship with overseas leaders and their countries; otherwise it is going to get worse still. It is as the European countries did fifty years ago, forming a sort of union to improve Europe, using the same money and the same passport; otherwise the same disaster would keep occurring. As long as we keep applying the same teaching methods, we will continue to lose vision of the modern world, and the same undesirable conditions that existed in the past and exist now will continue for generation after generation, one century after another, because they are a result of centuries of mis-education.

School officials must develop a modern method to give all citizens a new status; they have to modernize their school systems by having more interest in understanding the important task before them, and improving the situation for the underprivileged people that they are trying to reach. The modern teaching method should be towards actual education to develop everybody from what they are, rather than to only empower and influence certain groups. They should not try to influence students to leave their culture, origins, sexual orientations, ethnicities, races, religions or countries behind; they should develop these children and take every single one of them into consideration. How can homosexuals, blacks, Jews, Middle Easterners, Asians, females, average white males and others truly feel like equal, real Americans and have interest in learning while they are excluded altogether in the school system curriculum? In fact, the very little material that talks about them serves only to belittle and decry them.

They should have been included in the modern philosophy and literature more than the ancient ones because this is a modern time; the Greeks and Socrates should be paid less attention. The majority of modern students and citizens in this country and around the world should have been taught and encouraged to develop their own ideals of philosophy and beliefs rather than spending most of their lives studying those who died hundreds of years ago. The modern students who have been excluded in the school curriculum should have been taught and trained, in a sense, to delve into their backgrounds, to know and understand their past rather than others. Irishmen, homosexuals, Jews, Africans, Italians, Asians, Middle Easterners, Haitians, Jamaicans and others should have been taught to understand their own linguistic histories and philosophies: why they do certain things, why they are underdeveloped, oppressed or have certain beliefs, or are reluctant to do for themselves or contribute to their own culture, communities, heritage, and the world in general. These things are certainly more important for them to learn and study than what happened hundreds and even thousands of years ago. They ignore their own civil rights: students do not have to go to law schools to understand the U.S. Constitution. These are modern times; if they can use computers, they can learn their civil rights so they know when someone is violating them.

Education is the most important key to bringing citizens, races, religions, genders and sexual orientations together into harmony, loving and respecting each other. However, this arduous task can never succeed if the best and real teachers and professors are powerless while incompetent, narrow-minded and biased professors are the ones who emerge as the real educators, thinkers and people in charge of the school system. For example, on January 17, 2005, Harvard University president

Lawrence H. Summers said: "That innate difference between men and women might be one reason fewer women succeed in science and math careers." Allowing a man like Lawrence H. Summers, who has such bias and negative beliefs, to be the president of the leading institution in this country and the rest of world will always result in failure. Mr. Summers lacks any training or pedagogy to train modern students well, except to turn these bright kids sour and lead them to believe that it is impossible to make the world a better place. The system will be no different because he places every other race, all females, and the rest of this country in a position of inferiority. His teaching method handicaps the world because he was supposed to become a constructive force in the development of these students' minds and give them something new. Instead, he continues to teach them to regard an entire gender as inferior. And so, instead of these so-called leaders doing their parts by developing modern teaching methods of their own to better enlighten and educate our future leaders, they continue following the same biased and inadequate teaching methods which kill the young bright females' aspirations and doom them to function in the lower sphere of the social order. These leaders have proceeded on the basis that all citizens are treated equal and possess equal minds, but do the contrary. The main reason millions of children and adult Americans are incarcerated is because those who are called educators are not doing their jobs properly. Since their approach to teaching methods has been borrowed from the ancient Greeks and English philosophers, it leads them to believe it is impossible to improve the awful living conditions of blacks, Hispanics and others. They fail to realize that in order to do this, they must develop modern methods to deal with social and economical problems. As modern educators, they must not think like their predecessors, holding onto outdated ideas that females cannot do what men can do. We live in modern times, which call for modern solutions and remedies, rather than believing that blacks cannot do what whites, Asians, and others can do. Blacks, Hispanics, Asians, females, homosexuals and other marginalized groups will never be able to prosper and flourish if those so-called professors psychologically force them to live subjugated, in poverty, and as part of the lower social order. As long as the educational efforts and methods are used without the interest of all citizens in mind, it will always result in failure, because these biased professors and school officials unconsciously keep them from flourishing and getting ahead. Many of these imitators do not even know the real purpose and essence of education. They use education to empower themselves, to teach weak to see them as great achievers, thinkers and philosophers; furthermore, they also misuse the education to oppress and exploit a certain race, countries and certain groups of people.

In fact, they did not even develop this method on their own; it came from the Hebrews, Greeks, Romans and Teutons. Since many of these great ancient savants and philosophers lacked expertise with different races and genders, and did not really grasp the psychology and philosophy of blacks, females, Hispanics, gays, lesbians, Asians, and Middle Easterners, these so-called experts do not know how to approach them wisely, and cannot develop any modern systems on their own because they merely imitate. Nevertheless they continue to utilize their expertise, not to really educate the weak people and to develop them, but to extract more money from them for tuition and to teach blacks, Hispanics, gays, females and others to admire and respect them, to perceive them as savants and thinkers, instead of the mere imitators they are. And if the great ancient philosophers were so accurate, why are the people who used to be oppressed

(Italians, Hispanics, Irish, blacks, Asians, Middle Easterners and others) so dominant in the modern world? The past is past, and if the narrow-minded Harvard president was right, why are females more dominant than males in the professional sphere, and why are the best and the brightest leaders in this country females, for example, Senator Hillary Rodham Clinton, Canada Governor Michaëlle Jean, and Dr. Condoleezza Rice? Men like Lawrence H. Summers should never have been in the school system in the first place; Mr. Summers embodies one of the main reasons why such racism, bigotry, discrimination, hatred and sexism still exist. As stated before, racism, discrimination and sexism would never exist in the first place, if it were not started in the classroom. Lawrence H. Summers was never a real educator; he is just an imitator for all his life; his beliefs and ways of thinking are no different than the ones before, and those who still allow him to lead this educational program are no better than them. Senator Hillary Clinton should not blame many politicians for being incompetent and leading the black communities as if on a plantation; she must blame Lawrence H. Summers and many of the Harvard officials for connecting blacks very closely with life as it was.

The teachers and professors who lead the modern school system should be men and women who are passionate about teaching and who have distinguished themselves in the creative world. Many narrow-minded professors have many advanced degrees in social science, but that does not make them modern social experts, even if they believe so. They do not possess the expertise to solve social problems of today's world; if they were that confident about themselves and were great experts and educators as they label themselves to be, and really knew the true meaning of teaching, they would develop new teaching methods to reach out to these helpless children in inner cities and welcome any person who wanted to learn. They would teach regardless of their students' race, social class, economic status, gender, sex orientation and level of education, rather than overloading their classes with only the prepared and the fortunate students. Most of these teachers have never faced a true teaching challenge, and do not even know what is like to teach challenged children or adults, and have never had to turn hopeless students into great professionals and leaders, as many great inner-city teachers, state college and junior college professors and instructors have done. Any average teacher or instructor can turn a 3.0 GPA student into a professional, but not just any professor or teacher can turn troubled and lost teens and adults into great leaders. Nearly any average coach could have turned Kobe Bryant into an MVP because he was already a great player. He was already the all-time leading scorer in Southeastern Pennsylvania in high school; the only thing he needed was better structure. But not any average coach could turn Tom Brady into one of the best NFL players in history; it took a coach with a special mind and special skills. Brady was never the brightest and the best player at Michigan University; in fact, Brady was selected by the New England Patriots in the 6th round, 199th overall. But now, Brady is the best and most dominant quarterback in the NFL; he has won three Super Bowls and two Super Bowl MVP awards and is one of the best players in NFL history at a very young age.

By only teaching the fortunate and prepared students, a certain social class, gender and race, these so-called best teachers and professors have clearly demonstrated that they have copied the methods of Socrates and others. They have clearly illustrated that they never had any real teaching challenge experience, and that they lack the essence and spirit of real educators and do not intend to reach out to those Americans who have been wrongly left behind. These people who call themselves experts do not realize that in order for the world to truly advance and become a better place, they have to do their parts first, not as experts, but as humane and distinguished teachers and professors. In order for inner-city students, people on welfare, and non-violent inmates to elevate themselves, and for immigrants and poor countries to elevate themselves as well, these professors must develop modern methods to lead them down the right path. Otherwise these social, economic, immigration and other problems will only increase instead of diminishing. These people may not know how to read or write well; they may not be from the elite social class or wealthy countries, but they have dreams, and they are determined to better themselves, their families and their countries. Otherwise, they would not be in schools, in GED classes, break the laws or do menial work to support themselves and their families. They would not have immigrated to this country and others, leaving their children and loved ones behind; lost their manhood or womanhood, self-esteem, originality, and their native citizenship.

The reason these social and economic failures keep increasing is because these narrow-minded school officials orient their education more towards simply obtaining a diploma or taking a useless standardized test, rather than developing modern teaching methods to deal with the social and economic problems as they are. The teaching method tends more toward the social and economic benefit of a certain social class or gender, not the development of the world. They mostly train their students to be better than the masses, for instance: to get a degree, a better job, a mortgage, a better salary; and do not concern themselves with more. As a result of this inadequate training, our educational system will always result in failure, because students who have completed their Masters or doctorate have only learned from their inaccurate educational philosophy. This teaching method is not modernized enough to equip these bright students to really serve their people and their country. Moreover, most of the people these students have been trained to serve and empower are upper-class white males, not the disadvantaged ones from their communities. The biased and inaccurate teaching that these great students have learned will always lead them to lose vision of the modern world and lose touch with the common people. Because school officials have not yet developed modern creative teaching methods to reach out to those in situations such as the welfare system, segregated schools, gangs, and poverty, they have lost touch with the common people. Those schools that emerge as the best ones cannot truly reach millions of people who have never seen the light that their predecessors have sought since the beginning. Their teaching methods are based primarily upon what they know of the educational needs of upper-class white males, the richest European countries and a few wealthy Asian countries, while the inner-city, junior college, and state university teachers and professors are doing the real work by trying to become more creative to reach out to those who have been neglected and left behind.

Since most of these biased professors have not updated their teaching method for the modern day, they still cannot understand the psychology and philosophy of all human beings; they still adamantly believe only a certain race, gender, and group's students possess the mind to lead economically and socially. Instead of drastically lowering tuitions and welcoming any future leader who wants to learn about business and social methods, they only accept people who come from their own circle and have the same narrow-minded beliefs as they do. The fact is that they are selfish and biased, and their students end up biased and egotistic towards one another, the disadvantaged, and the world that they are supposed to serve and lead. Such education will always result in a huge failure, and inequality, simply due to loss of vision of the modern world.

Since these experts only have been imitators instead of great visionaries, they do not realize that in order for blacks, Hispanics, females, people on welfare, non-violent inmates and natives of third-world countries to be able to make an honest living and be productive, they have to be trained. Many who label themselves as great world business and social science leaders keep criticizing and decrying these groups for doing poorly economically and socially, while they teach their students and lawmakers to oppress and exploit them for cheap labor. If these people were noble educators, and wanted this country and the world to flourish economically and socially, they would help teach these Americans stuck in the welfare system, who break the law as an occupation, how to support themselves, leave the welfare system and stop being repeat offenders. In addition, they would go teach third-world countries about agriculture, because these countries have sufficient land for their natives to make a living on the soil. Most of the things these professors have taught these lowly people are to despise the business opportunities in their communities or in their native countries, so that their students can continue to take up the business opportunities in these communities to grow richer themselves.

For instance, many Hispanics, blacks, Asians and others have worked their way through college and university by working in their own communities. But when they graduate from business school, they refuse to go back to their communities and countries to build their businesses or to make the small businesses bigger, mainly because most of the professors have trained them exclusively in the psychology and economics of Wall Street. As a result, these so-called experts have led their students to waste business opportunities in their communities. If they had done their jobs properly as real educators, by developing better modern business methods, instead of criticizing blacks, Hispanics, homosexuals, Asians, immigrants and others, the graduate students from those communities and countries would go back to develop their communities and their countries economically, and go in search of other opportunities. If such an educational system existed, large numbers of these groups would not have to resort to break the laws regularly, and many immigrants would return to their native lands, or would not immigrate in the first place. Instead of these professors developing modern business and economy teaching methods to bring all citizens in this country and around the world together to uplift themselves and their countries economically and socially, the professors turn them against each other. They teach some that they have a natural right to control others; or that they do not work, respect, or treat others fairly because they are inferior and subhuman due to their skin colors, social status, culture, customs, genders, sexual orientations, or other absurd reasons. Many of these biased and untrained professors criticize the black and Hispanic communities for doing so poorly economically, all the while teaching their students to oppress and exploit them for cheap labor. Furthermore, these imitators are blaming and decrying immigrants for all of the immigration problems in this country, while their teaching methods are causing it in the first place. They call themselves critics or experts, but most of these professors never taught any of their own thoughts; even their anti-immigrant critiques are not original; they copied these critiques from eighteenth century English writers who used to criticize Italians, Catholics, Irishmen, Jews, and others for immigrating to this country.

Since these biased and narrow-minded professors never developed any modern business teaching methods, they still strongly believe that white males are smarter and brighter than the other races and genders, Europeans are smarter than Africans, Hispanics, Asians and others, and that males are smarter than females. If they had developed modern business philosophy teaching methods, as real experts and educators, to reach out to people on welfare, non-violent inmates, blacks, Hispanics, Asians, homosexuals and others instead of imitating the ancient incompetent ones, they would come to their senses to realize that Ivy League white male students succeed in the business world not because they are smarter, brighter, or better, but because opportunities are only created and offered to them. All communities, countries, and continents can do well economically and socially; McDonald's, Burger King, and others became billionaires nationwide and internationally by just selling burgers and French fries; 50 Cent, and Jay-Z have built their multimillion- or billion-dollar empires based on hip-hop; and Hustler's Larry Flynt became a billionaire by selling porn. Therefore, there are plenty of opportunities in other communities. Furthermore, these poor countries and continents would be richer by now if these narrow-minded professors were doing their jobs instead of demeaning females, blacks, Hispanics, homosexuals, and others. Their methods and philosophy need to be modernized; otherwise this country will face immigration and deficit problems the likes of which we have yet to see. We need great educational leaders to deal with the current economic problems; leaders like Lawrence H. Summers and the rest of the narrow-minded and biased, powerful and influential Harvard officials, are not useful for modern times. Most of them are still teaching the future world business leaders about Socrates, Aristotle, Plato, Marsiglio of Padua, and Wall Street, while millions of Americans are on welfare, while newly released inmates are prohibited from working, while immigration problems, crime rates, poverty rates, and illiteracy rates are increasing. Third world countries call us greedy, selfish, and self-centered, while they are dying due to poverty and civil war, and meanwhile Ford and GM are on the edge of going out of business for good.

Creative people who barely finish high school or college are becoming independently rich, while these narrow-minded and biased professors who label themselves as real educators and experts refuse to develop modern teaching methods to teach their bright students. They avoid teaching people who cannot afford college, or did not finish high school, and these people turn to the welfare system, or break the law regularly, rather than learning how to conduct a successful business, make an honest, decent living, and be happy, or how to establish business and economy schools in the poor countries for the same purpose. If these narrow-minded and biased professors had developed modern teaching systems, the world would never have had such economic deficits in the first place, and immigration and other social problems would have diminished instead of increasing.

Many call themselves distinguished professors; distinguished perhaps for Wall Street or for the white elite male upper class, but not for blacks, females, average Americans, Hispanics, Asians, homosexuals or others, and certainly not the rest of the world; otherwise, the world would see a better light, and develop economically and socially. In fact, most of these professors have chips on their shoulders; if they were truly the excellent educators they say they are, they would not increase the economic problems, and they would develop modern solutions and remedies to fix

33

economic inequalities. Many American citizens are enrolling themselves in the welfare system and breaking laws, and immigrants are coming to the U.S. or other countries because they became too despondent and hopeless. How can these immigrants advance in the world if the school officials are not doing their jobs? If these Ivy League school officials had spent less of the taxpayers' money on incompetent researchers, worn-out business theories, false traditions, and less time teaching and training bright students to benefit upper class white males, then blacks, Hispanics, Asians, homosexuals, and poor countries would invest their money and energy in their own communities. Those narrow-minded and biased experts who are in charge of the business school systems are not doing anything better for the average Americans, blacks, Hispanics, Asians, and others; they only brainwash, misuse and mislead these groups so they can keep throwing business opportunities away and so the same white male elite can keep growing richer and richer. And they wonder why this country never advances, why only the rich get richer, why the prisons are mostly filled with blacks, Hispanics, Asians, and uneducated whites as they were a hundred years ago, why the world still hates us and calls us greedy, selfish, self-centered Americans, why immigration problems are still worsening, why poor countries remain poor and why wars exist in nearly all countries and continents.

These narrow-minded professors should be developing modern business teaching methods for blacks, Asians, Hispanics, homosexuals so that wealthy people can invest in their children, communities, states, and the rest of the world. Instead, they keep modifying the same inadequate and biased business system created by their predecessors, the oppressors, in order to continue manipulating people who are willing to do anything for their children, their race, their communities. The professors mislead them so they can continue to exploit them, by investing their money in Wall Street stock and luxuries. This way of thinking will always lead to economic failure, because the poor will never be able to produce for themselves; no person, community, or country can truly develop or advance if they have not learned to produce for themselves. When these untrained and biased professors see blacks, Hispanics, Asians, and uneducated whites' businesses failing, closing, and filing for bankruptcy, and third-world countries begging for economic assistance; they write negative reports, smear them in the media, or tell their students: "these people do not have what it takes to build a successful business, because they did not graduate from Ivy League schools". Meanwhile many corporations and businesses that these professors have worked with, have already filed for bankruptcy and Chapter 11, or are about to do so or close their doors for good. A large number of their graduates are corrupt, breaking the law, oppressing and exploiting the average Americans, the weak races, and the poor countries for selfish purposes. If these narrow-minded professors were real educators instead of being imitators and critics, they would create new methods to give these people some remedies and solutions to make their businesses grow strong, and be able to survive through any crisis. The biased and inadequate business and economic curriculum these minorities have received has led them to believe their communities and the countries can never succeed in the business sphere. In fact, most of the professors who teach such things, and have written so many biased books and articles, have never experienced for a moment what life is like in these communities. But they think they are great experts merely by listening and watching these conservative reporters, who do not have anything good to back up their arguments.

Furthermore, these professors do not even realize

that by dissuading blacks, Hispanics, Asians, and others from investing in and developing their communities economically, it will always cause a huge deficit. In their little minds, they may think they are eliminating competition, but the fact is they are destroying the world economically and socially. Since the people who have taught to control the natural resources and to build businesses are less than ten percent, as a result, more millions of people will sign up for welfare, be incarcerated by the next generation, and more millions will try to immigrate to this country as well; therefore, the taxes, high cost of living, and social problems will inevitably increase. If these professors were genuine world business leaders and educators, they would develop new teaching methods so the natural resources and the production of raw materials would not be monopolized by greed and self-centeredness; they would be controlled for the common good. And, by doing this, the United States and the poor countries alike would move upward in the economic sphere. The only reason that the blacks, Hispanics, Asians and others are still having such economic debasement is because the powerful and influential business and economy school officials refuse to modernize their teaching methods to do the task better; and if these great countries and the rest of the world leaders do not intervene to make these narrow-minded professors improve their teaching methods, the immigration problems and huge deficits will continue to increase instead of diminishing, and the rest of the world will continue to dislike us.

These professors are not going to do the impossible or perform miracles, because most disadvantaged people may have poor business knowledge and skills, but they do have a lot of interest and really love business. We just have to develop modern business systems to reach out to them and provide them with good business structures, psychology, and philosophies. Most of them already have owned small businesses in their communities; unfortunately, many of them are also doing what they learned from life in the streets, but they would leave these types of business in a second if they had real business knowledge or training. However, in order for these people and the world in general to improve, these professors have to develop modern systems so they can gauge the psychology and beliefs of all human beings, not just a certain class, gender, or race. They would have to forget the biased things and untried theories that they have learned from their professors. Certainly, they would have to love the citizens of the world as a whole. These things require much sacrifices and work, but only then could they begin to confront and solve the immigration, social, and economic problems the world has been facing since the beginning of time.

Business school officials have placed far too much emphasis on business administration and human resources departments in colleges or universities. With no disrespect intended to these facilities, most of the blacks, Hispanics, homosexuals, Asians, and others who graduate from such departments are pretty much useless as far as the development of their communities. These bright students spend most of their time and money to study trifles instead of studying the economic problems that are killing their communities. Instead of these great business professors and leaders developing modern business and economy teaching methods so these students can be prepared to confront their economic problems in their communities and countries, they keep teaching them the salary, the benefits, and what to wear when they are going to seek employment. The point of view and the business philosophy these students really need is to seek business opportunities, learn good business methods, learn how to improve and rebuild businesses in their communities and in their countries. These students are not really trained to think or build businesses; they are trained in the exclusive psychology, business, and economics of Wall Street, which will always result in a business failure for lack of vision, courage, and confidence to go build their own business empire. But businessmen are not supposed to believe in personal gain and large paychecks, because the great success and reward in business is to produce and create opportunities, to build their own industry instead of begging others for a chance or raise. The small percentage of the elite class cannot feed everyone and do everything, but by misleading others instead of educating them, world's deficits, high cost of living and other social and economic problems will invariably keep increasing. Blacks, Hispanics, Asians, homosexuals and others have to learn modern methods of commerce, and build their own industries for their people and their countries, not for the entire world; they must help one another, not oppress one another. We must all learn from world business experts how to increase commerce and build their own industries on our own lands and support our own businesses before anyone else's. Every race and country must learn to produce for themselves and their countries; otherwise, if these professors and world business leaders keep being selfish, and want education to never change, then immigration and the resentment towards this country will never go away. We cannot afford to let the same self-centered professors continue to manipulate the system. They cannot keep blinding and misleading us in order to allow the same people to exploit and oppress the world. If they continue to teach these students that this country can own the world, it will only result in failure. During ancient times, instead of kings leading and developing their countries and the rest of the world, they owned slaves, and by trying to own the rest of the world, they lost all their empires, and their countries today are not even among the ten most powerful in the world. Adolph Hitler believed that white males and Germany could own the world. but the bigger Germany's empire got, the more they lost. Even historians cannot say with certainty what happened to Adolph Hitler; even at this moment, Germany is still suffering for it, because they are still paying other countries for the damage caused in World War II. Englishmen chose to own blacks during the 16th through the 19th centuries, instead of helping them, which causes this country to still suffer great economic and social problems. The country continues going backwards instead of forwards. And now, instead of these professors modernizing their business methods, and teaching their students to expand production of raw materials and the oil industries around the world, they are still teaching how to manipulate the system and monopolize natural resources, industries, and agencies. As a result of these professors' selfishness and incompetence, this country continues to suffer greatly; millions of our children and elderly go hungry because they cannot afford food; millions more of them suffer cold nights because oil and gas are too expensive. In addition, millions of elderly and children get sick and die due to their economic status; these same status problems keep causing immigration problems, resentment, and hatred towards this country, not because we are Americans or the most powerful country in the world, but because our business leaders are trying to own the world, as the selfish and self-centered people before had done. They do not realize the folly of controlling all the natural resources and production of raw materials around of the world; they fail to realize the potential benefit of developing and expanding them. While their students make huge profits in oil, our country is sliding backwards because many kids are losing their parents, many husband and wives are losing their partners, parents are losing their children, and many soldiers' deaths could have been avoided. If these narrow-minded professors were real educators, they would develop modern business teaching methods of their own to teach the present CEOs how to use oil and the other natural resources industries across the world instead copying other methods, and millions of lives could be saved. Moreover, many experts have stated the main original motivation for the war in Iraq was control of the oil industry for selfish purposes, not for the world's general welfare. Business school professors with similar impressions of life are weakening the world economy; they certainly are not good leaders for our bright students because they have lost vision of the modern world.

By teaching our great students to control the world economy, to oppress and exploit undeveloped races, communities, and poor countries instead of developing them, it will always cause the same economic deficits, immigration, and many war problems. But if our business and economy professors or leaders developed business methods to better use our natural resources, and improve the productions of raw materials for all communities, then poverty, crimes, and welfare would decrease drastically. Immigration problems would cease, because when the illegal immigrants see their native countries doing well, they would voluntarily return. Other countries would never even call us greedy, selfish, or self-centered. In fact, our leadership would never be compromised or in jeopardy, and our land would never be at risk because the rest of the world would love, respect, and admire us. Not because we are Americans, or the most powerful country, but for our great business leadership to the world. Business schools cannot proceed only with the methods of gigantic corporations; they have to also teach all citizens who want to learn how to organize their communities. Most people in poor communities have interest in developing their businesses, but they do not know the methods and the business field in which they operate. Many people who started gigantic corporations were just like them; most did not have an MBA and Ph.D in business, economics, or finance. In fact they did not even have a lot of business experience, but they had dreams, interest, conviction, and desire to make their small enterprises into gigantic industries. People in poor communities have much in common with these major business owners: they have the same mindset, want their businesses to flourish and have the same ambitions. Since they cannot afford college, are restricted to segregated poor quality schools, have no quality business training, are unable to get access to quality business literature, and have no training at all to study the market which they depend on, their businesses tend to fail. This is not because these people are not as bright and smart as the successful businesses, but because they are not sufficiently trained to do these things. Business school officials must develop modern teaching methods to prepare men and women to do such tasks; they cannot keep using the same old business teaching system to keep blacks, Asians, Hispanics, homosexuals and others operating in the dark, or misleading them about the psychology and philosophy of business. They must secure our bright students' intelligence and guide them to develop businesses in their communities. Our future world business leaders must teach untrained businesspeople to see when their businesses are outgrowing their ability to supply, and becoming too unwieldy. They must update their training or their staff before they start making errors of judgment and allowing oppressors and exploiters to take over their businesses. Educate them about the real psychology and philosophy of business; they must create their businesses to serve the customers, their communities and their countries; they must always keep prices low, and they must take care of their customers and employers, they must stay close to people they depend on; and they must help their communities. Certainly, they should not try to own their communities or try to be social kings by wasting money on cars, mansions, jets, boats, jewelry, and vacations.

Almost all the social science professors have imitated the ancient Greeks, the Romans, the Hebrews, the Teutons, and the Socratic philosophers, and those philosophers and savants had distanced themselves from females and peasants. They had not written any works about other human races or social groups other than elite white males. So the most influential and powerful social science writers ended up biased towards certain races, sexual orientations, genders, social classes, and countries, because the education methods they copied excluded the interests of most citizens in their countries and the rest of the world. Since many of these ancient philosophers dismissed the other human groups as inconsequential, these philosophers' imitators, who called themselves educators or experts, became biased against these groups. These communities count on professors to create programs to solve their social problems, but instead of remaining where these social problems are manifested and out of control, writing better and more modern philosophy books, and developing new programs to confront these communities' social problems, these professors became as unsuccessful in the development of the modern world citizens as the previous. They copied ancient philosophers who had never actually taken or developed accurate philosophy courses or read any books, and did not know much about social groups other than their own. Since they were not properly well-informed and educated about these groups, these professors who labeled themselves as social science experts were socially limited as well, because they followed old biased philosophies instead of developing modern methods of their own to really know and understand the people they are serving.

Instead of these professors developing better modern social courses and programs to make people feel confident, happy and secure about themselves, they do the contrary, by still teaching us to admire and highly respect the biased philosophers who created racism, war, discrimination, and inequality in the first place. These are the same philosophers who wrote that white males are superior to females; and that whites are superior to blacks, Asians, Hispanics, Middle Eastern, homosexuals, and others. But World Wars I and II were both caused by whites, millions of whites have enslaved, lynched, raped, and oppressed millions of black people and others, exploiting and oppressing blacks and other races. Teaching bright but disadvantaged students to follow these biased philosophers will result in nothing but social and economic failure for their communities. Only a small percentage of white elite males would always succeed in this country and around the world, because they believe only they are entitled to success. They continue to be told today that they are naturally smarter and better than any other social group, and therefore, must believe that the world belongs to them. That small percentage of white males would always manipulate the systems and agencies of the world to place disadvantaged groups in a position to be convinced of their incapability and inferiority. They place and oppress these social groups where they can never develop to see a better light. With this way of teaching, no other race, gender, communities, and poor countries can really go forward, because these incompetent professors are turning bright kids who could be a constructive force in world development to oppress the other races, communities, and the poor countries where they can never flourish. They are turning out bright youths to despise, exploit, and oppress the world, instead of turning them out to become bright leaders to develop the world for the people. This method of teaching is a sort of destruction and damage to the world, indeed.

It is unfortunate that these professors do not modernize their teaching method, because they are really destroying and damaging this great country and the rest of the great world socially and economically. For instance, by neglecting and refusing to develop modern accurate psychology and philosophy of all human beings, these intelligent and bright young people will always be restricted and segregated in the poor quality schools. Therefore, the majority of them have to be crammed in the welfare, criminal, and other undesirable systems; furthermore, they have to kill and oppress one another, rather than protecting and developing themselves, their communities, countries, races, and genders to a higher status. In thus neglecting they are destroying and damaging many communities, many families, this country, and the rest of the world socially and economically, merely because they believe those ancient philosophers were right about their ridiculous and biased theories. Millions of these great minds could become great assets for their races, communities, this country, and the rest of the world; sad to say, they became corrupt. If these powerful and influential school officials or experts lived up to the faith and belief they profess, such as to better all races, all communities, this country, and the rest of the world socially and economically, they would lower the tuitions drastically, and welcome any race, citizen, gender, sexual orientation, social class, and any poor countries' native to come to learn how to make an honest living, how to better themselves, their communities, this country, and the poor countries socially and economically. By imitating and copying off the ancient philosophers, disadvantaged groups have to show no promising future economically and socially. And when these humble people and these countries show no promising social and economic future, the United States themselves have no promising future as well, no matter what the conservative scholars and reporters state. This country's deficit and social problems will increase rather than diminishing, because the government officials will have to keep spending more billions in the welfare system, more billions to fight crimes, more millions to incarcerate inmates, more billions for the inmates' medical expenses, more billions to support the inmates' children and their families, more trillions to support illegal immigrants, fight immigration problems or securities, and more trillions to make sure the lowly people and countries do not go forward. Moreover, more trillions to support the poor countries when they have catastrophes and disasters such as Asia's emergency Indian Ocean earthquake and tsunami in December 2004, Haiti's hurricane, and other countries; in addition, on this land, such as New Orleans and 9/11. Since the school systems, which is the most important agency and tool to advance and develop the world socially and economically, are controlled by a bunch of narrow-minded, biased people and philosophers' imitators, who offer the females, blacks, whites, Hispanics, homosexual, Asians, others, and the poor countries natives no opportunity in the modern world to flourish, unfortunately, this great country and the rest of the world have no chance as well to go anywhere, where they ought to be.

Most of these professors and educators segregate themselves from the people and the countries that desperately need their leadership and their expertise, people who want to leave the poverty, the welfare, and criminal systems for good, people who want to be men and women as they were supposed to be for their families, their communities, this country, their natives countries, and the rest of the world. Why do not people who are supposed to be educators, teachers, and instructors live up to the faith they profess, go look for the uneducated people and teach them how to be more civilized, respect and tolerate one another's opinions and differences; how to function better in the business world for this country and the rest of the sick world? This is a modern time; therefore, the females, males, blacks, Hispanics, Asians, others, and the poor countries' native must learn how to do and to depend on themselves. Everybody in the world can be a great thinking man and woman and can do for themselves; this sort of teaching is a modern sort of destruction , indeed. The scholars and the experts have stated the main reason that a large number of people are in welfare system, in poverty, and in jail, or breaking the law as an occupation, killing one another and the poor natives are causing immigration problems is because they are poor and uneducated. Certainly true, they know these lowly people's problems and circumstances, so why do not they go to educate them, and do their jobs. These scholars think being an educator and teacher is merely based upon the schools and the degree which they went to and have received. Being an educator means a lot and carries a lot of responsibilities in the modern time, because they have to teach anybody who wants to learn and to be educated regardless of their economy, social status, sexual orientation, their race, and their religion; these are not options or up to them. Most people who are in charge of the school system are sellouts and inconsiderate indeed; they treat education as an auction, the people who can pay it, can get it. The majority of them already have been bought; they disgrace the education system; the only people they allow to get a quality education are people who can afford it or can do something for them, while everybody wants to be great achievers, successful, and have the potential and ability, while this country's deficits, poverty rate, crime rate, and immigration are out of control, and while the youths and citizens in this country and outside are dying, in jail and killing one another simply due to lack of education or modern education. This country cannot develop and see a better light because those so-called experts or educators do not even know the true meaning of educators and teachers; they think educators and teachers can chose whom to teach and whom not to teach; they still have not realized that a true educator has to be creative, passionate, unbiased, and unselfish. As long as this country's leaders keep allowing the same narrow-minded and imitators to be in charge; sorry to say, this great country has not seen hatred, immigration, social and economic problems yet, because most of them believe an MBA or Ph.D or certain school made them real educators. All these social and economic problems exist in the first place in this country, because they have copied a teaching method from the ancient time, and use it in the modern time, instead of doing what they are getting paid to do, which is to be creative and develop their own works and teaching method for the interest of all citizens and this country, and the rest of the world, not for a certain social class, race, gender, or group, country, and continent. The experts seem to have more interest in studying the old philosophers, passing a test, criticizing poverty and other social and economic problems in this country and overseas rather than manifesting any interest to see what has caused them and how to overcome them for the general welfare. This is a modern time, which requires real modern experts to prepare our bright children for the uplifting of downtrodden, oppressed, and exploited people and countries. Many of these narrow-minded imitators do not even know how to be an expert in the first place; they naively and absurdly believe that real experts are people who are from certain social classes, schools, genders, races, countries, or ethnicities or continents; people who mostly remain in their offices, classrooms, and copy off the previous incompetent and biased writers; in addition, have a higher score on the SAT, GRE, LSAT, and MCAT, memorize certain facts to pass their examination to complete their degrees for jobs and for their walls; and pay little attention to humanity's crisis. This attitude of educators would be good if everything was going smoothly, but the reality is not working socially and economically. For instance, the numbers of black, Hispanics, Asians and other college and graduate students have multiplied, and apparently are in better positions and circumstances than ever, but their communities, this country and the poor countries show almost as much backwardness as they did a hundred years ago or even thousands. Supposedly, the best institutions are located mostly in the cities, where the social and economics problems are manifested, but the presence of these so-called experts, and narrow-minded are not even equaled in the cities, like the presence of Tarzan in the jungle. Because Tarzan was a great leader for the jungle, he was protecting the jungle and the helpless and weak animals; but these experts are not good educators at all, they are not helping or rescuing the lowly ones. In fact, they continue to dismiss the disadvantaged as nonentities, as the ancient ones did. Such awful conditions exist because officials from the most powerful and influential schools fail in their main duty while getting millions for researches or are respected as the former Egyptian and black geniuses for starting the first civilizations in history, and while the world are getting worse in the economic and social spheres. Many hopeless and helpless people have stated, they got left behind because they do not have the right skin color, or connection, or came from the wrong places. Absolutely not, the reason these weak people got left behind, mistreated, abused and neglected as citizens of this country is because these so-called educators are purely imitators; if they were real educators, they would be creative as well. They would develop modern teaching methods to reach out to all children and all citizens who are tending downward to a level of disgrace, and they would not rest or give up until they worked out a plan or found remedies and solutions to lift such unfortunate students, or citizens, or countries' natives to a higher ground where they would find the light. It is really sad indeed, the average Americans are making less than fifty thousand; the leaders in this country do not intervene for the college tuition to decrease drastically. The education is the only tool to better the masses, the world's undesirable conditions, but if they can not afford it, where will be the future be for our unborn children: in jails, wars, poverty and welfare, as with us in the modern world. They have turned education into a business aspect, for instance, in order for the children to get finance for their educations, their parents have to have good credit, own properties, have a lot of money or assets; but what do these things have to do with receiving an education? These narrow-minded have stated: this is life, everything is hard, expensive and tough; the reality is everything turns out to be expensive because they are not doing their jobs as they ought to do. The middle class, the masses, and poor countries would never have existed in the first place, if they had owned major businesses, had great credit, and had a lot of wealth. These children who are about to become leaders of tomorrow cannot have their dreams and future shattered away from them because someone cannot make profit off them; they have to become leaders to accumulate the wealth for their families, communities, this country, and the rest of the world. By denying these children their natural rights to become great men and women, and to develop themselves sufficiently, will always affect them and this country drastically. If these disadvantaged people had a quality education, this country would be doing much better socially and economically. By oppressing, exploiting, restricting and high jacking the tuition when they feel like it, publishing the old biased books in a new edition, the disadvantaged people and countries' natives will always negatively effect this country socially and economically. Educators are not supposed to be narrow-minded, imitators, selfish, and inconsiderate; they thought that they were doing a great job by oppressing and exploiting a certain race, communities, countries, but the fact is, they thought wrong. All these economic and social problems in this country lay with causations; the narrow-minded and biased so-called professors and leaders think it was right in the country's interest to segregate blacks and Hispanics, Asians, and the others from receiving a quality education. It is not; yes, it is true, that the jail, prisons, the guns, and liquors industries CEOs and VPs are making trillions off them, but this country is going backward instead of forwards. Because the crime rate is out of control, and getting worse, the prisons and jails are overcrowded with inmates; most cities are overcrowded with gangs, delinquents and thieves. While they could be great leaders and assets for this country and while we as modern people desperately need better leaders, doctors and other professionals, those so-called conservative scholars and reporters still believe these lowly people belong there; otherwise, they would pressure the politicians and the leaders to modernize nearly all the systems and agencies in this country and the foreign policies, rather than wasting more trillions in useless foreign policy and immigration laws. Yes, it is true that the world business leaders send their students to go exploit and oppress these poor countries for cheap labor and more, instead of teaching their students to be world business leaders or experts to go to help other countries to develop themselves economically and socially, so their citizens can live and be happy on their lands. None of the so-called world experts think or realize doing the contrary would backfire with immigration problems, hatred, and more social and economic disasters in this country; again, most of these so-called experts never thought ahead and this is why they have lost vision of the modern economy-world.

The best professors and teachers who possess sufficient knowledge to develop their students, their poor communities, this country, and the poor countries socially and economically have failed because they are dominated by the thought of people who call themselves experts. Since the powerful and influential school officials manipulate the school system so the best and caring professors and teachers can remain behind closed doors, or to be powerless and to drift away from the people and the communities that desperately need them, as a result, the students end up in the hands of school officials who cannot develop a better doctrine and procedure of their own to better these kids and this country's future. These school officials are not there to really educate and develop these children's minds; they are in the school system to make use of the dogma of the white elite males as means to an end.

Frankly, they do not really care whether these kids receive what they need to have a bright future, or if they are serving their purposes in these children's lives. They know the school system is not working for the inner-city students, but they never tried to develop any modern system to reach out to these kids. The main reason for that is because they are not thinking for these children's or the country's interest; they are only thinking for themselves. These schools officials split off the school system like the old days; they have placed Hispanics, blacks, the poor whites, Asians, and others in the school system where they cannot go forwards in any professional sphere, while these kids are the children of this country, and place the whites in the best schools systems. Afterwards, they have the nerve to blame these children for been underachievers, for joining the gangs, breaking the law as an occupation, ending up on welfare or in the prison system. These kids have difficulty getting into college and having a bright future, not because they are black, yellow, purple, green, white; but because the most powerful and influential school officials are biased towards them, and not doing their jobs properly as they were supposed to. For instance, they would never enroll their own children in these poor quality schools; they place the disadvantaged citizens' children in these schools because they do not really have any interest in bettering these kids' lives. At the same, if all the school systems were united into one, the parents could choose which schools to send their kids; they would not even need that many jails or prisons for inmates, and the government would not need to waste that much taxpayers' money for the welfare system. Sincerely, there is no need for different school systems in the modern world; each school has the same interest and serves the same purpose for this country. By separating the school system, they also create disunion, racism, discrimination, and hatred among them and us as people; how can we as people respect, love, and tolerate one another for the greater good and as brothers and sisters, if we have been divided from infancy unto an adult. Those school officials think they are doing a great job in these children's and our lives as people and in this country, but they are confusing and dividing them and us as people. The school system began this way to cripple a certain race and due to lack of wisdom and vision, but now in the modern world, it is not only destroying a certain race; it's also destroying many communities, states, lives, this country, and the rest of the world. Many school officials have justified school segregation, while they were supposed to fight and defend the disadvantaged children and people and see only their interest. But at the same time, the only thing most of them are doing is rationalizing their actions by drifting away from righteousness into an effort to make wrong seem to be right. These school officials must be held responsible for destroying many communities, many lives, this country, poor countries, and the rest of the world; people have done things in the past based on their level of education, circumstances, and beliefs. Therefore, they should not altogether be blamed for causing so many social and economic problems at this present time. Thoughtless people who have followed and copied off them in the modern world should be blamed for causing such problems. Since most of them have been so busy imitating the originators of this nonsense, they could never stop for a moment to think about the meaning of these things or if their approaches and method of teaching are helping the modern world or crippling us as people. These school officials must know, copying people's works has two outcomes only, good or bad, but copying off unprincipled men and failures will always result badly. In the present time, it is bad, unlike the old times; black children or citizens died or injured or black countries natives died and other natives died, who cared, they were just properties or less people to worry about. But this a is modern time, many communities, countries, and millions of blacks, Hispanics, poor whites, Asians, others lives that have been destroyed, could have been saved, and we do care.

Loss of Vision of the Modern World: Part II

The school officials who were supposed to develop modern philosophy and other social science classes to bring all children, races, genders, communities, and countries into harmony, love, and respect for one another and for the general welfare have devoted less attention to the dissension between races, genders, communities, and countries, instead of teaching these bright social science students that the previous generations were wrong for enslaving, abusing, mistreating, restricting, oppressing, and exploiting certain races, genders, communities, and countries. The white race is doing better than other races in the modern world, not because they are naturally better and smarter than others, but due to the fact that the previous white males' generations had exploited and oppressed blacks during slavery and now, as well as the black countries and others' countries. Therefore, as a new fortunate generation, they have to do their part to assist the other races, communities, gender, and countries that are behind in their general welfare. But these school officials have chosen to do the contrary, in fact, they have not changed or updated any philosophy and other social science courses or program at all. As a result, the hatred and injustice that existed a century ago, among whites, blacks, Asians, and others, still exist, and the detestation that existed between countries is getting worse, nearly to the point of a World War III. Blacks, the whites, Asians, Hispanics, and others are still oppressing, exploiting, and fighting with one another. Unfortunately, the countries' natives and leaders are still oppressing, exploiting, and fighting with one another as well; and the small percentage of people who were making money or profit off them are still getting richer. It is sad indeed, that these professors do not realize that no communities, races, genders, countries, and the world will ever be able to flourish if they do not know and learn how to work together, accept procedure from one another, respect and assist one another. Not creating a better modern philosophy and other social science programs will always result in a failure, because the citizens are practically without support, respect, and love for one another. With such a teaching method and attitude; they will always turn against one another constantly, also, they will be handicapped for life, so the future unborn will be as well.

The leading institution bright professors in the world could develop modern social science teaching methods, so each race, gender, religion, community, and country can aid one another, and tolerate each other's differences so they can cooperate in the world for the common good. They have refused to do this; as the ones before had done in ancient times, they are modifying the same ancient biased books and writers to keep misleading and misinforming the children and the countries' leaders for denominational outposts, wealth, power, and to keep alive the biased system that the old kings and others had used to outstrip the other countries, genders, and races economically. By keeping the same teaching method alive, the whites, Asians, Hispanics, the others, and the countries would always have such disunion, hatred, and detestation among them. Therefore, these school officials have lost vision of the modern world, because they have not advanced their thoughts and social science programs to become working principles. Many of them may have many degrees, but they are not qualified to conduct any institutions in the modern world, because they are turning these bright social science students to imitate the ancient ignorant oppressors. Their methods of teaching are influencing these students who were about to become future leaders to look down on a certain race, sexual orientation, gender, communities, and countries as the previous and present ones. Instead of equipping the present leaders to help the disadvantaged people and countries, again, most of these conditions in this country and the world are due chiefly to the teaching methods these leaders have received. Honestly, only misguidance and inefficiency can be retained under this way of teaching. These school officials refer to almost all of these ancient philosophers as great men in history, while many of them are the causations of the past and the present social and economic problems in the world. Most of the social science professors devote most of the time teaching their students to appreciate and admire many people who used to oppress, exploit, murder, and restrict different races, lower social classes, genders, and countries for wealth and world power. It is nearly impossible for the students, who have been taught to admire and respect the selfish ancient oppressors, to support and do well by the unfortunate people, communities, and countries. Why should they help and respect the females, different races, homosexuals, communities, and countries? While these professors continue to glorify and refer to the biased ancient philosophers as great men in history, frankly, most of the philosophy and other social science classes their students have taken, have no good purpose in the modern world. Their students will always be selfish, self-centered, degraded, and mean with one another. Instead of teaching them to help each other, they have been trained to follow many of the unprincipled men who had wars with unoffending and helpless men for wealth and world power.

Many of the professors have given no attention to the racism, discrimination, and hatred problems that blacks, homosexuals, Asians, Hispanics, Middle Eastern, and other poor countries are facing on a daily basis. But they do not realize that telling the modern students and people to memorize the old philosophers' phrases or others will not give them the solution for these biased problems; in fact, it will turn them out to be ineffective and more biased. These kids are still prejudiced and selfish towards one another, because most of the social science classes they have been taking have no bearing upon the modern life, such as teaching them how to respect, love, care, and help their female, homosexual, black, Hispanic, Asian, Middle Eastern, and poor countries' native fellow classmates. Since the school officials have not modernized the philosophy and psychology teaching methods, when these kids go to a different race's, ethnicity's, or sexual orientation's communities, states, and countries, they cannot relate and feel connected to them. If these kids do not understand, relate, and care for one another, they cannot respect and tolerate one another's differences such as sexual orientation, social class status, gender, origins, and race. Since they do not care, know, love, appreciate, and tolerate one another, they will demean one another; if they degrade one another, they cannot work together. As a result, the world can never go forward, because the hatred and detestation between blacks, Asians, homosexuals, Latinos, whites, and others never got any better, not because we as the people are naturally born racist and biased, and not because we truly hate and detest each other, and not because the other countries hate us, but merely because our most powerful and influential school officials have lost vision of the modern world.

Therefore, by not modernizing the philosophy classes and other social science programs, all the citizens and the countries will never appreciate one another; unfortunately, this great country and this great world will keep going down, not because all races, religions, genders, sexual orientations, and all countries cannot tolerate and work with one another, but due to the fact that these officials are just ancient philosophers' imitators, not real educators. The lack of modern teaching methods and better quality of instructors have led large numbers of disadvantaged groups to fail to develop enough force to do very much for themselves, their communities, this country, and their native countries. These people's communities, this country, and the poor countries are sinking deeper and lower in the social and economic problems sphere, because the teaching method is not strong enough to influence all citizens to advances their ideas and thoughts. Since the educators have copied and imitated the wrong philosophers, these people, communities, and poor countries are led by social science professionals and many leaders who can scarcely help and understand themselves. But at the same time, these professionals do not realize that what they found in these ancient books cannot help them to work out constructive programs or find the remedies for the modern social problems. Since they have not updated the social science programs so they can reach out to the disadvantaged kids, homosexuals, poor communities, and poor countries, they blame them or blame different things or place fault at these people's, communities', and countries' natives' doorsteps, or say this is the end of life or the world, because everything is out of control; but in fact, life just has begun, they just lost vision of the modern world.

When these social science professionals see many young teenagers are getting pregnant or catching a transmitted disease, these experts turn around and blame their communities, countries, their parents, the music they are listening to, or the movies they are watching, the games they are playing, or their friends they are hanging out with, but they never stop for a moment to blame themselves as educators. As educators, they should realize this is a modern time, unlike before; if a couple teenagers had a baby, or caught a transmitted disease, they would be outcasts from the society, disgracing and shaming their parents. In the modern world, this occurs often; therefore, they have to deal with the situations as they are, such as to create more modern social science classes to teach them about safe sex, how to reach out those who got caught up or accustomed to the welfare system, or in the justice system. For instance, establish daycares in the universities or school campuses, or high school campus; teach these kids how to be great parents, how to provide for themselves and their families, regardless of if these school officials want to, but deal with those situations as they are. When they see the crime rates are increasing in the cities drastically, again, they turn around and blame the masses, the uneducated people, everything around them, and hip-hop, most likely, except themselves as educators, while these school officials and professors are the ones who are losing touch and ground with the modern world; in fact, any professor or teacher who criticizes hip-hop, doesn't really know too much about American art. Hip-hop is the true American art; it came from jazz, and the jazz is the only true American music. They criticize the whole hip-hop in general, illustrating that they do not really know too much about this country's heritage and culture; even so, a few hip-hop lyrics are bad influence for our children, but most of them are great voices for their communities, like many hip-hop legends such as Tupac, B.I.G., Jay Z, Naz, Haitian raps such Original rap staff, Masters, Master Dji, Top AdlerMan, King Possi, more, and other countries' raps. The majority of rap's lyrics are telling these kids to do the right things such as stay off the street, stay in school, educate them about the corruption in the justice system, other systems or agencies, countries, and in the democrat and republican political parties. Besides, if the education these kids have received were solid and strong, hip, hop would not have any influence or effect on them at all. Instead of these school officials decreasing their tuitions and developing modern methods teaching to reach out to these children and gang members, they cast them out of the society, as these kids choose this violent life that they are living, and see the fault in them; and leave them up to the biased justice officials and police officers to improve and rehabilitate them.

One free lesson to those who call themselves sociologists, criminal psychologists, and criminology experts: executions and prisons were never created to deter crimes in the first place. The ancient kings created prisons and executions to punish brave peasants who spoke out against them, or tried to overthrow their regimes. Therefore, not developing something of their own will continue to waste more taxpayers' money and innocents' lives. By supporting locking up disadvantaged children, or citizens, they are not helping the situations and this country at all; in fact, they are aggravating the situations even more. For example, by incarcerating prostitutes, drug addicts, petty thieves and petty drug dealers, without teaching them how to make an honest living or sending them where they can find treatment for their drug addictions or problems, these social science experts might as well use the taxpayers' money to buy bananas to throw at the monkeys in a zoo. Because by merely locking these people without giving them the sort of philosophy classes and education on how to do constructive things for themselves and their countries, these kids and citizens have to turn out to be vicious to their fellow inmates and the society upon their releases. Not because they want too, but because these untrained professionals led them psychologically to be in such a way and have such attitudes. For instance, when a petty criminal goes to jail or prison, which is a vicious violent environment, most likely, they are forever lost to their families, communities, and countries, because they would have to become vicious to the other inmates, and hurt other citizens when they return in the society. For example, while they are in the prison bus, they are thinking that they have to be vicious in the prison in order to survive and to be respected in it; therefore, as soon as they arrive, they have to hurt other inmates badly to send a vicious psychological message to the other inmates, so they will have to stay away from them. In fact, the more viciously and brutally they hurt the other inmates, the more power, control, fear, and respect they gain from the other inmates and correction officers, and more invitations they receive in the other gangs in jails. If they refuse to viciously hurt other inmates, they will be hurt and victimized themselves, or the other inmates will use them to do their dirty jobs for them, such as to hurt, stab, and kill other inmates and correction officers.

So, by refusing to teach these students to develop their minds so they would become productive citizens for themselves, their families, communities, and this country, they would develop their intelligence, mind, and techniques in another way, which is to run illegal activities in their communities, jails, or prisons anyway, because they have to support and feed themselves and their families. These social science professionals blame the inmates for becoming repeat offenders while they have received no constructive training and philosophy classes to give them the mental discipline to become law abiding citizens, to make an honest living, and to conduct themselves in the society and their communities. At the end, these kids are becoming the products that these school officials and social science experts turn them out to be. By denying or restricting blacks, Asians, the poor whites, Hispanics, and others from quality education, they will become this country's liability and the citizens' nightmares instead of great assets for their communities and this country. Due to the incompetence of school officials and social experts, the crimes, the inmates, and the welfare system rate have to keep increasing, not because these people are born criminals, lazy, or love to stay on welfare, and breaking the law as an occupation, but because the school officials refuse to modernize the school system so they can reach out to all citizens, regardless of their races, communities, and their social status, so the world can stop sinking lower and lower.

Furthermore, many social science professionals have stated that child molesters possess, or have, or suffer a sort of "mental defect". First, this thing does not exist; second, since these social science professionals cannot find the treatment and remedy for such behaviors from the ancient philosophers' books, therefore, they cannot cure or treat them; since they cannot cure or treat them, they say that these people suffer a sort of "mental defect." No one can say for certain if a group of people with a certain behavior and attitude suffer a sort of "mental defect," because in order to see if a mental defect truly exists, they have to examine all citizens, even those who do not act in such a way, which is nearly impossible to do. The social science professionals have to see that child molesters became problems or against the laws in the modern time; in the ancient time, many kings or officials used to marry children or had sex with minors; in fact, the slave master use to rape children for punishment of their parents. Furthermore, many polygamist leaders have been married to children in this country and many have been arrested or are about to be. Moreover, many countries still allow such behaviors or attitudes, since in old times such a behavior or attitude was acceptable and lawful, but now it is not. Therefore, they have to modernize their approaches to deal with this problem as it is. For instance, these social science professionals have to develop modern treatments, and remedies for people who have interest or are attracted to kids to come get treatment. In fact, the social science experts have to welcome them, make them feel as if is fine to have such feelings, because many people used to have them in the past and it was acceptable to. But it is a modern time; such behavior is unacceptable and against the law, therefore they have to come get treatment as long as they feel they have interest or are attracted to children. Also, they are welcome to remain to get treatment as long as they think they need and the urgency of such behavior has disappeared. If they feel this urge or sensation is gone and they want to leave, they are free to do so. However, if they feel the feeling is coming back, they have to come back to get more developed treatment. Their names would remain confidential and they would not be penalized in any sort of way for coming forwards, but if they go and abuse any children, they would get the maximum time, and their names would be posted everywhere. By welcoming these people to come get treatment and remedy for their behavior problems, and their names remaining confidential and letting them not be penalized, they would come for treatment, because they do not want lose their privacies, freedom, families and more; if they knew there were places they could go to get treatment when the feeling starts generating, then they would not have to go act it out on innocent children. But by only locking them up, not too much has been accomplished, because they are just taking a break from the outside world, and the urge for children will certainly keep increasing. And as soon they got released, they will go do the same things, because the urge is too strong for them to control; but by treating them they would be able to control themselves towards children.

Many of these social science experts are not measuring to the standard of the modern world; they wrongly label or cast anything they do not understand while many people, communities, and countries are going down in the mud. They do not find solutions and remedies for our social and economics problems, not because they are not smart, or competent, but because they would rather imitate and follow instead of being creative and original. Therefore, they seem not to know anything more about the present situations and nothing additional to what the old philosophers have written. Since the old philosophers gave no attention to blacks, the females, the masses, homosexuals, Asians, Hispanics, and the poor countries native background, they seem that they cannot surpass the ancient philosophers cleverness to find remedies and solutions for these lowly people, communities and countries, and the rest of the world that are sinking lower and lower in the crime, racism, poverty, illiteracy, war, economic, and highly fatal disease spheres. Since they cannot find the solution to better these people, their families, communities, and countries, they place the fault at these people's doorsteps, or they label the whole community, race, gender, and country as incompetent and inferior. But the fact is such things do not exist among human races and genders at all, because any race can do what another one can, either gender can do what the other one can, any community can do what another can, any country can do and achieve what another can, and no one is better, smarter, or worse than another. Unfortunately, nearly all citizens believe otherwise, because those narrow-minded and biased school officials have followed and taught us what others had done centuries ago. Therefore, we as the modern people end up believing inferiority and superiority exist between us, our communities, countries, races, genders, and sexual orientations. They continue to spend most of their time to mislead and misinform other races, genders, communities, this country, and other countries about their inferiority and other silly criteria while the deficit, crime rate, and other inefficiencies are increasing significantly in this country and around the world. Due to the loss of vision of the modern, smart and skillful people are unwilling to go forwards, because their minds are controlled by these oppressors. The lowly feel, why should they embarrass themselves to try to produce for themselves, their communities, countries, and the rest of the world, or why should they be friends with one another for the common good. Since negativity has been drilled into their minds by these so-called best experts and scholars, they assume that they are going to be laughed at and fail anyway. If these schools officials were serving all citizens, they would have taken the goods from what they have found in these ancient books, and use them to work out a better program and school system for all citizens in this country and around the world; not for a certain race, gender, social class or country. They would understand the people whom they are serving and the countries that they are dealing with more, and they would certainly become real experts in solving vexing problems in all communities and countries. These people would be better educators and school officials if they taught the disadvantaged children, citizens, and countries' natives to devote most of their time to harmony with one another, and to the development of themselves, their communities, and their countries, rather than cramming their minds with extraneous matters from the old social science writers, which have no bearing on the racism, discrimination, war, high cost living, and social and economic problems which lie before them in the modern world.

Very few quality and caring school officials exist in the modern time, therefore, undesirable conditions have to exist in the modern world; the majority of the influential and prominent professors and scholars have trained their bright students as their missionaries to do the same thing to humanity as before, such as oppressing, exploiting, and restricting the weak people, races, gender, communities and countries. Since the majority of the prominent school officials are biased, selfish, and corrupt, the official positions cannot be opened for honest people, school officials and leaders who are artistic, imaginative, creative, and inventive; those who have interests and desires to develop minds only, instead of their pockets, gender, race, and social class; those who truly love all children, all communities, all races, all religions, and all countries. Unfortunately, the prominent positions open merely for people who have connections, came from a certain social class, school, race, gender, and sexual orientation, since the school system is controlled largely by certain narrow-minded people, practically all incompetent, self-centered, and biased, and the exploited people who have been barred from other powerful and influential positions of their states, this country, and the rest of the world by lack of connections or intelligence or economics are overcrowded into the school system for the oppression, restriction, and control of certain races, genders, social classes, communities, and countries' natives. The fact is, the most powerful and influential school system positions are filled up with such officials; the great caring, loving, creative teachers and professors who can change this country, the entire world, and humanity are powerless, and have to remain quiet; otherwise, their positions would be revoked. By having the school systems filled up with such officials, no better jobs can be done for the disadvantaged children, communities, states, this country, the poor countries, and the rest of the world. Many honest people, including President George W. Bush, who are trying to better this country socially and economically by reinforcing the policy that "no child should be left behind," have found their task too difficult and impossible to succeed and achieve. Unfortunately for the masses, the weak people, homosexuals, weak communities, and poor countries, those who are in charge of the school system have no interest, intelligence, and no vision to develop and assist them in any sort of way; in fact, they already dismiss and restrict them to a nonentity's status. Even if those school officials say otherwise, they already have strict regulations to prevent people who have different mindsets, or from different races, genders, schools, or communities to establish any new better policies, while the wrong mindset, bias, exploiters and narrow-minded are them. Those school officials are fully aware that Hispanics, homosexuals, blacks, Asians, the others found themselves, their communities, and their countries deprived of influence in the professional sphere, and held down to the lowest order of the society. Not because they are mindless or natural born imbeciles, but merely due their economic and social circumstances; but they never tried to become creative for once or try to develop a new program to prepare these bright children and citizens adequately to participate in the professional sphere or better the circumstances their communities and countries found themselves in. These school officials know that education is the most important thing for the uplifting of the poor communities and in the poor countries. But they continue to manipulate the whole educational system so these young Americans can end up only in the poor quality schools, since they end up there, they will always enable to find the way out of these undesirable difficulties. Most of these school officials have thoroughly demonstrated that they do not care and have no sympathy or interest to better these kids and those citizens' lives, communities, and countries. If they modernized the schools in the cities to be as efficient as those in the rural and the suburbs, this country and this world would definitely go forward and the light which they have been looking for since beginning of time would be found. These school officials are not only incompetent, biased, racist, and self-centered, they are also true cowards as well, because they are only doing this thing to the underprivileged children, weak races, communities, and countries' natives that cannot fight back against them. If these narrow-minded and biased school officials were going to do something good for these lowly children, these communities, and these countries, they would have produced men and women qualified to lead and develop them by now. Most of the narrow-minded school officials and Ivy League officials control all the school administrations to raise money only for their institutions, and nothing for the poor quality schools officials who do not have contacts. Clearly, this depicts that they are extremely self-centered, and they do not have an interest in uplifting the disadvantaged Americans who are left behind, are they not? And refusing to touch the masses, the poor communities and the poor countries, also shows no promising future, indeed. If these professors were willing to work with the school officials, citizens and leaders of poor communities, it would certainly be possible to achieve business improvement and public welfare. Again, by them refusing to intervene, the masses have to get wider, and the immigrations problems have to increase drastically. Frankly, all these social and economic problems are rapidly widening because the leading world experts have lost the vision of the modern world. All citizens, communities, and countries' natives can be great assets for their communities, genders, races, religions, countries and this world, only under harmony, and under honest leadership of all intelligent leaders in it.

The large majority of educators today are still doing nothing for these disadvantaged children, citizens, and countries, except to keep making them respect and envy the upper class. They have abandoned the people, communities, and countries that need them the most. These people could have attended schools in preparation for college, but narrow-minded school officials do not see them as future leaders and assets because of their skin color, social class status, religion, gender, sexual orientation, or country of origin. Since they are not regarded as future leaders, schools do not endeavor to educate and train them as such. With the world's backs turned on them, these neglected children turn to unproductive lives of smoking marijuana, drinking alcohol, selling drugs, having sex, prostituting themselves, and killing each other; since they cannot be good, they have to turn out terrible. Most of these people's futures have been predetermined largely by what these narrow-minded and biased school officials make left them out to be.

The disadvantaged continue trending lower and lower in the social and economic spheres because most of these school officials are simply narrow-minded imitators. They have learned from the biased and oppressive writers who used to oppress and exploit the weak for their wealth and power. Instead teaching these people how to make an honest living and be happy, the educators teach them how to specialize in begging and criminal behavior. Educators are supposed to be sympathetic, understanding, kind, caring, sensitive, considerate, selfless, noble, helpful, gentle, responsive, and thoughtful people. Unfortunately, most educators exhibit none of these qualities to the disadvantaged; in fact, they are colder and harsher with them. As intellectuals, educators are more corrupt, biased, and selfish than the average men in the street; they form their own groups of biased, narrow-minded, self-centered, and dishonorable people who call themselves conservatives. In a way, they are conservatives, like the old biased and ignorant oppressors. In fact, most of the corrupt and shameful things they have done are not for the greater good; otherwise, they would be acclaimed heroes. But they have done these things purely for self-interest, to feed their egos, or to please other narrow-minded people. Perhaps their morality and principles are borrowed from their predecessors, because they have not done their jobs any better, and they certainly have not raised their standards any higher than the oppressors and exploiters of the past. The disadvantaged are screaming for help, but the experts do not help them uplift their communities for the common good. Instead they return from visiting poor communities and decry and belittle them to their families, students, and colleagues. Why would any genuine person do this after seeing that their fellow citizens are suffering and dying? What good are their Ph.Ds, MBAs and other degrees if they cannot provide a solution for these disadvantaged people and their fatal social and economic problems? The higher their degree, the more selfish, self-centered, and egotistic they turn out to be toward other humans.

Ancient civilizations would kill each other in the name of money, but people die and money remains; where are the old civilizations now, and where are their countries? Exploiters and oppressors have no heart or compassion for the weak and humanity in general. And most of their students have turned out the same way due to the lack of quality education. Many leaders that could be great, are instead the products of these narrow-minded and biased people. Far too many get their education, and social science knowledge from these imitators who have lost vision of the modern world and humanity; and who certainly confuse education with exploitation, oppression, and enslaving minds. The disadvantaged are still wondering why they are always the victims. The answer is simple: these narrow-minded and incompetent professors or school officials who are in charge still refuse to modernize the school system, and they are not bright enough to overcome the teachings of the old ignorant oppressors.

Another reason that poor communities are not uplifted socially and economically is because religious leaders refuse to create conducive programs for the people they are trying to serve and lead. In fact, most of these church leaders are connected to their communities solely for personal gains and political reasons. Many church leaders are not the great assets they should have been because they refuse to modernize theological teaching methods to reeducate disadvantaged children and citizens. As with leaders in many other areas, prominent religious leaders use religion as a tool to exploit and segregate the people among themselves, instead of enlightening them to love and respect one another and Christianity. Since most of these leaders do not live up to the religious faith that they profess, they cannot help the unprivileged and undeveloped people who see themselves as enemies of each other. Instead of the church leaders developing modern theology methods to guide the disadvantaged towards a better path, they brainwash them and try to control the world and one another. These prominent religious leaders have misinterpreted and manipulated the literature of nearly all religions in order to exploit, demean, exterminate, and segregate, and mislead the people instead of creating modern programs for them to respect each other's gender, sexual orientation, race, religious beliefs, their communities and their countries. For instance, prominent Catholic leaders have trained their people to say "God save the king," while Henry VIII strayed from

Catholicism due to his lust for women.

Most religions were founded by unprincipled men interested only in exploiting and segregating their people. Today, churches crowd into poor countries or communities like neighborhood liquor stores. The relationships between Jews, Muslims, Methodists, Catholics, Baptists, Muslims, Islam, Judaism, Jehovah's Witnesses, and others are deteriorating because their leaders are more interested in money collection, world power, wealth, and charity than harmony, peace, faith and preaching their religion. If these leaders were in harmony with one another, they would respect one another's religious beliefs; therefore, they would need fewer ministers, fewer preachers and fewer supervisory officials, and would be united for the greater good. If they were united with each other, they could understand each other's religions and attitudes better as well the real purpose of their religion. They would not need a hundred churches in each state or millions around the world. They could use each other's people and houses of worship for their services and ceremonies, and they would have more time and money to establish productive and practical programs for people in need instead of having to specialize in "amen, hallelujah, sexism, war, racism, violence, and hatred." These religions do not need millions of churches or bishops, because they are all teaching the same faith and belief. Theology professors believe that their religious leaders need their own bishops or churches because they are imitating and duplicating the beliefs and works of the founders of each religion, who thought they needed have their own bibles, literature, beliefs, and establishments. Theology professors fail to realize that they are causing a major schism around the world by misinterpreting the psychology and philosophy of Christianity; this failure will always harm people and cripple the world. By misinterpreting the religion, they continue to lead the citizens of the world into disagreement, and kept these disputes unresolved; this will cause Christians to divide and to harm each other. Christian agencies divide people, which leads to tension; people can never improve and uplift the world as brothers and sisters, because they cannot tolerate the differences between denominations and accept them for what they are. Unfortunately, the disadvantaged have to suffer and pay for the consequences of the thoughts, systems, and beliefs of ignorant despotic men, due to this lack of knowledge and loss of vision of the modern world.

Religion was supposed to be an institution for well-educated, wise, loving, caring, and peaceful people to gather together. Unfortunately, the churches are controlled and populated mostly by child molesters, adulterers, addicts (sex, porn, alcohol and drugs), and selfish, biased, narrow-minded and exploitative people. Most of these people have not and cannot influence any other societal systems. Since they have a lack of finance and education to ease and comfort their lusts, they use religion as a tool to provide them with what they cannot get elsewhere. The church leaders have many opportunities and freedom to provide poor communities with what they really need in order to develop. But sadly, they choose to do the contrary, by exploiting, oppressing, and segregating their people. Instead of professors educating and training religious leaders to be better leaders and to create better programs for the masses, they still use the same centuries-old teaching theories to mislead and poorly train their people. They also still allow theology professors and scholars, who can barely understand and develop a better doctrine of their own, to be in charge of the course of modern religion. As a result, today's theological professors are doing the same thing as before: teaching their students that religion is just religion, nothing more or less, and teaching them the dogma of their religion as a means to an end. Prominent religious men are supposed to oppose war, racism, sexism, terrorism, segregation, and lynching, but they turn a blind eye to these things or even help them to continue. Before any country goes to war, a chaplain comes to bless the soldiers who are about to go kill or be killed, instead of rationalizing and stopping both sides from attacking and killing each other. Today, these leaders are mainly making what is wrong to seem to be what is right. Instead of developing modern theology or religious systems to come together as Christians to improve the situation of poor communities, these leaders follow their predecessors and abuse, mistreat, exploit, and divide their people. And by imitating their predecessors, they are keeping the poor communities too weak and confused to overcome the social, disunion, hatred, and economic problems that characterizes them.

Instead of prominent church leaders in the wealthier communities joining those in the poorer communities for their general welfare, they only intensify the social and economic divide. As a result, religious leaders and their people end up lacking harmony and respect for each other; therefore, they cannot take orders from each other. And if they cannot work together, they can never properly serve and enlighten their people. The church leaders do not even realize that they are the ones who are still encouraging hatred and division among the people that they were supposed to enlighten spiritually. The people of a particular religion only love, respect, admire, tolerate, and listen to other people or leaders from their religion. If a preacher has an problem with another church leader, the people of that church would end up resenting and distancing themselves from the people of the other church. Religious leaders with such attitudes should never have become preachers in the first place, and do not preach in the spirit of Christ. Moreover, if the church down the street closes their doors due to financial reasons, the other pastor or preacher would be happy because his donations and influence would increase, even though many people are left without spiritual leadership. The theology professors or prominent churchmen who train leaders to have such attitudes are crippling them, this country, and the rest of the world instead of bringing us to the light of salvation. If all prominent churchmen tried to bring all people and church leaders together, they would find resentment, hatred, racism and discrimination among them. But as long as they refuse to do this great task, we are all but lost.

Furthermore, religious leaders can not even find among themselves a small percentage of people qualified to run, lead, and serve the weak, because most of them are propagating biased and worn-out theories that narrow-minded oppressors created in the past. But it is not altogether the fault of the church leaders that there is a lack of services for the poor; it is due mostly to the system or organizations to which they belong, and to the type of Christian education and training they have received. Many are sincere and honest people; they went to theological school to obtain a quality education and training. They got their diplomas, certificates, and licenses, but most of them are inefficient at reaching and serving the confused and the weak because many have never received any other education to make a decent living, and theology schools or religious training never taught them the true philosophy of Christianity. Thus, they are not well educated in the first place, and are practically poor, but they expect to make a decent living while preaching; the only possible outcome of this lack of training, education and vision is inefficiency. Because these church leaders have not been properly taught how to help and work with one another and how to reach the masses, all they know is to memorize psalms, phrases, or scripture references, all of which mean nothing to those who are looking for direction. The majority of the lessons and speeches people hear about polytheism, monotheism, and the doctrine of the Trinity are practically useless to them in the modern world, because the only thing that can be derived from it is the devotion of one's life to dead languages and millennia-old events. Most of the philosophical and biblical beliefs behind theology are the dogmas, domination, and multiple wars of ancient white kings against peasants and weak countries. And the masses they attend are not worth studying either, since they do not know people and situations discussed, so the sermons have no effect on uplifting people or the world in general.

When students go off to theological school, their minds end up full of unnecessary trivia rather than useful lessons about people, love, and true peace with one another. When these graduates return to their communities, they cannot understand their own people anymore, and as a result cannot serve them or reach out to them. This means that these people can ultimately not be reached r elevated; they end up having little interest in church, and eventually stop attending. When the preacher or the pastor or the priest stops seeing these people and their children at church, the church leader lays the fault at their doorsteps for not coming. But how can these people be willing to come to church while the theologians have not developed any modern program or study to reach out to them? Church leaders open their door five days a week or even more, including multiple Sunday services. But at the same time, they could open up their churches three days a week for mass and use the other two days for service to poor communities. They could unite and condense the entire Methodist church, Catholic church and other churches in a united establishment and decrease the amount of preachers, pastors, and supervisory officials drastically. They could ask the educated people in their churches to teach the illiterate how to read and write well it. Furthermore, they could establish after-school programs in their churches and assign bishops to help the disadvantaged and underprivileged children with their homework, tutor them, and give them direction in life. They could provide lessons about their civil rights and their constitutions so they would know when the government is violating them. They could teach the adults who are forever lost in society to regain their dignity and their rights, how to make an honest living, and how to become assets for their families and communities instead of being liabilities. This would give them mental discipline and direction so they would be able to love, help, respect, tolerate others' opinions, and be happy instead of resenting, despising and killing each other.

Many youths are leaving churches nowadays because what they find there is not strong enough to hold their interest; there is no doubt that what the church leaders are preaching has no bearing upon the lives they are living. Many youths in church end up getting pregnant, quitting school, smoking, drinking, on welfare and in the criminal system; the youths simply end up souring on life. An influx of youth in the church could make for great leaders and provide great assets for the modern world; in fact, many of the world's greatest leaders were God's servants, such as Dr. Martin Luther King, Malcolm X, Carter G. Woodson, Gandhi, and Nelson Mandela.

The principal reason why modern youths in the church are out of control is because their leaders fail in their responsibilities to organize modern programs or good teaching methods to reach out to these children who are spiraling into the world of crime and poverty. Due to this neglect, the churches are forever shrinking; if they do not enhance their programs and their approach, as many churches will close doors in the future as have done so already. The only youthful attraction in the modern church is the band, but what about youths who have in interests in catering, technology, industrial work, social sciences, medicine, art, and others? Many great singers in the world have found themselves in church such as Whitney Houston, Michael Jackson, Stevie Wonder, Wyclef Jean, Jacques Sauveur Jean, Joseph Dieudonne Larose, "Missile 727," and many others. Perhaps if the church had other youth programs, they would produce great leaders in other aspects as well. By neglecting to refine and modernize their theology programs for the modern world, the church fails millions of youths in offering motivation to do anything for themselves and their communities. These youths who could advance far in professional and leadership fields are instead sinking lower and lower for two reasons: first, theology professors have not updated and advanced their studies and thoughts for the modern world; and second, theology professors and the prominent churchmen have lost vision of the modern world.

Loss of vision of the modern world is a new sort of epidemic in communities around the world; unfortunately, by allowing those who have lost vision of the modern world to teach today's youths, many of their students become unproductive and unsuccessful citizens. These churches are led by people who do not understand the modern "talented tenth," but they think they are going to find good sermons or speeches in the ancient books and Bible. Excellent preachers would take the good from the old books and build on it; they would be much better examples to the youths and others. They would devote most of their time to outreach to the people that they are trying to serve instead of thinking how to extract money from them and filling their minds with extraneous matters that have no bearing on the situations they face. By not updating and modernizing the theology methods, churches are filled with incompetent, vicious, and narrow-minded leaders who have been shut out of other careers because of prejudice, lack of education, lack of connection, and the economy. Many rush into religion and churches for political reasons, to become communicants in name only, and to exploit and divide a certain social class, to retaliate against another person, or slander another group's or country's leaders or natives. The bar is low to enter the ministry; regardless of a person's education level, beliefs, and their contributions to others, nearly anyone can enter. Many pastors and preachers have stated that they have a certain restriction and requirement, but this is that they only allow people with the same mindset as them to fulfill the prominent positions in church.

In fact, most of the lessons of the church to the modern "talented tenth" are precepts and examples written by biased and narrow-minded white males. Most of the present narrow-minded and biased people do not fully understand the old Christian spirit, psychology and philosophy, and cannot hope to understand the new ones. While the youths are taught to specialize in "praise the Lord and hallelujah," they are also learning to hate other races, ethnicities, nationalities and religions. These narrow-minded and biased church leaders, who have lost touch with the modern world, seem to forget that everybody is equal in front of God. These churchmen consider themselves principled men because they hold a Bible and can memorize a few psalms. But they have so much more hatred for others in society than the average person. The modern world is still as confused with irrationalities and absurdities as they were in ancient times, because the current church leaders are merely followers of the old ones, and cannot overcome the performance of the religious leaders to truly serve the world. Everything that modern religious leaders are teaching their people is not new; they have borrowed from the previous oppressors, who in turn borrowed their ideas of hatred and killing from the ancient unprincipled philosophers and kings. These leaders are teaching the modern "talented tenth" to hate, despise, and destroy each other and humanity, instead of loving, caring, and rebuilding their country and the rest of the world together as brothers and sisters. These biased churchmen are passing their sins, vices, and corruption to these bright children, meaning the future children can never see salvation. These poor communities have mostly seen and learned betrayal, deception, hatred, extermination, and perfidy from their religious leaders. When these powerful and influential leaders go to poor communities, they are more interested in gambling, expensive restaurants, drinking liquors, illicit and underage sex instead of bringing their people something new. It is sad indeed; the majority of children and people in the modern world learn to hate, despise, harm and kill from the Bible or their religious leaders. These leaders were supposed to teach humanity, harmony, morality and peace, how to worship and connect to each other, and protect humanity and the world.

The trend that medical school officials and professors take towards disadvantaged patients who need medical attention in the modern world is despicable and inhumane. In ancient times, peasants who practiced medicine were quite sincere. Their aims were to serve and treat all who were sick or medical attention. Their mission was to enlighten and treat the sick, and to develop medicine as a science to help their fellow citizens. But these people had more enthusiasm than actual medical knowledge; the majority of them did not fully understand the treatments and diseases before them. When they saw that their fellow citizens in their villages were ill, their approaches were more towards remedying the symptoms of the injury, wound, or disease; they had no interest and were not well enough informed to categorize and treat the disease or affliction itself. But they paid little attention to the sick person's social status, background, race, gender, sexual orientation, and their origin; their main goal was to simply treat their afflictions, to provide and do the best they could for the ill citizens or children. They paid more attention to the malady itself, less attention to a person's background, and practically no attention to factors such as compensation, for these people simply to develop and practice medicine for the common good. Unfortunately, these people and their heart, aspirations, and vision, are far removed from the study of medicine at the present. They had no interest in using medicine as a tool to kill, exploit, and dominate the sick. These great creators and inventors are uniformly eliminated from medical teachings or any other type of science; these great originators and visionaries did not take the MCAT, did not have a GPA, a Ph.D, an MD, or any other type of expertise in the field of medicine. But they had enough enthusiasm, passion, and concern for the people of their villages, to use the little knowledge they had about science to serve them efficiently, and to create treatments using natural resources. In the early advancement in the medicine field, these people invented poisons for hunting and blended plants and other objects for pain relief or to cure diseases. It is shameful and sad that these great creators and visionaries who were supposed to be inspirations for the modern medical and nursing students are mostly forgotten or omitted, while modern school officials forcing their bright students to learn from ignorant oppressors who use medical science as a tool to exploit and suffocate the weak and disadvantaged.

Most powerful and influential medical school officials and professors are not sincere, honest, or helpful. They have shifted the purpose of medicine from providing, serving, helping, and treating the ill to exploiting and exterminating them. They educate and train their medical students to only serve and the insurance and pharmaceutical industries, the upper class, their institutions, and the wealthiest countries. They are also trained despise and disregard the disadvantaged and the poor who are dying due to lack of quality medical knowledge and training. These lowly people are studied in medical schools only as problems, and viewed as a heavy load for the world. Students are taught to see these deaths as salvation to humanity. Instead of school officials using tax money wisely to teach disadvantaged communities how to confront and cure AIDS, HIV, and other deadly viruses, they misuse it to finance research for their institutions and pharmaceutical companies. Many medical students and young physicians know how to treat and cure many sick children and deadly viruses, but for lack of money, they refuse to help and educate the patients that need it the most. They turn their backs to the millions of sick children and adults who are dying on a daily basis, because they were educated in a system that dismisses minorities and the disadvantaged as less than human.

These medical students are taught and trained almost exclusively to treat, help, and serve the white middle and upper classes of the wealthiest countries, and in such a way as to despise helping, serving, treating, and educating poor communities and the lower social classes. At nearly all schools, these disadvantaged groups are studied only as problems, but not to be solved. Many medical books and classes guide these medical students to only work for the benefit of the white upper classes, insurance companies and pharmaceutical companies, and to dismiss the weak and disadvantaged even as they are dying in large numbers. The thought of becoming rich and serving only one group is drilled into their minds in almost every class and every book they study and read. Then by the time these students go take their medical state test, their attention is set more on the riches they will earn, instead of the great services they will render to the sick. As a result of this biased education system, the majority of physicians come out worthless as far as treating minorities and the disadvantaged. If these schools' officials were doing their jobs instead of filling their students' minds with trifles, modern physicians could offer something new to these people and their communities, teach them how care for and treat themselves medically. These physicians could develop modern ways to educate others about medicine, and would invest in their own pharmaceutical companies so that drugs and treatment would be extremely affordable. In fact, precious few physicians become constructive forces in the development of poor communities. Since underprivileged people are dying by the second simply due to lack of medical skills, this makes many medical school officials and professors seem to emerge as imitators of Adolph Hitler, who thought he was doing the world a favor by killing millions of Jewish children and citizens. These professors and school officials also believe that they are doing the world a great favor by letting the weak die on a daily basis. This sort of teaching method in the modern world constitutes a vicious crime, not against the underprivileged, but against humanity. It is shameful that the powerful and influential activists around the world have not risen up against this injustice. This is even more important than the antiwar crusade, since in the last ten years more people have died due to deadly viruses and lack of medical attention than by war.

No medical providers should have the right to let a group of people suffer and die simply because of their economic and social status.

Medical school officials that are more concerned about tuition, GPAs, and MCAT scores than about human lives, should have been removed from their positions because they are not serving this country and the rest of the world. The attention paid to money and statistics is not going to solve the medical weakness and injustice that the world is facing today. They seem to be even more useless in the modern world than ever before, because do not solve any medical problems, nor do they lower medical costs or provide decent medical coverage to all. People from third-world countries are still living longer and healthier than Americans, while we have the best medical schools in the world and spend trillions on medical treatment and research. Many of these schools' officials seem to have no interest in dealing with medical matters and the injustices that confront the underprivileged, because most of what these professors have taught their students is only applied to the white elite classes, the pharmaceutical and insurance industries, and the wealthiest countries. Otherwise, the medical insurance companies would not have such fancy and expensive buildings and the best experts on their side, while the average people cannot see a doctor or medical provider, or have a decent and affordable medical clinic in their communities. In fact, in medical schools, minorities are denounced as inferior while being reminded of their roles as carriers of deadly viruses. Many claim that AIDS and HIV came from the black, Hispanic and homosexual communities of Haiti, Jamaica, Africa, and other Latin countries, but many of the whites who have these viruses never had contact with these people. The main reason for this prevalence of these viruses among the disadvantaged is their economic and social status, and their lack of quality medical education and training. The only time when these so-called world physicians and experts place emphasis upon or develop a cure for a disease is when it threatens white people. All the narrow-minded and biased professors wrongly blame the underprivileged for everything that is wrong with the world, while they are the true cause of these problems.

Since what is true about medicine and other types of science has been distorted by so-called experts ever since they were created by the ancient peasants, the approach of medical providers is crippling humanity, instead of bettering and enhancing it. As a result, clinics and hospitals only serve the rich minority of the population, and those who need medical attention in other communities are dying because they receive extremely inadequate treatment in comparison. And the narrow-minded and selfish physicians who label themselves as experts hold their studies and findings back in order to sell them to the wealthiest pharmaceutical companies or treat and help the rich. Modern medical students have been misled as to the psychology and philosophy of other races and social classes by their own professors and school officials; their teachers justify the extermination of other races, genders, sexual orientations, communities, and countries as a salvation to the world, so the majority of graduates of such schools have no better mission for these sick people. When these young physicians learn of places where diseases and viruses are epidemic, they do not help or even suggest helping them. They simply let these ill people suffer and die while untrained and unqualified local doctors are doing the best they can to keep these sick people alive for any length of time, or at least ease their pain before they die. Another result of these medical students training so exclusively in the psychology of medicine is that they bypass the opportunity to start their own small community clinics, or to make house calls to patients without medical coverage or who cannot afford hospital treatment. Also bypassed are the medical students and young physician who try to become as visionary as the ancients by developing their own medicines and treatment with natural resources. The selfish and narrow-minded people who call themselves businessmen bribe politicians to prohibit the sale of these medications among the poor communities, because they are interested only in using their clinics and hospitals to overcharge for medical bills and put their patients into lifelong debt, ensuring a constant cash flow. Many pharmaceutical companies grow richer in this way while not even giving anything back to these communities, let alone better quality hospitals so the sick do not have to wait for hours just for medical attention or even pain relief, or, establish college funds for students who have interest in pursuing medical or scientific careers.

Unfortunately, once medical students from poor communities have completed their requirements in medical schools, they have been equipped mostly to serve the white upper classes and the wealthiest European countries, not their countries of origin or the those in extreme need of medical attention. Before they take their final exams, their professors persuade them to work for major hospitals, clinics, and pharmaceutical companies, and to demand bigger salaries, bonuses and benefits. The underprivileged people that these students had intended to serve, have been so belittled and criticized so much by their professors, that students no longer have interest in serving them medically. These medical students consider their professors to be noble and distinguished, and thus end up imitating them. The education they have received continues to lead to failure for this country and the rest of the world because they have been led to believe it is impossible to help the truly hopeless, which is contrary to the development of medicine through the ages.

By changing the true purpose and the essence of medicine, tomorrow's medical students are doomed to be as sour as today's; they will handle the sick with dishonesty and corruption. Instead of teaching and educating their students to help those who are suffering because of illness, lack of medical attention, or lack of training, these narrow-minded physicians instead blame the disadvantaged for their own problems. These medical professionals are educated and knowledgeable in medicine and science; they must know that the fault lays at the hands of medical professors and officials for refusing to train and educate these people. An equal amount of fault lays with pharmaceutical CEOs, for refusing to cut the price of their medications. Since these narrow-minded professors and medical providers receive large sums of money, big bonuses, stock options and memberships in country clubs from these companies, they are afraid to attack them, for fear of losing their reward and their inner-circle access. So they turn upon the disadvantaged, who are simply doing the best they can to cope and live day to day, all the while believing that they are the most sincere and distinguished people on this planet, helping humanity because they have a high GPA, a good score on the MCAT, make six or seven figures a year, and have many diplomas on their walls. These professionals fail to realize that they are not doing any better a job for humanity than convicted murderers, since they are the ones responsible for many deaths by taking curative drugs away from the sick and dying. These people should never have been accepted in medical schools in the first place because they are not helping the ill and certainly not helping humanity; they are killing them. If a robber is guilty of murder because a security officer shot a bystander while trying to prevent a robbery, these doctors and businessmen should be guilty of people's deaths, and their injustices against humanity. The robber may not have pull the trigger himself, but his actions, and those of the doctors, have led innocent people to suffer and die. One may have an advanced degree while the other has a handgun or knife, but neither is helping to improve mankind.

The selfish and narrow-minded medical professors and school officials do not want to teach other social classes how to flourish; in some respects they are right. For if the disadvantaged and underprivileged were to become influential, they would be able to treat and help people from their own communities and countries medically; these institutions and professors would end up losing their contributions and big bonuses. Many of them publish articles and books in the American Medical Association, but a rare few of them find fault with their peers, colleagues, and the pharmaceutical companies; they carefully word their arguments and findings in a way to concede that they are sincere and helping humanity. Why should they have interest in helping humanity? They live in million-dollar mansions, get free stocks from these pharmaceutical companies, they get invited to fancy corporate parties, and receive college funds for their children. Many professors and school officials claim that they are not narrow-minded and biased; but if so, why are the underprivileged still dying from lack of medical aid or training? Many treatments and cures are on the market, but the medical system is manipulated to restrict access to them. How can Canada provide medical coverage for all their citizens, be they black, green, yellow, purple, immigrants, naturalized citizens, or citizens by birth? Why are we the richest country in the world, with the best medical schools and experts, but still lack medical providers and treatment for the poor, while Cuba, a small country facing a generation-long embargo, has a surfeit of medical professionals? How is it that over fifty million Americans lack medical coverage? Are they not Americans too? Why do we have to wait hours in an emergency room to see a physician? If medical professionals are not biased and racist, why is medical treatment plentiful in the suburbs and scarce in disadvantaged communities? We are supposedly equal in the Constitution, are we not?

Medical schools made it illegal for minorities to pursue a career in or study medicine in the past, but now these medical professionals refuse to accept the duties of their oath to treat everyone equally. These physicians emerge as educators and leaders while refusing to treat, help, serve, and educate children who are dying. As long as these school officials base acceptance to their schools on GPA, MCAT score, gender, race, and social class, we cannot expect anything better from our medical system. If this system were working, people would not have to file for bankruptcy, thousands of Americans would not go elsewhere for better and cheaper medical treatment, and millions of American children would not get substandard treatment for lack of medical coverage. Due to the lack of honest and quality reputable medical providers, many corporations cannot pay their employers well or expand their businesses. They have to pay exorbitantly for medical coverage and many times they almost file for bankruptcy because of it. The Ford Motor Company and GM both have to pay almost a trillion dollars a year for medical coverage for their employees, all while facing bankruptcy. Many of these professors do not realize that by continuing to offer inadequate medical education and prolonging the ineffective medical system of this country, millions of people have to suffer and die, millions of Americans fall into debt from medical bills, many employees have to survive without medical coverage, and millions of children and elderly have to suffer and die.

Moreover, many corporations have to deny employment to those who want to leave the criminal and the welfare system; they cannot expand their businesses because of the high medical costs associated with new employees. In the end, the country has to cripple and handicap itself further because it cannot advance; this country may be the wealthiest country in the world, but its people are economically strangulated.

The majority of people and corporations find themselves restricted and deprived by high medical costs; they cannot invest elsewhere or repay the debts they owe the government. The government, in turn, is paying trillions of dollars in coverage for children and the elderly but not recouping their debts. The medical system is one of the major components of any country; if it begins to falter, the whole country will suffer. The school system is manipulated such that underprivileged classes are unprepared to flourish. Medical treatment should not be hard to obtain, and the cost should be low; by clinging to an outdated medical system, we as humans are losing ground. Because all citizens need and depend on this system to live healthier and longer, it should not be regarded and treated as a luxury. If school officials were doing their jobs, everybody would have a basic knowledge of medicine; everybody should know how to cure a headache, a stomachache, deliver a baby, etc., because these tasks were common knowledge ages ago. Most of today's medical students learn about things that have no bearing on the modern world. Medical school officials accept only certain races, genders, social classes, GPA levels or MCAT scores, but they are still unable to turn out graduates who make a difference in the world. What is the point of doing all this, if millions of people are still suffering and dying in the modern world, just as they were a century ago? These professors and school officials make it hard to accept different races, genders, social classes, and sexual orientation in their schools, and their graduates still cannot sufficiently serve the sick. These students can better serve their country and humanity in general, but the medical education they have received has led them to think this is impossible to achieve. These professors and school officials proceed on the basis that the requirements to be admitted to medical school are important and effective; this thought process would be good if the medical system were working, or if treatment were inexpensive, or if they were finding effective treatments or cures for deadly viruses. But the medical problems in poor communities are getting worse while these narrow-minded physicians think only that driving an expensive car and having a nice office make them excellent physicians. They refuse to advance their medical knowledge for the greater good, and at the same time condition the common folk to admire and respect them, to believe that they are right, and to believe that there legitimate reasons to overcharge for medical treatment. Most of the world is dissatisfied with their medical system or services, but they refuse to stand up to these school officials, the modern Socrates. It is very clear that the medical education the students have received is not improving the society; it is no better than what it was a generation or more ago, and it has certainly not solved the medical problems it was expected to solve. Those that may claim otherwise, must have never have had any experience in an underprivileged communities, to see how many millions there are suffering and waiting to die, or leaving their loved ones behind merely due to the lack of quality medical education and training. Sadly, many of these sick people see death as a solution and relief to their pain and suffering even though they are leaving their loved ones behind.

Instead of these professors teaching the students the true purpose of medicine (so that their graduates have the passion and enthusiasm to help and enlighten the sick and the poor communities), they continue to teach the contrary. They teach them in such a way as to let their own people, communities, and countries suffer and die, and to use their expertise and knowledge to turn millionaires into billionaires. They teach these medical students that medicine is all about money, power, and wealth; what kind of Mercedes-Benz or Porsche to get after completing their medical schooling. By teaching them in such a way, these medical schools are not preparing and encouraging these students to go help, treat, and serve the greater good. The appeal of these professors and school officials is primarily to wealth, power, and economic and social status. How can we offer relief to those who are suffering and dying be relieved while medical students are concerned more with expensive cars, wealth, and power than saving lives or reducing medical costs. The lack of quality medical training and education reverts this country and the rest of the world back into more medical problems and injustice; no good can be expected from our young medical graduates when they were only trained to extract money from the suffering and dying children rather than treating, helping, and serving them. These doctors develop less and less interest in treating patients who are suffering and dying merely because they cannot afford the services.

The high cost of medical bills, however, is not altogether the fault of the physicians and nurses; it is also due to the medical schools overcharging students for tuition. Many doctors want to bring about medical reforms in poor communities, but financial support is not forthcoming—not from the inadequately supported school system, nor the communities, nor the politicians. The so-called American dream turns into a nightmare, because everything is about money in today's world.

Politicians, leaders, and businessmen get into business and the government to make money and to live a lavish life, never stopping to think about the future of their country. They create ill-conceived policies and laws to improve the country for their own children's benefit. They allow banks to become wealthy off college loans. The schools are more concerned with the high interest that they are going to make off these graduates with loans rather than making them assets for their community. If a community were to prepare these students adequately and finance their education, they would be much more productive for that community. Medical graduates would worry more about long-term employment than manipulating the medical system to overcharge patients so that they can pay their loans off sooner. Every study they participate in would be primarily to serve the interests of the communities that financed their education. They would resolve to fight the problems of high medical costs, and stand behind the community that financed their education. Furthermore, they would give the taxpayers what they want and need, becoming a constructive medical force against medical injustice and for the development of their communities. They would love their state for paying for their education and be willing to sacrifice for their taxpayers above all others. The medical problems, injustices and high costs could be dealt with, and they would be confronted not by doctors or physicians who try to profit from ill or dying children, but by passionate and caring medical providers who would have a mission to improve a community who helped them achieve their dreams and goals. They would only concentrate on the medical needs of their communities rather than pharmaceutical companies and other corporations. The trillions of dollars that states pay for medical bills for children, pregnant females, the elderly and other citizens would not have to be paid, because they would receive better treatment. These doctors would share their medical knowledge to make medications cheaper for the residents of their communities, and they would gladly train them to identify and treat medical problems that they find. They would not need or try to charge extra money to these people they love and respect; They would place the citizens and such a state above all; they would no longer think of themselves, they would think of the state and their patients, rather than their loans and interest. They would not even have to be concerned about higher salary elsewhere, or work for pharmaceutical companies, or get bonuses from them and dishonest attorneys, or be deceitful with the ill patients, because the thoughts of these things. They would develop medicines, which they could then sell at a small profit in other communities that did not invest in their education. The communities would have competition among them for advanced, quality, and inexpensive medicines or treatment. This would help the other communities facing undesirable medical conditions, and the world of medicine would be much better off for everyone. At the end everybody and other countries would love this great country's leadership, and they would do anything to keep protecting this nation's leadership. If a catastrophe were to befall us somehow, other countries would assist us, because they would see a great nation in trouble - not because we are Americans or this country is the most powerful country in the world, but because of our great leadership to them and to the world; they would do anything in their power to work with us as leaders. And instead of the medical injustice and disadvantages this nation had been facing, we would develop stability and the capacity for growth in this country, the world, and all of humanity.

Loss of Vision of the Modern World: Part III

Today's minorities have not influenced the professional sphere much, if at all, due to the lack of support from school officials, the government, and their perception by the modern world. Most research has been done by biased, racist, and narrow-minded scholars and researchers, who placed the world's faults at these oppressed people's doorsteps. In fact, they decry and belittle minorities for being socially and economically undeveloped while the same researchers and their ilk are actually oppressors. These people never used common sense or the little intelligence they have to see that these weak races and people have been barred from the professional world because of their skin color, gender, origin, ethnicity, or their social status. Too many systems, agencies, and institutions are controlled by a small percentage of white elite males, who manipulate them such that other social classes cannot ever benefit or flourish in the professional world. The numbers of minority physicians, attorneys, architects, pharmacists, politicians, dentists, and social science experts have not increased greatly because of their economic status and racism against them, in addition to the viewpoint, drilled into their minds at every turn, that they cannot succeed in the professional spheres. From pre-school through college and beyond, narrow-minded and biased schools officials have never given these disadvantaged people enough support so they can develop their minds enough to become influential or successful. These self-centered professors do not even know the true philosophy of their field, but they oppress other social classes to make themselves psychologically and economically dominant so that the disadvantaged perceive them as noble and aristocratic rather than the oppressors and imitators that they are. And by manipulating all the systems, agencies, and institutions in such a way, the oppressors discourage and frighten the disadvantaged away from these professional fields. Few have succeeded professionally, not nearly enough to remedy the injustices towards their social classes and communities. Nearly all underprivileged people need to study the civil rights in high school, so that they know when their civil rights have violated. They need this because civil rights violations occur daily, not only by biased and racist judges and police officers, but also by leaders as well. As a result, the same disadvantaged groups keep being victimized and restricted behind closed doors. In the past, it was illegal for certain social classes to attend law school. Things have not changed much in modern times, because those who need it the most are still psychologically and economically blocked from studying law and becoming part of the government. Inner-city school systems have been manipulated so that their students will not be prepared, and they made it impossible for people with a different skin color, social class, gender or religion to even be considered for or admitted to law school. As a result, these social groups make up the lowest social levels of the modern world. By restricting these people from knowing their own laws, these school officials are destroying and handicapping them and their communities. How can the weak protect themselves and their communities from biased politicians, corporations, and judges if they do not know their civil and political rights? One of the most important things these people need to know, is instead taken from them, and as a result they are not a part of one of the most important systems they need to be a part of. Law school officials might as well just reinstate the previous laws that barred minorities from law schools, because only a small percentage are still allowed to enter. These officials know that the main reason most minorities are barred from political offices, mistreated, wrongly profiled, and in put prisons, is due largely to racism, economic status, and their lack of education. These prominent and influential officials are fully aware that over ninety percent of these people are abused, mistreated, wrongly convicted, incarcerated, and confess to crimes that they did not commit, due to the fact they do not know their civil rights and cannot afford an attorney. Butt if these people are not able to learn and study law, as the oppressors have stated, why do so many of them study law in prison and have their cases overturned, retried, or dismissed because their civil and federal rights were violated?

Furthermore, minorities must know the law because they still cannot move freely even today. Many times they have been wrongly overcharged by banks, or pulled over by racist police officers. Most white attorneys do not care or have any interest in remedying the injustice towards these people and their communities. Many of these professors label themselves as law experts while millions of innocent people are in prison, or on death row. Corrupt and racist businessmen overcharge them simply because of their skin color. These people never experience real justice in this country. If these so-called scholars spent less time labeling themselves as geniuses, and more time educating their students about how to confront injustice in their communities, we would be living in a better world.

A few generations ago, African Americans were regarded as mindless. But Thurgood Marshall became an attorney who won many cases before the U.S. Supreme Court and changed the system to better this country, and

Johnny Cochran won high honors for being one of the best criminal and civil attorneys. Making any minority group feel inadequate is not helping them or this country; we can never move forward unless these social problems are resolved. When people in positions of power make these biased and ignorant comments, minorities believe them to true, because they perceive these people as noble and distinguished. These professors rely on worn-out theories, and biased data to prove that they have reason to oppress and restrict the weak. They have learned from other biased and confused teachers, who wrote books about "Logic," and "Ethics," all while oppressing, restricting, and dismissing their own minorities, and killing others. Instead of these law schools professors teaching minorities how to strengthen themselves and their communities, they spend most of their time teaching them how to cite cases, defend a flawed system, overcharge their clients, and accept that they can never succeed and become influential in law and politics.

This injustice continues to increase towards the same groups as before, but the law school officials refuse to modernize their teaching methods to prepare these students for such a task. They have drilled into their students' minds that their people belong in prison, and that their communities and countries belong where they are; they do not even try to improve them because better opportunities do not exist. How can they provide better opportunities and overcome this injustice if they have not been taught and trained properly how to do so? These people are out of legal circles because law school officials psychologically force them out. They teach their students to bring democracy and justice to other countries, something their own country lacks. It is an insult indeed to us as modern people, that of every twenty-five attorneys, one is black, one is Hispanic, one is homosexual, one is Middle Eastern, and one is Asian, while all others are Americans, with the same rights, abilities and minds. These untrained law school professors must not lecture and teach people and other countries about democracy and justice while their fellow Americans have never experienced them in their country; the only thing these oppressed people have always experienced since day one are torture, mistreatment, racism, and hypocrisy.

These social groups have not been dominant in certain fields, mainly because they are still oppressed and restricted from them; the "experts" keep teaching their students to manipulate the system so that these groups can never gain influence. These narrow-minded men copied this method from the ancient philosophers who used to oppress and restrict other social groups. It requires only adequate training and education to be a lawyer, but these biased and narrow-minded professors claim that the white upper class elite males dominate the field because they are smarter and brighter than others. A free lesson to them: an elite race does not exist; there are only two types of people: trained and untrained. Someone who has a certain talent or gift still needs discipline and direction to thrive and succeed; they may only need a little, but they still need it. Minorities have not prospered in law as much as upper class white males because the education they receive does not prepare and develop their minds for it. The only thing it prepares them for is disgrace and humiliation. Only a small percentage of minorities have achieved greatness in the legal field; meanwhile millions of them are killing each other, fighting wars, paying taxes, and simply being Americans. The non-segregated schools have taken sufficient time to train and prepare their students for college and graduate schools. The salvation for these minorities is to provide the same adequate education for them, and for any child to be able to go to any public school they wish too;

otherwise, they will only poverty, vicious criminals, immigration, racism, and inefficiency.

The surest way for the world to see and experience real justice and equality, is to retrain or replace incompetent and biased professors retrain with better and more open-minded people. The current legal teaching methods will always be a huge failure for plenty of reasons. Law school officials are mostly white males with a lack of vision and interest for most minorities. They are more concerned with a specific social class and wealth than the welfare of the country. Many are reluctant to offer a bright future for these social classes. Instead of supporting them, these officials repeatedly tell them that they have no future in law. And since the majority of people in this country are failing socially and economically, the country itself is failing from within. Instead of these professors living up the equality and democracy they profess, they allow biased laws like affirmative action to handicap the majority of people in this country. How can females, homosexuals, blacks, Asians, Middle Easterners, Hispanics, and others break through barriers, stop this ordeal, and live at the same level as the rest of America? If they are treated as unequal and inferior, they can never succeed and flourish in their own way, and if they do not succeed, Americans as a whole cannot succeed. After all, they are all Americans; the more successful they become, the richer and wealthier this country becomes; it does not matter who makes it because we are all Americans; oppression will always backfire on this country in the long run.

If upper class white males were judged and graded by what they accomplished, they would be the ones who would need controlling. By letting the oppressors control the system, this great country will waste away over the next few generations. How many incremental editions of a textbook can a law professor churn out without changing anything? Because these officials have lost vision of the modern world, they cannot see that minorities have no admiration or appreciation for their law texts or their foreign policies, because they cannot relate to them and they have no good purpose in the modern world. Furthermore, since these law school officials have lost vision of the modern world, they still believe that they are living in an era of power like the seventeenth and eighteenth centuries. They make it practically impossible for other races, genders, social classes, sexual orientations, and nationalities to better themselves, their communities, this country, and the rest of the world socially and economically.

In the past, biased and narrow-minded politicians criticized and ridiculed great politicians, including Congressman Oscar De Priest, for distributing copies of the U.S. Constitution to freemen, Hispanics, Italians, Irishmen and other European immigrants. These disadvantaged people and their children were prohibited from learning Thomas Jefferson's and James Madison's opinion that the U.S. government should derive its power of the governed from the consent of the people. Throughout history, politicians have killed bills that would have given the underprivileged more knowledge of civil rights, political rights, and their Constitution. They were opposed to these bills because if the disadvantaged had studied the U.S. Constitution and other legal documents, they would have fought for their civil rights. So, by keeping these lowly people in the dark, they would not know when their rights—guaranteed under the Declaration of Independence or the U.S. Constitution—had been violated. How could these disadvantaged people and children pay any attention to such matters; why should they not trust the people who took an oath to enlighten and protect them, and their rights? Why should they assume that their leaders were manipulating the system to continue oppressing them? Quite simply, to keep minorities and the underprivileged where they would never develop. By oppressing, restricting and denying these people their natural rights, they would be forced to live in the lowest levels of society

Instead of creating laws to help the underprivileged and their communities, law professors teach and educate their students to regard the people that they were about to serve and protect as inferiors, opponents, enemies, and outcasts. They created or sponsored bills to restrict, oppress, exploit, and control the disadvantaged, and created a biased foreign policy to exploit and oppress other countries instead of developing them. By controlling a large number of people and systems, they do not have to worry about them ever flourishing. By treating and making these people feel inadequate, incompetent, and inferior, they will not even attempt to get ahead in the world, because they are already convinced of and accept their inferiority, ineptitude, and incompetence. As a result of this brainwashing, members these groups do not even attempt to get into politics, because they are convinced they do not belong there. At the same time, they have developed a sort of fatal dependency on upper class white males to improve their situations. And poor countries have developed the same fatal dependency on this country and others to improve their own. But the things that are happening today are not new; they are merely history repeating itself. If all political science and law professors continue to use their books to mislead and misinform their students, it will always bring this country backward, instead of forward. Many of these biased and incompetent writers simply rewrote past events in their attempt to become great politicians, thinkers, and heroes. But they are as biased and racist as their predecessors, because they copy people who banned females, Irishmen,

Italians and blacks from owning property, influencing the professional world, and voting. Many of the politicians, leaders, and writers that modern scholars have copied, wrote that they respected Asians, but they imprisoned thousands of them after the attack on Pearl Harbor, and said that it was a huge mistake to let these people free and to treat them as citizens. In the modern world, these fanatics continue to manipulate the systems so that minorities and immigrants always feel inadequate, unequal, and remain part of the lowest order of the world.

Instead of preparing their future leaders to respect all people, and to work together for the greater good, these professors keep teaching the same shopworn theories; the same approach and faith still exist even in the modern world. Today's minorities have still never experienced equality and justice; "justice for all" applies only to the elite, not the majority. These professors refuse to embrace the modern world; they keep teaching from the same biased point of view as their predecessors instead of teaching them to direct their attentions to the problems of today. The old and biased methods prevent the world from ever being taught about true democracy. Otherwise, these biases, racism, discrimination, oppressions, restrictions, and exploitations would vanish, and this country would be able to take turn for the better. For these concepts to disappear, professors have to do their part by refining and modernizing their teaching methods; they must teach nothing but the truth. When the truth comes out, citizens and future politicians can build on it to make the world greater for generations to come. By simply teaching that all races, genders, social classes, religions, and countries are getting along well, or that we are on the path to improvement, is not enough. It worsens our problems, endangers us as people and discredits our teachers as first-world citizens.

In order for the underprivileged to resolve the

hate and racism in today's world, political science and law professors must update their programs and bring all social groups together to serve the people. They must be more than professors and lecturers; they must be leaders and philosophers. They have to modernize their teaching approaches and methods first; many may refuse, but for the interest of this country and of the world they have to train their students to treat all citizens equally. If they only teach world leaders to create laws that benefit a certain social group, the results will be nothing but failure. There is no way this country and the world can go forward if only social group is prospering. Our leaders have to see the world as a great and expensive car with a flat tire; since the car has a flat tire, it cannot be driven, no matter how strong and great the car is. If the owner tries to drive it without fixing the flat tire, he is only doing more damage to the car. The owner has one duty: repair the flat tire so he can enjoy the car again. The same theory goes for the rest of the world: all citizens must work together for the benefit of this country. And for the world to run smoothly, leaders and citizens alike must respect and help one another's territories. Teaching these bright students to oppress, restrict, and exploit the weak people, communities, races, genders, and countries will only further cripple and destroy this country and the world.

People have never really experienced and sensed true democracy; many great leaders who were trying to speak up have been assassinated, such as John F. Kennedy, Martin Luther King, Abraham Lincoln. In modern times, people with different religious beliefs, sexual orientations, races, genders, and origins have been frightened to discuss political matters publicly, despite having the same rights as everybody else. Many people who try to speak out against unfit politicians have been labeled as troublemakers and terrorists. School officials have taught their students to oppress and restrict people who speak out against the injustice that they are facing on a daily basis, rather than teaching these future leaders to listen and fix their problems. As a result, the majority of citizens in this country end up accepting silence on these matters as a fixed policy, and those who refuse to be silenced end up watched by the federal agencies or have their civil and federal rights violated.

Many biased reporters and leaders have said that many Americans and foreigners do not like this country because they destroy and terrorize their cities; they burn the American flag when they are fed up with injustice and see that their voices cannot be heard. They do like this country, but they do not like the leaders of this great nation. When black people destroy grocery stores in their communities over twenty to thirty percent price increases, the so-called leaders do nothing; the conservative reporters convey nothing good to the public either. Blacks and other minorities should not be blamed for the social problems in this country, because the political system—as all other systems—has only ever served one side. Our so-called leaders have offered no remedy whatsoever. Police brutality and racism occur on a daily basis; many biased politicians working with corporations to keep blacks and other minorities in the mud. Why else would only black and minority communities be teeming with liquor stores and guns, but have poor education systems? Why did it take FEMA three days to start rescuing blacks that were dying in New Orleans after Katrina? Blacks are not still considered property in the modern world, are they? Senator Hillary Clinton was right: the House of Representatives runs black communities like plantations. These disadvantaged people end up taking matters into their own hands, because these narrow-minded and biased school officials have continued to teach and train their students to deceive the people who have voted and elected them into public office, instead of serving them efficiently.

At the same time, these professors do not realize that teaching their students to only serve and protect one social class will jeopardize world peace and lead to social problems, because other social groups that have been intentionally neglected, oppressed, or exploited will develop to retaliate against their oppressors. Since the oppressors do not live among them, innocent people will end up victimized, because the retaliators destroy the peace by any means necessary: destroying properties, communities, lives and the country itself. As a result, this great nation will never be able to thrive because their professors have lost the vision of the modern world. The conservative media have labeled them as terrorists rather than working with them to solve the national nightmare. These law school officials could have taught their students to listen to the citizens, have a great relationship with them, and to serve and live among them. Instead, they teach their students to dismiss them and see them as inferior troublemakers. How can national and world leaders love and serve all communities when they have been taught to do the contrary? When a large number of Americans criticize the administration and burn the U.S. flag, such remarks and behaviors should not be dismissed or taken lightly at all; if we dismiss these problems instead of fixing them, it will continue to cripple and handicap this country rather than the people who are making money off these dreadful situations. In fact, why should the upper class complain; they are making huge profits even though the deficit is getting worse every day; as far as they are concerned, everything is going well because they are getting richer every day. The only time the rich complain is when they are paying taxes; many of them place their businesses before the country's best interests. These narrow-minded school officials have never taught how to serve and uplift, but instead how to oppress, restrict, and exploit the weak. Rather than teaching their students how work together for peace and to respect other nations, they teach them to sweet-talk business leaders for contributions, and to extract votes and trust from the lowly and oppressed people while leaving them to face the injustice and ordeals that they have been facing since the beginning of time.

Due to the unspoken restrictions and bans on minority groups from political office, the members of these groups end up with no interest in state or national politics. Since political officials have kept the teaching system the same way, also keeping the political system the same, U.S. Congress and other political offices are still overcrowded with biased, sexist, corrupt, and imbecilic white upper-class men. The decent, well-qualified men and women who could change and better their communities, have been overlooked as part of the political sphere. These sincere people have distanced themselves from politics, not because they could not do better than those in office, but because the so-called law experts and political analysts continue to teach and train their students to restrict and oppress them. These people grow up without knowledge of the political matters that affect their lives, their communities, and this country in every aspect. It does not require a Ph.D to understand politics; otherwise, most of today's politicians would never have entered politics the first place. They have taught and trained their students to misinform and mis-educate the underprivileged, to keep them where they cannot observe or participate in the affairs of bureaucracy, government, and foreign policy. And as a result, many men and women who could fix the world's problems, instead continue to distance themselves from politics.

But if these school officials taught and educated their students to welcome and support the underprivileged instead of restricting and oppressing them, the world would be a better place. Since the disadvantaged believe that the political system is biased and corrupt, they do not even bother to vote; many times large numbers minorities simply do not vote. The largest numbers of voters are middle and upper class, heterosexual, Catholic, or Baptist. Not because these people are the only ones with the right to vote, nor because they love this country more than other social groups, but merely because the laws and the politicians protect their interests, businesses, and their communities instead of the whole country's interest. Therefore, this country remains where it was in the eighteenth and nineteenth century: minority communities are still overcrowded with guns/drugs/liquor stores, while they do not even make these products. The minorities would not be harassed, killed or wrongly jailed by racist police officers government officials on a daily basis, and the laws would not continue to mean one thing in the white community and a different thing in another community. What do those so-called modern politicians and leaders do to fix the situation? Life in prison or death row, and the same segregated school systems. What do these politicians and leaders do to these dreadful corporations? Give them huge tax breaks and more immunities so they can escape liability for pain and suffering in minority communities. Hillary Clinton was absolutely right in saying that the House of Representatives runs these communities like plantations. These politicians spend more time fighting among themselves, protecting the interests of corporations and their political party, rather than serving, protecting, and leading this great country under the oath they took.

These school officials and professors do not even try to encourage and stimulate their students to develop equality for all citizens. They teach and train their graduates to oppress and restrict the underprivileged to the lowest levels of this country and the world, and to dismiss them as they did a hundred years ago. When these weak people ask their leaders for the tools they need to uplift themselves and their communities, such as quality education and economic support from the government, they get mere lip service. There is no money or support. The institutions that turn out these leaders keep receiving trillions of dollars from taxpayers for the same worthless research and worn-out theories, and all the while they are making six figures for doing next to nothing. It is sad indeed; the hardworking inner-city teachers, firemen, and others have to strike and protest to receive fair salaries for their hard work. Future world leaders cannot get the things they need in order for themselves and this country to get ahead, such as quality updated books, computers, and other resources, to convert this American nightmare to a real American dream. Their great parents have worked and spilled their blood for this great country, but these so-called law experts and political analysts train their graduates to reject them.

The majority of these laws that students learn to honor and protect are the ones that are holding us back. Such beliefs, attitudes, and knowledge of politics are antiquated, because other social classes are not benefiting from them. These professors must know that this country is out of control because it was created as a one-sided system since day one, and such a system cannot work in the modern world. When this country was founded, only English and German men had rights, not females, Italians, Irish, Jews, Asians, Native Indians, and certainly not blacks. But this is the 21st century; everybody must be treated equally and given the same rights so they can contribute to the world. Teachers must modernize and update their teaching methods to deal with a multilateral system, whether they want to or not. By teaching their graduates to deprive the disadvantaged of their freedoms and privileges, they will lose interest in accomplishing great things and contributing to this country, and the social and economic debasements will only get worse. America is a luxury car missing its tires; it has no chance to move towards success, not because the owners do not possess the intelligence to learn how to repair it, but because the mechanics refuse to teach the owners how to do so. If professors asked every citizen the names of their state senators, the number of members of Congress, and how well they know and the people who are serving them know them, most would know practically nothing except that they are a bunch of corrupt white males. They would know nothing about their local and state governments. Since it is difficult to find minority groups that benefit from the system and wish to contribute to it, it is difficult for the country to move forward as well. Law school officials are failing this country by refusing to prepare and teach their students to better the systems for all, to teach all citizens about how the government and its members function. Most minorities lack knowledge about these public servants; when they encounter them for the first time, they are usually in for bad experiences such as tribunals of injustice, vote fixing, and property repossession due to unpaid taxes. Since these poor citizens are not taught about the assessment of taxes in their communities, and in this country, and they do not learn how their tax dollars are used for improvement, many ignore their duty to pay taxes, because they see that the social and the injustice problems still remain in their communities. Firemen, policemen and teachers cannot get a decent salary for a reason, and the elderly who have worked all their lives cannot even get their pensions or quality medical coverage.

These school officials do not even realize how

unfortunate it is to eliminate or cast out homosexuals, females, blacks, Hispanics, Middle Easterners and others from politics and other governmental systems. Because the majority of people who control the system are from small social circles and specific institutions, they have not been trained to strive for the interests of this country and all of its citizens. They have been trained only to benefit their own race, gender, and social class. Politicians have shown little generosity to other social classes, not because they are insincere, but because they have been trained to be that way. How do these narrow-minded and biased school officials expect others to contribute and succeed if they teach their students to oppress, exploit, and restrict the underprivileged? In order for these groups to stay above homelessness and crimes, they need positive, conducive systems, programs, and quality education to stimulate them. As long as the educational system and other systems are what they are today, we cannot expect to rise up above poverty, homelessness, and crimes. Unfortunately, nearly all the systems in this country and around the world are corrupt, simply due to the fact that many leaders were trained to be that way. As a result of all this corruption, the load is too heavy and inefficient to go forward. Because the country and the rest of the world has no chance to uplift themselves, and the professors who are getting paid to find remedies and solutions refuse to make any effort to modernize their teaching methods, the future leaders will be inadequately prepared and trained to restore equality, peace and justice to the world.

Politicians and leaders can also not serve the people because they have been trained to take contributions from corporations. Since the wealthiest people and corporate CEOs are the ones who can support these politicians financially, they bribe them to manipulate the system to put their interests above the rest of the country. The politicians pay more attention to their corporate donors, such as granting tax cuts, while the average workers pay far too much in taxes. The wealthiest corporations have the most powerful and influential politicians on their sides, and we as the people are left out with nearly none. As soon as a corporation gets large enough, the CEO wants the most powerful politicians on their payrolls. This method of political teaching can never serve the non-elite sufficiently, because most people cannot afford the most influential politicians, who are not supposed to be for sale in the first place. These politicians are supposed to protect and serve the entire country. As a result of this inadequate system of politics and teaching, the laws that were intended to serve all people are deterring them instead. The people that these systems are serving are the small percentage of white elite males and their corporations. How can these politicians be great patriotic leaders and public servants when they have been taught and trained exclusively to support, serve, and protect the interests of one group? This political system is a source of destruction and damage to this country and other countries in the modern world, and the teaching methods that lead to it must be seen as something that cripples this nation and the world.

These school officials refuse to develop a modernized system; the majority of presidents of leading institutions of the world fall into this trap. These people who were supposed to support and encourage the underprivileged to pursue and be influential in their chosen professional spheres, especially politics, are doing otherwise. These professors know that many of their students are not helping the underprivileged, but instead using them for their campaigns and rounding up their votes. After they have won the campaign, they ignore their constituents and eventually abandon them for good. Or, when they make up their personnel administration, they carefully chose one or a couple minorities for their staff, only to treat the underprivileged with the same contempt as their predecessors. These narrow-minded and biased professors and school officials have seen that these weak people and communities have been abused and humiliated for centuries, but they still refuse to train and these disadvantaged people to turn them into reputable leaders and create a new system to uplift them. It is sad indeed, when these disadvantaged groups see token members as part of the administration; they become complacent with only one person representing their group. These people do not realize that the administration would not choose any of them at random; the person that they chose to be a part of their staff has to have a negative attitude towards his or her own group. In order for that person to rise to their position, he or she has to restrict her or himself in all social and political matters concerning his or her status. Before that person can serve his or her race, gender, sexual orientation, and community, he has to serve the administration or the party's interest first; not the country's or the people's interest. And for that person to be a great a staff member or an American, he or she must, above all things, be a good homosexual, black, Hispanic, female, Middle Easterner, or Asian, or other first, and then that person must learn to stay in his or her place. For example, Dr. Condoleezza Rice remains powerless when her race or community needs her; she despises and distances herself from her own race, heritage, culture, and community, and intentionally lies to the American people constantly merely for her political party's interest.

The professors had many chances to educate and train their graduates to enlighten the weak people, communities and countries' natives about political knowledge to empower themselves, and to become influential in the modern world. But they chose not to because they want the weak races, genders, and those of other sexual orientations to always be controlled, oppressed, restricted, and to feel as inferior as ever. By keeping them in the lower order in society, it makes it impossible for them to become self-dependant and self-sufficient. Therefore, they have to stay out of the most powerful and influential positions in this country and around the world.

Another injustice these law and political science professors and school officials taught their students is to regard and dismiss minorities and adults in the inner cities as gangsters, corrupt people, and troublemakers, merely because of the way they dress, act, and carry themselves. In the meantime, the real corrupt people in their communities, in this country, and around the world are their former students, whom they have equipped to continue to manipulate and corrupt nearly all the systems, the agencies, and institutions so the disadvantaged people in this country, poor countries, and the rest of the world can continue to go backwards.

Again, the main reason different races, genders, religious practices, social classes, homosexuals and other countries' natives are in the lowest order of society—and are regarded as enemies, opponents, inferiors, and terrorists in their own country and the rest of the world— is because these school officials have trained, taught, and equipped their students to keep oppressing and using them as a means to an end. Unfortunately, these people, communities, and countries' natives are still seen and considered in the modern world as inferior and incompetent, while these biased and narrow-minded professors still teach their students to place them in the position to feel and act in such a way. When a few oppressed people, communities, and other countries' natives try to make noise and scandal about the injustice towards them and their lands, they end up being crushed by their own kind, which have been bribed by the oppressors. In order words, the oppressors carefully pick a few people from the oppressed group or land to defend the biased and corrupt system, and tell them that the faults are at their doorstep. For example, if they worked hard, they would be dominant in these spheres as well. The sellouts do not realize they are playing a part in the destruction of their people, race, gender, community, and countries. They recruit different races, nationalities, sexual orientations, and social classes to assure and guarantee votes and other support from their communities and countries for their campaign and administration—not because they want to recruit these people, but just for political gains. It is unfortunate and sad that these professors do not realize that they are crippling and handicapping their and our own countries and world due to the lack of vision of the modern world and common sense. History shows that when the political strength of a country or world is only present on one side, the country always ends up failing and crashing eventually. These professors must know that the small percentage of white male upper class cannot solve all the problems and better this country and the rest of world by themselves. Therefore, relying on and teaching only a small percentage will always result in failure for us as people, this nation, and the rest of the world, especially when their agendas for the campaign are based entirely on empty promises, their party and their pockets' interest. By misleading and misinforming these bright students from learning the accurate psychology and philosophy of politics and foreign policy, they always end up restricting and oppressing great thinkers and countries that could be great assets. The old political system will never work in modern time because many of the ancient leaders had a lack of vision, intelligence, and had no interest in their own people, countries, and humanity. Again, that is the main reason they lost their ruling positions in the ancient world; the fact that modern scholars and professors are teaching us the same things as before—such as giving all attention to power and wealth, and none to this country, all other countries, and humanity—will make history eventually repeat itself. Teaching our present and future leaders the same old method will always jeopardize our nation's leadership of the world because they will keep ignoring the weighty problems of the world.

Gain of Vision of the Modern World

In order for us to see the light that we have been looking for since day one, the school system has to prepare and train students and the rest of the citizens adequately to battle against these odds in our society, our country, and the rest of our world. Students and adult citizens can no longer be trained and educated to be followers, oppressors, and exploiters like those before them: they have to be trained to be leaders, and to develop their minds in a way to see the impossible things as possible to achieve. Everybody has a clear conception of what they want for themselves and their lands. And the only way for them to achieve that is to have respect and to work together in order to drift towards an idealistic world. We have been taught and educated as people to lack foresight in the modern world. The education that we have received as people was supposed to better the relationship among ourselves, lead us down a better path, and give us excellent direction and structure so we can rejoice as a human race in the modern world. Unfortunately, a large part of the education we have received turns us as people into a perfect device to oppress, restrict, and destroy each other, our countries, and our world. And those school officials who continue to be satisfied by such an educational system should be immediately removed and demoted from their positions because they would continue to teach us to cripple and handicap our country and our world even more.

In the modern world, we as people have prolonged struggles among ourselves, our country, and the rest of the world. All of us as people and citizens in the modern world find ourselves inconsequential regardless of our different races, sexual orientations, social classes, and ethnicities. None of us as people can find a piece of land, country, or continent that we can settle on to be truly happy and safe, and live abundantly. Each country or continent has a malfunction or breakdown in some way—either too much poverty, disease, crimes, war, destruction, segregation, hatred, racism, sexism, or oppression. In the end, we are the ones who are doing it to ourselves. We are the ones that are destroying and deterring our own lands, world, and humanity as a whole. Again, the world belongs to the citizens or the people that live on it, not to blacks, Asians, Hispanics, whites, females, yellows, greens, purples, homosexuals, Middle Easterners, nor to any other country or continent either. However, in order for us to settle on one side of the world to live happily, and be comfortable and safe, the leader of each country and the world has to be trained adequately on how to do their parts first. For example, a family that was trained to have great parental leadership would always keep flourishing no matter what happened in the family. They would always get through crises because that family has a strong family leadership, harmony, and love. The children from that family do not have to be told to go to school, join the family at the table for dinner, do their homework, go to college, and not become criminals because the leadership the children have received already teaches them and prepares them that way. The leadership that the kids would receive would lead them to do the right thing without being told to do so. However, if the parents did not have great parental leadership, the kids would not do any of these things. In fact, they would do completely the opposite. They would disrespect their parents, not be connected to them, not care too much about them, assault them, steal from them, be vagabonds, terrorize their neighbors, classmates, and others. They would probably start drinking, smoking, and getting pregnant at an early age, come home late at night or not come home at all, end up in jail, prison, or even on death row. If any unfortunate things happened to their parents, they would probably be happier because they would end up inheriting their properties, life insurance money, or other things. These children that could be great children and assets, and make their parents proud would end up hurting, shaming, and disgracing themselves and their parents, not because they are bad, or were born to be bad, but merely because the parents did not have a great leadership to give the kids excellent structure and guidance. Instead of the parents modernizing their parenting methods and approaches to reach out to their lovely and helpless children, they turn around and place the blame upon them, disrespect them, decry and abuse their children physically, psychologically, and verbally. The only things these kids were desperately looking for and needed from their parents were great love, guidance, and parental leadership. As a result, this family would be handicapped and crippled for life; even if they were wealthy, educated, and from the best schools. The problems for this family would keep getting worse because these kids would end up doing the same things to their children. So the next generation would keep doing the same thing; in the end, it would be just a fatal cycle for that family.

Unfortunately, we as people cannot live happily on our lands because the world educators and professors do not develop any modern system to reach out to all the citizens and countries, so we as people can live happily and comfortably in the modern world. These professors and school officials are not born narrow-minded, biased, greedy, selfish, racist, and sexist; they just followed the same cycle that has existed since ancient times. Therefore, they end up doing the same thing that the others were doing; they do not even realize that they handicapped and crippled themselves, their own country, and their own world forever. As a result of following these unprincipled people, the same immigration, war, social, economic, sexism, racism, and other problems still exist in the modern world. In fact, they will get worse and worse. All these problems—such as economic, social, high cost of living, medical, hatred, racism, sexism, and war—have to get worse, not because we are incompetent and unintelligent as modern people, but because we have not gained vision of the modern world. Therefore, we as modern citizens and philosophers have to gain a vision of the modern world so that we will be able to deal with these problems as they are.

In the modern world, we as citizens must not be content and accept many things as a way of life. We as modern people and citizens have to stop using these expired and worn-out theories that were created thousands or hundreds of years ago to separate and distance us as people from each other, and to make us hate one another for no reason. As modern people and educators, we have to change them and improve them for future generations. These professors and school officials have to modify their teaching methods and their approaches to teach us as citizens and leaders of this country and the world to treat the citizens and leaders of all nations as we want to be treated, equally and fairly, because we as modern people and leaders cannot be biased or sexist, or despise one another based on what others have said since the beginning of time. We as modern people have to look for social and economic equality for all citizens in this country and around the world. Since everybody in this world has a mind, and can be taught and learn to do for themselves, their communities, and their countries, modern professors and experts have to develop modern teaching methods to prepare them for such a task. The leader of the world, which is this country, has to work for the interest of the citizens of this country and the citizens of the rest of the world. And the world's leaders have to treat all citizens and leaders of other countries equally, and not be allied with any country in the world. because a great leader cannot be biased and partisan. Leading the world in such way jeopardizes our leadership of the world, indeed. Therefore, a leader should not deem anything that relates to other communities, races, sexual orientations, genders, social classes, religions, and countries as a matter of indifference to them. When any race, sexual orientation, gender, community, and country has a problem with another community or country, the leader must step in to be impartial, unbiased, and fair to both sides, and have them settle the matter among themselves peacefully, so that no race or religion or country would get ready or prepare for destruction, war, or so-called terrorist acts. This country and the world leaders must listen to their problems, and deal with them as they are. They must have the matter between countries televised so world citizens can be the third party. If the people are the third party, they can see who and what caused the conflict. If the countries' leaders are not happy with the outcome, they should be able to appeal the matter to a higher court. Again, the founders of this nation said that the government should derive from the people. The leaders are the people; before any organization and corporation are satisfied with the ruling, the people have to be satisfied first. History shows when the majority of people in a country or the world are not satisfied with a result, progress cannot be made. Therefore, if the majority of people are not content with the result, a new system has to develop until they become satisfied with it. If they ask for the government's leaders in the office to be replaced, such a request has to be followed up and granted because the people's interest has to come first. By refusing it, nothing good can ever come out, except more damages to them, us as their leaders, and humanity.

We have way better and wiser educators and philosophers in the modern time than the ancient time. Therefore, they have to be more creative, better visionaries, smarter, and brighter educators and professors to surpass the ideology and intelligence of those before them in order to help the world to advance. Without attaching to and working with one another, modern innocent children and we as adults have to be biased, prejudiced, sexist, racist, and harsh towards one another and life itself. By studying, following, and imitating the old biased and racist philosophers and leaders, we as modern people will never be able come together as brothers and sisters, or to work for the general welfare of all. We are all brothers and sisters, and together we must learn to do what is best for our country, world, and humanity. To continue to teach students in the modern world to be divided and distanced from one another and humanity will continue to tie us to more consanguinity and destruction. As modern professors and educators we cannot let war, poverty, racism, sexism, disease, and economic debasement keep increasing. We have to develop modern teaching methods to confront these things so they can start flourishing as they are supposed to. If prominent school officials and leaders refuse to do such a task, they have to be frank as educators and leaders with the people in this country and around the world. They should step down as genuine leaders to let people who can turn the impossible into the possible step forward. Frankly, it should not matter which race, gender, social class, creed, and sexual orientation gets the job done for the people; the only thing that should matter is that the job gets done. As great leaders and educators, we should not continue to let our children, elderly, and other citizens keep suffering from the same war, poverty, oppression, disease, racism, and discrimination due mainly our egos and selfish purposes—it is not an ego contest. We as modern educators should not have more interest in our pockets being heavier, while in our country and the rest of our world deficit, debt, crime, war, terrorist acts, fatal diseases, poverty, and illiteracy rates keep increasing drastically.

The professors and school officials have to modify the school system so every American in this country is treated like and feels like an American, and has the same rights and privileges. And to teach and train foreign policy officials and diplomats to respect, treat, and protect all other countries' citizens and leaders in the world in the same way. All races, religious leaders or servants, genders, sexual orientations, and social classes have been victimized in the modern world in some way. All of us, or our ancestors, have shed blood or died or worked for this country in some way. Therefore, all of us must benefit from this country as any other Americans. If the world were to end from nuclear war, all countries' citizens would be victimized and be at a huge loss. Therefore, a new system has to be developed for each country's natives to live on their piece of land peacefully and abundantly. We as educators and citizens of this leading nation have to formulate a well-thought out program to deal with war, immigration, high-cost of living in this country, and other social problems and economic problems as they are, and we must work until these problems are resolved. These problems are not going to disappear on their own. We as educators, modern philosophers, and citizens have to modernize our ways of thinking, so these problems can go away for the next generation to rejoice in a better nation and world. Everybody in this country and around the world has to be trained adequately to stand and to battle these odds in their countries and in the rest of the world. The fact is that all the different races in this country abandon their communities to settle in the white communities and live abundantly, which shows how much we have lost vision of the modern world. What the whites have done for their communities, they can do for their communities as well. The fact that the majority of citizens around the world want to immigrate to this country for a better life is even more sickening and threatening to this country. The citizens of poor lowly communities have not really failed; neither have the citizens of poor countries. These oppressed and helpless people have failed in the modern world because prominent school officials and lawmakers have failed them. Since these leaders have followed the educational system and other systems that were created to only serve a certain race, gender, sexual orientation, country, and continent, these humble people have no choice but to fail in the modern world. The modern professors and educators have to know such social and economic debasement problems exist because they have used an education which was created to oppress and exploit blacks, Hispanics, Asians, Middle Easterners, and others. The bottom line is that these systems were not working then, and are not working now. If we do not modernize them, the same failures will continue to get worse for future generations. In order for this country to bloom economically and socially, all races, genders, sexual orientations, social classes, and poor countries in the world have to do well first. Therefore, trying and forcing this country to succeed without them will always cause more damage to it. For example, if you have a car with a flat tire, and instead of fixing it you install a T.V, nice shiny rims, and nice leather seats, the car would certainly look nicer, but it doesn't mean the car would drive. Not only that, but forcing the car to drive without fixing the flat tire would cause more damage to the car. By not trying to modify the teaching method so we as people in this country and around the world work as a team, sorry to say, the damage to this country will have to get worse. Crime rates, welfare, and the number inmates in prisons have to keep increasing, and the deficit in this country will have to keep increasing as well. By not developing modern foreign policies to help poor countries to get back on their feet socially and economically, and to create a world peace movement among all countries around the world, immigration, terrorism, and other international social and economic problems will continue to get worse. No matter how much money we spend on homeland security or other resources, in the long run this country would be the one that would end up paying the heavy price as the world's former rulers.

The modern political science and law school officials have to modernize their teaching system to teach students who will become the leaders of this nation and the world to be better leaders than our modern leaders; for them to develop a great relationship with all the citizens in this country and around the world, regardless of their sexual orientation, gender, social class, religion, customs, language, and culture. In order for the leaders to serve the rest of the races and countries efficiently, they have to know them; have friendly and mutual dialogue with one another. Face it, these races, religions, genders, sexual orientations, and countries can never be served adequately and appreciated by world leaders if their direction and interests are aimed at one race, gender, social class, country, and continent only. In order for these people, communities, races, religions, and countries' citizens to be comfortable with their leaders, they have to have a great relationship with them first, and their leaders have to respect and look out for their interests as well. A special holiday has to be created for the world leader and all other countries' leaders around the world; mainly to get together, enjoy each other's company, culture, music, food, beverages, and other things. By creating such a holiday, they would know each other more, and respect and enjoy each other's company more. For example, in any great successful company, there is a special day for all the employees, including the CEOs and VPs, to enjoy each other's company and to celebrate the success of the company together. A better relationship among the people means a better environment and more success for the company. Likewise, a better relationship among the world and its leaders means a better world environment and more success for each country in the world. Modern students have to learn that great leaders should not hate, isolate, and oppress each other; they should work together to serve the people and the world well. Future leaders cannot be taught to accept segregation, division, hatred, and more as ways of life because these sorts of beliefs, faiths, and conceptions are what is killing us in the modern world. The professors have to train and educate our future bright leaders to find the ultimate solution to these problems at hand, and the only way the problems in this country and the world can be solved is by teaching them to really embrace, respect, and work with each other as brothers and sisters and for true democracy. We as modern people have been accustomed to all these social and economic problems and these injustices, because the present school officials have never really educated us how to better these undesirable conditions. In fact, school officials have never taught us as people how to really overcome immigration, war, poverty, terrorism, racism, sexism, segregation, hatred, and economic and medical problems; the only thing they have taught us as people to do is to accept them as final and just.

Again, our bright children have to be trained to rethink life and humanity well. Afterwards, each country around the world would be able to see their predecessors' dreams come true. They have to teach to have these bright citizens turn the impossible into the possible so all these hatred, war, poverty, high cost of living, immigration, sexism, bias, and racism problems that still exist in the modern world merely on false tradition and worn-out theory can be trounced. Asians, blacks, whites, Hispanics, Middle Easterners, homosexuals, lower class, and others refuse to work with and help one another based on the false traditions and worn-out theories that they have learned from one another. Due to loss of vision of the modern world, such as the stereotypes that Middle Easterners are terrorists, blacks are lazy, Jewish people greedy, Italians are gangsters, the poor countries' natives are inferior, homosexuals, Haitians, and the Africans are inferior and germ carriers. In the modern world, children are supposed to be taught to appreciate, respect, and work with one another because in order for each country in the world to stop fighting one another and sinking lower and lower in the nasty mud, they have to learn to appreciate and respect each other's land socially and economically. Otherwise, the next generation will be liabilities to each other instead of assets like us today in the modern world. The leaders of these countries have to refine their approaches so all future students in this country have the same opportunity and privilege because they have a chance to grow up to become assets to this country and the rest of the world, instead of threats and liabilities. Their aims have to lead and support these bright kids to become great assets of this country rather than liabilities. By them becoming assets, crime, welfare, and poverty rates will have to decrease drastically because they will be educated and trained, and will not have to turn to breaking the law as an occupation. This aim would definitely benefit this great country for two main reasons: first, this country would be safer and the tax rate would have to decrease. And by them becoming professionals, this country will be richer because there will be less crime and more taxpayers. On the other hand, if these kids become "threats or liabilities," they would become content with breaking the laws, or with menial jobs and drudgery. They would be more violent towards one another, their communities, states, and the country itself. More likely than not, they would end up in prison for life. Therefore, the tax money would have to continue to increase drastically to support them, their families, and their medical care. Moreover, their communities and this country would have to train more policemen and women to fight such high crime rates. We as tax payers would have to pay to support them in jail, for their medical care, their kids and their families' welfare, who will probably end up in the same system and created by the same cycle as them.

The students who have an interest in becoming leaders of this country and the world have to learn to advance and better politics and foreign policy studies, and approach them a lot better for future generations. And we as the people also have learn and be educated by school officials, teachers, and leaders to elect the best men and women among us so these jobs will get done. They have to teach us efficiently to know who would be the best candidates to better our nation and world. We as people must not be trained to elect candidates mainly based on the certain schools they went to, or the family or social class they came from, or their races or genders, what sexual orientation they have, or the religion they practice because these ways of thinking are what keep us in this mire. We as modern citizens and voters have to be educated to see who has the potential to help and lead us to overcome problems of immigration, war, racism, sexism, high-cost of living, and hatred that we have had since day one. We must not think like our ancient ancestors, not because we are better than them, but because we cannot really relate to them. As modern philosophers and citizens, we must accept that many things they did would be despicable in the modern world. Therefore, our approaches have to be modernized. Things such as exterminating millions of disadvantaged Jewish children, females, elderly, and the rest of the citizens for no reason, enslaving millions of blacks and others mentally, psychologically, economically, and socially for no reason, oppressing and abusing females physically, verbally, and psychologically for no reason, having millions of children start to work at an early age for no reason, murdering millions of weak people and citizens of other countries merely for wealth and world power, and being more concerned with maintaining the supremacy of a certain race, gender, religion, social class, sexual orientation, and religion rather than working for the common good. We as people have to learn to respect each other's territory, in business and socially, and to join one another to work together as people to stop the world from sinking into this nasty mud. In fact, we as modern people have to learn to maintain the supremacy of this country, the rest of the world, and humanity before all.

The prominent modern political science and law professors and officials must teach and prepare our next generation to include all citizens, races, genders, sexual orientations, social classes, and religions in the councils of the party and the government. They must be taught as citizens and people in this country to not stand around and watch as their country and world are deteriorating while they have the potential to do something about it. And they should not just give the impotent communities and immigrants donations because it doesn't really help them in the long run. Otherwise, they would be living in heaven, and so would we. Instead of giving the poor people donations, establish constructive programs for them. For example, if you give an uneducated person a million dollars, in a couple of years such a person would most likely be in the same circumstances as before receiving the money. He or she would go and spend so much money on clothes, cars, and jewelry, and eventually waste every single penny. But give an average kid a quality education and strong support, and the kid would be extremely frugal; he or she would save some money for college, try to start a business, and eventually the kid would grow economically and socially. To be more explicit, let us look at Mike Tyson, MC Hammer, and many others. These people waste money as if there were no tomorrow, while others develop and grow well with the little they had. So, if the citizens in this country really want the property price to drop drastically, and want the high cost of living to disappear forever, they have to be more than citizens, they have to be trained as world citizens and humanitarians first. People have to know and learn that mailing millions of letters to their congressman and presidents will not solve their problems, because politicians cannot do everything by themselves and they certainly cannot better this country and the world by themselves. Every citizen who wants their children to have a better future and to live in a better world than we do has to learn to do their part. For instance, instead of buying pepper spray or a handgun so they won't be mugged or to be safer, complaining about high taxes, criticizing, and oppressing one another, they, as the people, could visit the poor quality schools in their communities and help out, again, not just giving donations. They could start their own after-school and tutoring programs to assist the disadvantaged children with their homework and more. They could go establish better creative programs for those on welfare and recently-released inmates, and other places the masses are getting wider. By teaching these impotent people how to do for themselves, respecting and helping each other, they will eventually develop themselves and become productive citizens in their communities, states, and country. With such a method this country would end up flourishing more instead of deteriorating, because less crime would be committed, less tax-money would go to the welfare system and other government support agencies or organizations, and more people would be paying taxes. As a result, better hospitals, school systems, police and fire training would be created, and certainly, the common people would have to pay fewer taxes. Why would people mug, steal, sell drugs or become prostitutes if they could provide for themselves and their families financially, and why would they want to move to other neighborhoods if their communities are well situated and safe? Everybody's community and state school systems would be working. Therefore, property taxes in the suburbs would have to decrease as well. By having one side have a quality school system, the tuition cost, crime, poverty, immigration, and high cost of living problems have to keep increasing instead of diminishing. In the end, we as a people and country itself would end up suffering.

Furthermore, this country is the leader of the world. It's not just the president that has duties to help the world, but we as world citizens also have duties to help the world, especially if we really want other people to love, respect, and admire us for our leadership to them, instead of despising us. If we as Americans really want immigration, wars, terrorism, and high cost of living to disappear in this country for good, we have to assist in this struggle as well. We cannot solely rely on George Bush and congressmen and women to fix everything in this country and around the world. If we cannot be great examples to them and better than the ancient ones, are we any better than them? We as American citizens and leaders have greater responsibilities to the world as Americans; yes it feels good to be an American citizen.

But, it also comes with American responsibilities as well. We are not the leaders of the world merely because of who we are and the color of our flag. We became the world's leading country to better the world and humanity. Copying ancient world leadership would put us in the ancient world's position and danger as well. We have to be great citizens to our fellow world citizens. They have to love and respect us based on what we do for them, for the world, and for humanity. Therefore, we have to be trained and taught as great humanitarians, so the hatred and all the social and economic problems in the world can finally go away. For instance, instead of prominent school officials teaching us as citizens to encourage our leaders to exterminate, oppress, despise, and hate citizens of other countries, they could teach us to see, help, and work together as brothers and sisters. In fact, they are our brothers and sisters because each one of us in this country, or our ancestors, came from a different country around the world. The professors have to modernize their teaching method, and get rid of the false traditions and beliefs so we as modern people can form a new relationship among ourselves. Instead of us attacking a country or it attacking us, leaders could request an unbiased meeting to see why such hatred and detestation started. If they want us to leave their lands or our country's businesses to leave their lands so they can grow their economy, such methods have to be followed through. People have to respect others' lands, and leaders have to respect other leaders' lands. If they have a product they want to sell, they are entitled to do so. No other country's business tells our country's business leaders what to sell and how much, so why should we try to do it to others? Again, such an attitude will always result in hatred and resentment towards this country— then war. The death of our troops and innocent children in this country and around the world are laid with causations. Therefore, we as modern citizens have to learn and educate our children to deal with the problems as they are.

Millions of poor people from other countries are breaking the law to immigrate to this country and other countries merely due to a lack of knowledge and skills. And those so-called scholars, intellectuals, and experts have done nothing to teach them about how to create and patronize businesses in their countries and to live abundantly. Other so-called civil rights activists and humanitarians have never pressured the leaders of major corporations and others to step out of these countries' business markets so theirs can flourish. Then, they still wonder why other people hate us, call us greedy, and want to exterminate us. None of them ever come together to develop a great world system so each country and continent can develop their lands socially and economically. We as their world leaders and humanitarians have to do our part first by educating them on how to better their school systems, grow their own industries, develop agriculture on their soil, their technology, and build their roads. By having such an approach, our land and leadership to the world would never be at risk; these aims and approaches would have better outcomes for plenty of reasons. First, the citizens of these countries would never have the interest or need to immigrate to this country or others. Secondly, all the taxpayers' money that has been wasted to fight illegal immigration, to keep immigrants in jail, for their deportation, medical costs, and others would be going into something more productive for this country and its youth. And we still wonder why our property and other taxes are so high, why many schools have been closed, many funds have been cut and why our deficit has increased. By helping them to produce, to get what they need on their own, they would be extremely happy in their countries, and in the long run it would benefit us as their leaders. Again, this country and other wealthy countries' debts, social problems, and economic problems have causes; and the cause is a loss of vision of the modern world.

Millions of illegal immigrants are prohibited from making a legal living; therefore, millions of them have to turn to breaking the law as an occupation. As a result, millions of them end up in jails, on welfare, in the school systems, and using other government support, which is funded by taxpayers. Regardless if we want to or not, or if it's legal or illegal, they would make a living. These impotent people are in a position where they cannot be reasonable and kind people. Anybody who expects the property tax, crime, welfare, medical injury rates, and other social and economic problems to diminish has to be naïve. And anybody who expects them to speak the English language, and be productive and supportive to this country has to be more than an imbecile. How can they be these things or have such feelings for this country when they are denied all these accesses and rights to become productive, while their countries and those in the U.S. are exploited for cheap labor and others by the U.S and its leaders? For example, if a person has a dog, but never feeds or trains the dog how to hunt, eventually that dog would be out of control around the house, and vicious to the owner. These poor illegal immigrants are not bad at all. We as their leaders place them in a position where they have to act upon us and our lands in such a way. And refusing to accept the blame and our faults as their leaders clearly shows that we live in denial, and would damage our land, other lands, and our world even more. The high cost of property, tax, crime, number of people in prison, immigration, welfare, high medical cost, and hatred problems towards us and our land are increasing on a daily basis, not because they were meant to be that way, but merely due to the lack of common sense and loss of vision of the modern world. For instance, the cost of property in nearly all major cities in this country are way too expensive for the average American to afford, mainly because these cities and states are overcrowded with poor people and illegal immigrants. Way too many people have needs and want to inhabit such a small area. Therefore, the price has to increase fast; there is too much demand for property. Millions of people immigrate to this country and millions of babies are born on a daily basis. In fact, it is a joke for us to expect the cost of property, tax, and high cost of living to go down while millions are coming every day, and none can stay to work in agriculture, textile, and other industries in their countries. It is unfair indeed for the average American to pay half a million dollars for a small piece of property, have a thirty year mortgage, and work two jobs for these basic things, while the country belongs to them and they can improve their conditions. The average American should not have to work two or three jobs to afford a small of piece property on their own land. By working that hard, they pretty much become the modern slaves for the major corporations. The average American works three hundred fifty mornings, days, and nights in a year to meet their basic needs, while these narrow-minded prominent school officials, CEOs, VPs, judges, and politicians work fewer weeks, days, and hours, but still enjoy the American dream. No wonder they turn the average American and the poor against one another.

If the world leaders, experts, and professors were doing their jobs as they were supposed to, they would teach us as Americans, or the citizens of other wealthy countries, to develop the average citizen in these countries instead of voting for them to oppress, restrict, and exploit the poor for cheaper labor and others, because in the long run, again, we will suffer too. And certainly, they should learn not to waste our taxpayers' money on phony immigration reforms, or waste our time on the Mexican border. The world experts must be taught that they have that prestigious title, not because they are from Harvard, Yale, Oxford, Cambridge, MIT, Princeton, and other leading institutions, nor because they are a bunch of narrow-minded white upper class males, or of noble status; but because of what they can accomplish as world experts for us as people, and for humanity. Therefore, when they see that a country, continent, and the world has a serious problem, they should not stay in their office and copy some worn-out theories off ancient writers and leaders to take advantage of it or to mislead us. As world experts, their main duty is to find a solution for it. They have to educate and train people to deal with a crisis as it is. For instance, instead of continuing to waste trillions in tax money on worn-out theories, treating disadvantaged illegal or legal immigrants, blacks, Hispanics, Asians, Middle Easterners, and others as criminals, and wasting other trillions on useless agencies, they as world experts and educators have to develop and to teach future world leaders and the citizens of this country to develop a world uplifting movement and peace program, so every country in the world can be united for the world's and humanity's interest. We as modern citizens cannot still believe that we cannot come into harmony with one another to save our country and our world. We as modern people must not accept and be content with such bad social and economic problems. Educators have to train and educate us as the human race and humanitarians to put our differences aside, to respect each other's territory, culture, heritage, and customs, and to work together as people, as brothers and sisters, to confront this country's and the world's poverty, fatal diseases and germs, and high crime rates with the best tools. Instead of investing our hard-earned tax money in nuclear weapons, invest it in a modern education system, so future generations will look for peace and harmony instead of war or nuclear weapons. We as world citizens must say yes to peace, harmony, respect, love, and development for all rather than some, because we as modern people are more reasonable and kind than our ancestors.

In order for these great things to be accomplished, we as modern-world humanitarians and leaders have to be well educated so we can forget and reject the worn-out theories and false traditions that we have learned from ancient civilizations. We as the leaders and leading citizens of the world can no longer believe such terrible worn-out theories and traditions about our brothers and sisters in this country and around the world. Therefore, we can no longer be taught and trained to remain content when our brothers and sisters that we were supposed to be friends with, loving and caring as neighbors, want to exterminate us. The leaders and the citizens of the world must be taught to include all countries' citizens and their leaders in the world and peace movement, and leave that policy that we copied from ancient people to favor and treat a certain group, gender, social class, country and continent better than others. We as people and students have to learn such foreign policy is unacceptable and improper in the modern world because it leads and forces us as leader of the world to stamp a badge of inferiority and enemy upon the people and the citizens of other countries that we were supposed to serve and lead. We as modern and educated philosophers and leaders cannot accept such doctrine as settled, and abandon the people that we were supposed to lead in the modern world as nonentities. In fact, this sort of national and foreign policy method that we have learned as modern citizens and leaders leads to oppression, segregation, restriction, and exploitation of one another in our country and the rest of the world. As a result of these so-called laws and foreign policies, we as modern people end up re-enslaving and damaging ourselves, this country, our world, and humanity without knowing that we are the ones, as people and citizens, that are doing this to ourselves and our lands. Not teaching our leaders and ourselves as the people of this country and the other wealthy countries to teach and help the leaders and the citizens of the countries that are doing badly socially and economically to uplift themselves in those spheres, makes us no better than those before us. By teaching our leaders to do otherwise, we as the leaders of the world are opposing freedom for them, and for ourselves because we as leaders of the world always have to worry about them financially and socially, always have to support them financially and socially, always have to rescue them when they are having a crisis. For example, if we do not teach them how to grow business in their countries as their leaders and educators, how are they going to be able to do it by themselves, and how can future generations have a better life? In the end, we as the leaders made it impossible for them and the rest of the world to see what they are good for, and what we are good for as leaders as well. If we had been taught as world leaders and citizens to prepare them adequately to deal with the problems on their lands by themselves, to be in charge of their lands, let them be the women and men that they are meant to be, in the end, we as world leaders and citizens would emerge as a great loving mother to them and to humanity. For example, a mother that has a couple of kids, but refuses to prepare, support, and teach them adequately to be on their own. Eventually, mainly because she wants to control them, such a mom will end up having a bad relationship with her children, and crippling them as well, instead of developing them. In the end, such a mom would think that her kids were ungrateful, but not at all; her kids love her. They just want to be on their own as adults. They do not always want to do what they are told by their mother. If the mother did modify her behavior and attitude towards them, they would not end up acting that way towards her.

Such a foreign policy will always result in huge failure for poor people of other countries socially and economically, and for us as their leader as well in the modern world. For instance, if after the Egyptians had developed their civilization in ancient times, they went to different lands to teach others how to do the same things for themselves and their lands, the unskilled and uncivilized ones would have appreciated, admired, respected, and loved them, and they would have never lost their world ruler position in the modern world. And schools such as Harvard, Yale, Oxford, and other prestigious schools in the modern world would never be that dominant and influential. But the ancient Egyptians used their skills and knowledge in the old days to oppress, abuse, massacre, enslave, and exploit a certain race and gender for their wealth and other natural resources. Eventually, they were attacked, invaded, and lost their world power and status by the oppressed people. Those who came after them, including the Greeks, the Romans, Teutons, Socrates, and others did exactly the same thing. The same thing kept occurring and history kept repeating itself. If those in the past had respected each other and their lands socially and economically, put their differences aside and worked together as brothers and sisters for their general welfare, this country would have never become the world leader in the modern world. All these wars and battles that have occurred in the ancient time had causes, including World I and II, the Vietnam War, the Civil War, and others. All the ancient great countries lost their leadership to the world merely because of the foreign policies that they were applying. Many of them took hundreds or thousands of years to lose their leadership of the world, but eventually they lost it. In the modern world, our professors are making a great mistake, and certainly, place our leadership to the world in great jeopardy by continuing to teach and train us to admire and copy the laws and foreign policies of ancient kings and presidents who had lost their empires and started this mess in the first place.

Many countries that had great empires, such as France, England, Russia, China, and many more lost their empires and their world power as well. No leader in the modern world can be controlled and treated like a child; they are leaders. They might not be the world leader, but they are still leaders. Therefore, they must be treated and respected like any country's leader, no less and no more. Trying to control them will always result in huge failure for us as world leader and world citizens. In the modern world, we have to be taught as world leaders and world humanitarians. Otherwise, we will continue to keep suffering as leaders and people. The world experts and scholars have to be taught in a way to develop the world, so all of us as people can do well. The world experts and scholars expecting the poor people in this country and around the world to develop socially, economically, and medically without providing any support makes them look more incompetent. They should learn from history, not follow it. Following it endangers each of us in the modern world. For example, when children in a family are not doing well, the parents end up doing poorly as well because the kids always depend on their parents economically and socially no matter how old they are. They would have to depend on their parents for a place to stay even when they are adults, to take care of their kids or baby sit for them. The parents would have to go bail them out when they get picked up by the police, or go visit them in jail or in the hospital when they get shot for trying to rob a place, or by other thieves or drug dealers. And the parent would have to take care of their children when they get released on parole or probation, or take their grandchildren when they are doing time in jail or prison. If the rest of the world is not doing well economically and socially, all the countries that are doing poorly will become overcrowded or the people will immigrate to this country or another country, legally or otherwise. They will always have to depend on this country for natural resources that they could develop in their own countries, such as food, beverages, oil, and others. Therefore, this country and other countries, including China and Japan, provide goods for the entire world. The cost of living has to increase, and natural resources will always get more and more expensive as they decrease. Property will have to get more and more expensive, and this country's citizens will never be at peace or experience a quality life. Since the people who are coming over here are less likely to be educated or skilled, they have a greater chance to end up doing the wrong things rather than good things, such as overdrinking, smoking, breaking the laws, becoming prostitutes, hating the police, becoming dependent on welfare, disease, and crime rates, and plenty more. As a result, this great country will never do well because the rest of the world is not doing well.

The deficits of this country and the world have to increase, not because we are not smart enough, but because the majority of our leaders and citizens of this world have not gained vision of the modern world. Teaching us as modern people to restrict and oppress certain groups of people, countries, and continents ends up hurting us and this country in the long run because in the end, we are controlling, restricting, and hurting ourselves, our country, and our world. Controlling and oppressing the world is not good for anybody, or any country either. As modern philosophers and citizens, we have to perceive controlling and oppression as a way of re-enslaving ourselves, our country, and our world. If we as leaders and citizens are friends and respect all citizens of other countries and their leaders as we are supposed too, we would not need to worry about immigration, poverty, war, and terrorist attacks at all on our soil and in the world. All friends have disagreements and conflicts among themselves. However, if they cannot find a way to make up and move on to continue to make their friendship stronger and better, it is because they were not such great friends in the first place. The same analogy should apply to countries and world leaders. If they have a conflict that they cannot work out among themselves peacefully and in the people's best interest, they should not have been leaders in the first place. By helping to develop one another socially, economically, medically, and technologically, many of these modern problems would disappear. For example, kids in the street have handguns, not because they want to carry them, but because it is unsafe in the street, and they have access to them. The same thing goes for many countries. They have nuclear weapons not because they want to exterminate other citizens or countries, but because their countries and the world are unsafe, not because the world was meant to be that way, but because its leaders made it that way. As a result of looking for peace, professors are teaching their students to look to control other countries, and since the leaders and citizens of many countries do not want to be controlled, they have to fight with one another.

For instance, instead of these professors teaching us how to modernize our system for a world peace movement and development, they are continuing to teach us the same ancient system. As a result, we keep building more military bases in every single country, not to develop them and their country, but to control them. That system was copied from the ancient kings because they used to have their soldiers in every land to watch and control poor ancient people. When we need our troops for our own service, we cannot find them because they are all over the world. We as Americans cannot find our troops to rescue the citizens and the country that they were supposed to serve and protect. As a result, thousands of innocent people have to die, and this country's leader emerges as racist and incompetent to this country and the world. For example, hundreds of elderly, children, females, and ill people were dying and suffering in the New Orleans flooding catastrophe. And, the worst part, they had to wait for three days to get help from the government leaders and soldiers who took oaths to help when they were needed. Furthermore, the officials in other cities who have refused to let these hopeless people enter their cities have to be immediately removed from their places because they cannot be partisan in such circumstances. As for other citizens who support their unethical and vicious actions, shame on them too. How would they feel if that was them? If American leaders cannot help all Americans in a serious crisis, why should they be leaders to the American people, and why should such men and women be elected to a public office when they are doing more harm than good?

Furthermore, if the leaders and soldiers of countries are trained to serve their countries only for wars, or to abuse war prisoners—sad as it is—these people have not been trained adequately at all for their duties. If many countries are having natural disasters and countries are not offering their soldiers to help out, how human and kind are we? If these disasters happened as they have with the flooding in Haiti, and the South-East Asia earthquake and tsunami catastrophes, and they do not send help to assist, how can they expect the leaders and citizens of other countries to be compassionate towards them, help them, respect them, and admire their leadership in the world? If we or the world were at peace as real humans, soldiers would not be trained chiefly to kill or be killed, or to stay on military bases all over the world. They would be trained to help and assist their lands and their neighbor' lands.

If political science and law school professors do not modernize their teaching and their foreign policy methods for the modern world, they will not do good jobs, indeed. And we as the people of this country and as citizens of the world will never see a better day, except to keep continuing to distance ourselves from the people that we were supposed to serve, and to enslave ourselves more, socially and economically. In order for this ordeal and injustice to stop for future generations, modern professors and philosophers have to make more efforts to become free in all aspects. We cannot become totally free if we cannot disconnect ourselves from the methods of ancient people, forgive, and modernize our approaches, beliefs, and policy for the freedom for all races, genders, social statuses, sexual orientations, countries, and humanity as a whole.

Professors and philosophers have to teach to gain vision of the modern world. We as the people have to work for the equality for all races, genders, sexual orientations, and countries. We can no longer be taught and trained as people to clamor for justice while we are encouraging a part of the system to oppress, restrict, and exterminate other races, genders, homosexuals, religions, and the citizens of other countries. We as people and citizens of this country and the world have to be taught to feel comfortable in the presence of each other, feel comfortable to go into any neighborhood, state, and country that we wish to. If we as modern people and world citizens cannot do these little things, as nominally free men and women, sorry to say, we still are socially and internationally enslaved. If we as people cannot go to different places, communities, or countries then we clearly show that these false traditions and beliefs have turned us to hate and despise one another. We as modern people and citizens can no longer be afraid of one another. We have to come together to stop terrorizing each other in our world. Due to the lack of modernized approaches and techniques, the system that was supposed to better us as people and the world are making the world worse. Such a system has extended from security to violating our civil rights. We as people cannot just get on a plane and fly without being worried and scared. In fact, when we are flying, we as people have to be screened and searched from head to toe, have to take our shoes off, and have to turn off our phone, regardless if we have sick children and loved ones at home. We as modern people are terrified to travel, either by plane, bus, or subway. Furthermore, if any of us says anything out of place on the plane, we get removed, labeled or treated as terrorists in our own country, and even put on trial for it in the media or in the court of law. Unfortunately, many Americans and taxpayers find themselves hedged in and wrongly profiled merely by the color of their skin, their origin, and their religious beliefs.

This way of living is a modern form of slavery. We as people do not have any rights at all to do or be treated as we want to; we are in a country and world where many died for us to be free as people and citizens. These professors and philosophers refuse to prepare modern students and citizens to come together with other countries so the world can be developed. They refuse to teach us to help other countries to participate in world matters and issues, or let them be heard or speak out against their injustices because they are a part of the world. Those rights are not granted by any country or leader. We have to help them as world leaders and world citizens to participate in the higher things of life, because by not joining and helping them socially and economically, we are handicapping and enslaving ourselves and our lands. Therefore, as modern citizens and people we can learn from ancient great leaders to look for peace when there are problems between them. For example, the Japanese raid on Pearl Harbor on December 7, 1941 was one of the great defining moments in history. The great politicians had reached peace and settled the matters among themselves. In the modern world, Japan and this country have a great relationship. Therefore, by not trying to educate and train modern students to follow the great politicians of the past, these people as educators and professors are causing us as people to continue to enslave and handicap ourselves, our lands, and our world through systematic exploitation, oppression, and domination. The people of this country and the citizens of the world are supposed to profit from education and our leaders. We cannot be treated as a means to an end. We cannot learn to be happy, and smile while we are not safe on our own land, and are not able to afford a nice piece of our own land without working three jobs and paying a thirty-year mortgage. Modern students must be taught that citizens cannot be happy and comfortable with their nation if they cannot show them a better way to escape this miserable life. We as world leaders have to be trained in such a thing. Therefore, we cannot turn out to be unprincipled men and women when there is a country leader that acts inappropriately. We as leaders have to be trained to approach such leaders wisely and intelligently. When the leader of a country is out of control, the country's citizens have to be taught to vote them out peacefully. When there is no good result for their country, they have to call and depend on us to better their situation. If the leader is way out of control, incompetent, inefficient, and abusive towards the people who voted him or her into office, he or she can be removed from his or her office only at the request of the people of his or her country. Then, if such leader does not want to be removed, the people of such a country have to request for the continent leaders to intervene. If the continent leaders cannot do such a task, they call on the world leader—the United States—to intervene, and only at the request of the citizens of such a country, and the leaders of such a continent. If the foreign policy system were taught that way, we would not have to go to almost every country to remove people from power, and certainly, we would not have so many people hating and wanting to exterminate us. Since we have been called upon by the people of such a country that we are serving, now it is our duty to help the leader to step down peacefully from his or her power, and the leader has to remain in his or her country. Why have millions of leaders been exiled from their native countries, and not one of ours has been exiled even if the leader has stolen and murdered the people? His or her wealth has to be taken back from him or her and given back the government and country. Such a leader has to remain in the country to pay the consequences of his or her actions. Otherwise, they would just steal from the country and spend such a country's wealth in a different country, as have Haiti's former leaders and those of other countries as well. By calling the leaders of other countries and the world when they have a crisis on their lands, they would make us feel more comfortable as people. For example, if a mom has three children, when these kids are having problems, they should be comfortable calling their parents when they need them. Since this country is the world leader, other countries in the world should feel free to ask for help from this country when they have a crisis they cannot handle by themselves. When the leader of a country refuses to step down peacefully, the world leader has to take certain approaches before using force, such as sending a negotiator to talk to them, make him or her realize that he or she only serves the people, and if the people no longer want his or her public service, she or he has to step down. By refusing to step down, as a next step, bank accounts should be frozen and property and other goods she or he owns should be seized as well. Still refusing, the world leader has to teach the soldiers in such a country soldiers to go after them, and remove such a leader physically from power. And such a leader would have to be tried as well because leaders have to respect the laws. By refusing to step down, he or she is breaking the laws. How can they write laws for the people to follow if they themselves are breaking them? After he or she is physically removed and all her or his properties have been taken away, they invest in that particular country, and this leader has to be tried for such behavior. In the end, the people in such a country would always love us and depend on us for our leadership, not just because we are Americans.

For example, in the mid 1990's when the Colombian government had trouble with Pablo Escobar, the Columbian drug kingpin, and they could not get him on their own, they called the U.S government to assist them in the pursuit. The U.S government assisted them as a world leader by sending U.S. Special Forces, Navy SEALS, and DEA agents to train the Columbian army to move on him. That is how all countries in this world are supposed to feel and be treated. They call the continent and the world leaders when matters require a certain expertise that they never had or needed before. Therefore, when a government official does not want to be removed from power, the students who are about to become world leaders are not supposed to be trained to stay and watch matters out of their jurisdiction, or to place an embargo on such a country because it is not good for the citizens and this country in the long run. Such a leader would not suffer from the embargo because he or she controls the economy of the country and use it for his or her own purpose. Secondly, an embargo would lead the country itself to suffer socially and economically. No commercial planes and shipping would be allowed, and other citizens would be scared to go visit such a country, even its own citizens living abroad. Third, it would backfire on us creating more immigration problems. Let's look at Haiti and Cuba, for example. Such foreign policies have to be modernized because they keep countries out of desirable conditions. As a result of these methods or ways of teaching, many countries will always be confined to poverty, high crime rates, and violence. In order for these important tasks to be carried out, our bright students who are about to become the leaders of this country and the world have to be taught to move forward as people and world citizens, and work together in this country and the world as well. The leaders have to be well trained and educated to give the people what they really need, but not what the professors may think that they need. They have to give world citizens what they really need. They have to teach the citizens of the modern world to be independent so they can do for themselves, and not possess this fatal dependency on this country and others while they can do for themselves and flourish their own countries. Then they would not have to immigrate to other countries. This task is promising, but it is a long and hard task as well because they have to train and educate many citizens of this country and other countries who have never learned how to develop their mind properly.

Since our country is the leading country in the world, our bright students and future leaders cannot be taught to be biased, or serve just one race, gender, social class, country, and continent. Teaching our bright students to be biased and partisan towards a certain race, gender, social class, sexual orientation, and religion will always cause huge failure for this country, the world, and humanity itself. Having a one-sided system would have to make this country weaker and weaker because the country itself cannot be profitable, supportive, and comfortable with only one-sided support. A one-sided system causes this country to end up having more unpleasant sections, especially in the big cities and states, such as New York, Boston, Washington, Chicago, Miami, California, and others. By teaching our leaders to act in such a way, only a small percentage moves along, and a small percentage will never be able to carry the whole country. As a result, this great country will always end up sinking deeper and deeper in the mire. Also, teaching our students and future leaders to protect only their allies will always result in huge failure for this country, many other countries, and humanity itself because our leaders are only friends with just a few countries. Again, such an approach is unethical, biased, racist, prejudiced, and will always result in huge failure for us as modern people in this country and future generations as well because the men and women who were supposed to become world leaders are going to connect themselves and help certain countries, and control, restrict, and separate themselves from the other countries that they were supposed to serve and lead. In fact, no country leader in the world is better than any other. The so-called allies who are supposedly our friends because we, as Americans, are giving them something in return. In other words, they are watching out for their interests. Their country's products push this country's products aside. They make millions in this country on a daily basis. They are our ally as the world leader because they are watching and securing their benefits, not because they are better than the ones that are burning our flags and attacking us. They are not doing the same thing as them because our foreign policy system is working to their benefit. Since our foreign policy only benefits one side, the other sides that are left out have no choice but to retaliate against us, and the citizens of other countries who do not like this country's leaders end up cheering for them. In fact, the same thing happens in this country also when blacks, Hispanics, and others see that they have been victimized and the justice system either ignores or dismisses their matters as real people. Blacks and others end up breaking things in their communities and other communities, and hurting innocent people when they see a black person has been victimized by a policeman, and the justice department does nothing like justice, as in the Rodney King incident and millions more. In fact, Malcolm X was promoting violence towards the police and others as a sort of retaliation, revenge, and justice. The citizens of other countries do not hate us as American people, but since our leaders have been trained to serve and protect certain countries and continents instead the entire world, they end up hating and damaging us as a whole.

We as the world leaders never intervene to help them when they really need it. Everybody in the world knows the only time our leaders intervene in a situation is when they see their interest, or when we intervene in a crisis to support one side. The neglected side will retaliate against us eventually. But if we were really taught to be great world leaders, when we see that the leader of a country wants to occupy another country's lands, we have to intervene. We have to support neither of them with money or weaponry. By supporting one and letting the other suffer or die, the leaders are creating problems for us as this country's people. They are putting our lives and land in jeopardy. If the neglected ones were big and powerful countries, they would attack the country that occupied their lands, and sorry to say, they would eventually attack the other country that supports their opponents economically and provides them with weapons. And teaching our leaders the method of having allies instead of being great leaders to all countries in the world will always result in failure because the other countries would go looking for allies as well. Therefore, all countries would end up having allies, so when two countries have a conflict both rely on their allies for protection. For example, a kid has problems with another kid, but a kid comes out of nowhere, and assists one of the kids in the fight. Later on, the kid who was the victim has his friend with him, and he will jump the kid who supported the other kid to beat him or her up. All these things are happening in the world merely because of a lack of common sense. Since small countries are not big enough to fight us, they end up taking a sucker punch at us while we are not watching them. In the modern world, this is called a "terrorist attack." The other small countries, which have been neglected by us end up taking their side and cheering them on, again, not because they are bad as people, but merely because we have been taught by these narrow-minded so-called political analysts and experts to restrict, oppress, and keep them in the dust, by serving one side, instead of being the great leader as we were supposed to be.

Unfortunately, no matter how much money we spend on our security system, it can never really be safe because many of them are American citizens by birth or naturalization, well educated, and fade in to the system. The only thing that could make it a little safer is to put them in a camp as we did to the Japanese during World War II. But this is modern time, and therefore, such an approach is out of the question. Besides, that approach was unethical and illegal, and violated all the civil and federal rights of those citizens. They see many instances where we as world leaders could help them or vote to establish a world movement of peace among all the countries in the world, but we still refuse to include them as a part of the world. Many instances that we see where they are wrongly losing their citizens, or their citizens are wrongly incarcerated in other prisons, we do not intervene to rescue them as their leader. It is unfortunate that our professors have not realized that this crusade is not going to stop on its own because many of them who they label as terrorists have been captured by the Egyptians and others, and demand for them to be treated as prisoners of war. They also wrote many books to teach their children to view us as their enemies, and we do the same thing with our children. As a result of this nonsense, both sides think that they are at war, and no one really knows why. We are continuing to train our soldiers for war and they are continuing to train their people for war as well. Those that cannot have war with us would equip themselves with sophisticated terrorist's tricks. But the sad part for all of us is that nothing good can come out of this tragedy, except more millions of innocent children, elderly, mothers, fathers, and other citizens dying on both sides. While law school and political science professors do not realize that by not teaching citizens and young leaders to vote for a world peace movement so all countries can reach out for peace for their general welfare, these undesirable situations will get worse and worse because the countries that do not have nuclear weapons will seek to purchase or build one or more, or ally with those that have them. As result, the whole of humanity is in great danger. Remember that World War I was based chiefly on electronics. World War II was based primarily on technology, but World War III would not be based on either. It would be based mainly on powerful nuclear weapons. These professors seem to forget that some powerful nuclear weapons can really damage humanity and the entire world. For example, a country leader that might be at war may see all his or her soldiers and country are totally damaged and losing everything they had, and their people might be dying. The leaders of that country might say, "forget it, my people, my soldiers, and my country are being wiped out, so I will press a button and launch a powerful nuclear weapon." As a result, human ego and a lack of common sense would cause the whole world and the human race to disappear. Scientists just gave theories about the disappearance of the dinosaurs on this planet before the arrival of the human race, but none of these experts can say for certain why all the dinosaurs that used to roam this planet were just suddenly wiped out.

The best and brightest professors, school officials, leaders, and citizens in this country and around the world must know the present crisis will never get any better in this condition. We, as citizens in this country and around the world, have no programs whatsoever to find a way out unless we come together as people and put our differences aside because there are numerous comments that we hear from government officials that there is on attack on this land, or see in the media that others are getting prepared to attack us, or we as world leaders are preparing our soldiers to attack them as well. In fact, these things occur on a daily basis. Instead of professors developing modern methods so the future leaders can develop a better program on their own for this country and the world that they are leading, they tell or teach these bright kids they do not need different races, sexual orientations, genders, religions, social classes, and citizens of other countries because they already have the whites and the wealthy countries on their side. Teaching leaders such politics and foreign policy methods will always block them from trying to better the relationship that the officials in the government of this country have with other different races, homosexuals, females, social classes, religions, and countries. Instead of bettering their relationship and their behaviors, they would worsen them, because they have not been taught that the fault is with the system, or with them. In fact, these leaders have to be trained properly on how to have a great relationship among their parties and others in order for this country to progress. For example, if a mom sees her kids having problems among themselves or with the neighbor's children, she has to tell them to work it out among themselves peacefully if she wants to have a better relationship with the neighbors. If the kids' mom and the neighbor never tried to better the relationship between them, one day the kids and their mom might go out, and the neighbor might see her house is burning, and she might ignore it and not even call the firemen or police. As a result, she would lose her house based mainly on a lack of friendship, common sense, and ego. Therefore, the future leaders and the future generations must be taught to stop despising, hating, controlling, restricting, and oppressing other races, genders, sexual orientations, social classes, and other countries because all of us need each other if we want our country and our world to grow. They cannot continue to be taught to create or leave the opportunities only for one race, gender, a couple of religions, and the wealthy countries because by only doing such a thing they are increasing immigration, racism, high cost of living, war, terrorism, sexism, and more social and economic problems for future leaders.

Any leader and professor who wants future generations to be much better off has to gain vision of the modern world. They have to teach their future world sociologists, economists, medical doctors or other medical care providers, psychologists, criminologists, and other professionals to go teach the leaders and people of poor countries how to create more opportunities for themselves and their lands. These poor people have to learn how to maintain peace on their lands and with the leaders and people of other countries, how to lead and serve their lands, how to build and operate their industries and other machines in their countries, and how to sell natural resources and mineral goods among themselves and overseas at a fair price. These leaders would not teach them how to do impossible things because the poor have their own lands and minds just like everybody else. They just have to be taught how to develop them. Again, by preparing our country and world leaders adequately, this country and other wealthy countries would be better off: taxes would decrease, peace would be established, the economy would grow, and the high cost of living would disappear for good. The leaders of other countries would no longer depend on this country and other wealthy countries to feed them and their people because they would know how to use their lands and their knowledge to serve their citizens sufficiently. Our citizens would not need to work three jobs on their own land to buy a small piece of property or afford the basic things in life.

Gaining vision of the modern world is the only quality solution to better our ordeal. We as the people have to appeal to the brightest and most creative professors to step in so they can prepare leaders in this country and around the world for only great results. We as the world leaders should try to reach out to the leaders and citizens of all countries to be united, to better our relationship, and to offer each other something new as their modern leaders. We as world leaders have to do our parts first. We have the best experts around the world in every single aspect. We have to reach out to and look for those who have been lost forever to be our friends even in modern times, and educate, prepare, and train the poor in countries around the world so they would be able to function in important economic, social, medical, and technological spheres. These world experts have to be trained, since there is nothing we can do that they cannot do, just as there is nothing that they can do that we cannot do. At this moment, the professors, educators, teachers, citizens, and leaders of this country and others must begin to gain vision of the modern world by preparing to do the very thing that they have been taught that they cannot do. Big countries have to stop thinking about the large debts that poor countries have with them. They have to face the fact that they cannot pay them back, not because they do not want to, but because they are not able. By helping to establish them financially and socially, someday they might be able to repay their debts or find better programs to make their debts disappear for good. Furthermore, one thing that the wealthiest countries must see is that poor countries have been in debt for so long because the people of poor countries have only suffered and have been exploited and oppressed. One of the main reasons that they have been handicapped for so long—especially black countries—is that their country's leaders and citizens in the past have controlled and restricted the poor to a place where they could not grow at all because millions of their citizens have been raped, sold, tortured, murdered, and enslaved for over three hundred years. In addition, they continue to be exploited for cheap labor and other things by many oppressors in the modern world who label themselves as genius businessmen and women. Sincerely, the outcome of these countries cannot be any better than what they were and are at the present time. The rich in these countries have and continue to manipulate all the systems in the world so the poor will be always poor and worthless.

Any oppressor who wanted to get richer in the past, and even now, just went into a country, paid almost nothing for labor, took the products that these disadvantaged people made, and sold them in this country and around the world for a fortune. They do not give these impotent people anything back, such as a better medical center, roads, and schools. Many of the modern oppressors are the Uncle Toms, sellouts, and the house slaves. They are doing this injustice to their own people, blood, and countries of origin. They have got some nerve to label themselves as businessmen and women because they have a couple of lousy degrees, can bounce or throw a ball, sing a couple of lousy songs, and play in a couple corny movies to finally leave the projects, the ghetto, or poor countries, wear suits and ties, and have lunch with the white oppressors. They ask the black community and countries to support their music, films, clothing lines, sneakers, and other products, while the factories that make these products are not even located in black communities or countries. Many of them are complaining about paying child support for their own kids, spending five hundred thousand on cars and jewelry, but none give to black colleges or black countries. They do not even attempt to invest in developing their own products since the white males say they can't. So why should they try? Nearly all of them are all but worthless to black communities and countries, and they still wonder why the president of Mexico made such comments about them. They are spending five million dollars for a piece of property, but not to build a hospital, a school, or other productive things for the communities or the countries they or their parents came from. Not one of them tries to come together with poor people to develop the community that they came from, again, since the white males said that the black communities and countries cannot develop. Why should they try to prove them wrong? All the Ph.Ds, MDs, MBAs, and other degrees they have received are nothing but expensive pieces of paper. They spend thousands and millions on

European products, while they do not spend a penny on theirs. Otherwise, they would not have to ask someone for a job, or slave in this country or any other instead of creating something of their own. They are looking for national political power while they cannot help their own people. In fact, they are just graduate slaves, or million dollar slaves. After they make their money in the poor community, they leave the people and the communities that used to support them in the nasty mud, and go spend the money where they were prohibited to drive or to be seen. The schools that they went to have never received anything from them, not even a computer or college assistance for a couple of kids. The only thing they ever went back to those schools to do is to give a speech and flash their "bling-bling." They make their products so expensive while they are fully aware that most people who wear their products are kids who are from the undesirable conditions and situations like when they were growing up. And many of these kids have to break the law to be able to afford their sneakers and other products that they made. Many of them who call themselves or think that they are business geniuses are no better than the ancient slave masters who labeled themselves geniuses, and businessmen as well, while they were enslaving and exploiting their ancestors, and the other weak people for wealth and power.

In order for this country and the world to develop well, the future leaders of this country and the world must be taught and prepared to reorganize this country and the world in a sense to enrich the country and the rest of the world, not the wealthy people, because the richer these people get, the more debts and mud the world sinks into. Again, the professors have to develop new systems to deal with and confront these problems as they are in order for this country and the world to improve economically and socially. They have to modernize their

161

aims to provide the masses and poor countries with the solution that they really need, which is quality education, training, opportunities, and strong support. Jails and prisons would never be crowded that much if these people had received a quality education. If they had, then the number of professionals would increase, and the number of taxpayers would increase as well, and elderly people would be able to get their retirement money easily.

The CEOs of corporations are asking for tax cuts while many of them are making millions for pretty much doing nothing. At the same time, they refuse to cut their own salaries to expand their corporations, all while exploiting the weak races, genders, communities, and countries for cheap labor. Why should they get a tax cut? The average citizen is overloaded with taxes, and they still manage to pay them, and their corporations' truck drivers and cashiers are the ones who practically live at their jobs and work, and are making close to minimum wage. Instead of letting these CEOs continue to exploit the world, restrict them from exploiting the weak people, communities, and the people of other countries for cheap labor and others, because all these things reflect and backfire on the country itself. In fact, the future leaders of school officials in the world and continent leaders must be trained in a way to do their duties by educating school leaders in poor communities and the world, so the citizens of these poor communities and countries can be educated, and pool their earnings to improve themselves, their communities, and their countries. Especially in small countries, citizens usually are crowded in the center of a village or the city. School officials of the world have to teach the citizens of these poor countries that the best way to decentralize their country is by creating business in the provinces because if these citizens in poor countries do not get themselves established in business and socially as soon as possible, the illegal immigrants that are already in this country will continue to weigh it down with more loads by continuing to commit more crime, or use more medical care, or crowding the big cities. If the system does not improve vastly and soon, by the next generation the only Americans who would be able to afford a simple basement in Boston, New York, and other buildings would be the ones that will have a college degree, because the tax would go much higher. And the rest of this country that has not been crowded yet will be overcrowded. It does not matter if confused and hopeless American citizens stay on the border, or spend more trillions in immigration reforms to build walls and fences, poor immigrants will always find a way to come. Otherwise, deported people would not find their way back into this country. If politicians and school leaders do nothing about these matters, and still let the crooked people exploit them for cheap labor and others, by the next generation, there will be nothing left for the future citizens of this country.

The modern professors and school officials have to develop a better system so the weak genders, races, people, religions, social classes, communities, and countries can build their confidences back up. The main reason that poor people do not even battle to attempt to develop under these fatal oppressions and restrictions is the fact that their confidence to produce, develop, and build things has been taken away from them psychologically since day one. The leading experts in this country and the world have to build the confidence of weak genders, races, social classes, and the citizens of poor countries to build for themselves socially, economically, medically, and technologically. By teaching these people to manifest enough confidence in them, and properly support them, they would be strong and confident enough to build their communities, the masses, and the poor countries. Therefore, high crime rates, people in prison, and welfare rate crises would no longer exist, and the immigration crisis that has been causing this country so many social and economic problems would disappear. This government and the World Bank would not have so much money to withdraw and lend. In fact, they would have more deposits to make and invest because the world would flourish economically. These great professors and school officials have to develop these modern methods because this great country is getting weaker and weaker because most people depend on this country's economy to live. Almost all the countries around the world depend on this country for support. For example, no matter how strong a person might be, when all the blood in his or her veins has been extracted, that individual would not even be strong enough to stand on his or her feet. This country would begin to flourish as long as the weak races, genders, social classes, and citizens of poor countries have enough confidence to do for themselves, their communities, and their countries. In fact, these professors and school officials must emphasize confidence a lot more, because no person can succeed in life if he or she does not have confidence in her- or himself. Confidence for these people should be placed as top priority because it is one of the most important keys to success, even more than money because if these professors do not teach these weak people a way to rebuild and refine their confidence, they might as well just not teach them at all. Again, a lack of confidence is one of the major things that keep these races, social classes, religions, genders, homosexuals, and citizens of poor countries in such a mire. If the world's professors and school officials developed such modern methods, the rest of the people would end up having a new push on life to improve.

It is shameful indeed that we are deterring while only a small percentage of citizens are educated and trained for improving their countries and their world. Modern school officials and professors have to modernize their systems so their large number of citizens can be educated and trained to do for this country, their countries, and the world. These people can no longer be trained to worship others as Socrates, professionals, and creators, while their minds, souls, and bodies are as useful as the small percentage that is dominant. There is no way out of this mess in this country and the world if the majority of people are underachievers. Again, the world cannot only be supported, or be fed, by just a small percentage of people or a couple of countries. Education is worthless if they cannot teach these people how to better their races, genders, communities, this country, their countries, the world, and humanity, and if the world is waiting on a small class to find solutions for their problems, while the small percentage of the white male upper class cannot relate to each particular race, community, gender, social class, sexual orientation, and citizens of other countries. In fact, it seems that the more education the white male upper class gets, the worse off these races, genders, social classes, religions, this country, and the poor people in other countries are. It does not necessarily mean that the white upper class does not care for these people, communities, this country, and the people in poor countries, it merely means that the education that they have been receiving seems to have made them do the contrary because the more education they have received, the more they seem to be further from the other races, religions, people, communities, and countries that need their help and assistance. They seem as though they never had any aspirations to go help this country, the weak people, genders, and communities. The white male upper class seems to be concerned more about social and economic status than to awaken this country. As before, other world rulers had less than two percent wealthy people in their country, and in the end, they lost everything. By doing the same thing as those before, all these negative approaches may backfire on this country eventually. Again, this country would be richer socially and economically if the other wealthy countries were doing better jobs with their business approach, and if the upper class white males had been properly educated about business responsibility to a community, country and world because they are a huge part of the cause of immigration, high cost of living, high crime, welfare, terrorism, world status, war, and prison overcrowding. In fact, these things are worth more than money. The great school officials, professors, and leaders have to know that we as people, and the citizens of this country and the world, have to be well educated for our minds to develop, for us to see things in a better perspective for the common good. The mind of the modern human race has to be developed and trained in a way to sufficiently gain vision of the modern world by overcoming racism, terrorism, oppression, destruction, restriction, sexism, immigration, and poverty problems. The only way to do so is to forget what the ancient people have written or said, and to modernize our own prophecy for the modern world and modern problems, so we can become valuable as people and citizens for this country and the world for our brothers and sisters. We as people cannot be taught about being human by oppressing, controlling, restricting, and destroying one another because in the end, we as people are not doing it to ourselves. We are doing it to our countries and our world. No one should be excluded in this movement because all of us can learn to do our parts and repair the damage that the ones before have done. Therefore, all of us must be educated and trained in a way to become assets, and valuable for our races, genders, sexual orientations, social classes, this country, other countries, our world, and humanity.

Type of Leadership for the Modern World

We as the people and citizens of this country and the world find ourselves in an untoward situation in the modern world, mainly because the people who are leading and serving us have been educated and trained in a sense to control this country, the world, and humanity, instead of developing them. Since they have been trained to control and oppress certain genders, sexual orientations, communities, races, religions, social classes, and countries only, and not develop them, the majority of us end up in this country and the world as restricted psychologically as children. Because the majority of us in this country and around the world are restricted mostly only to small things in life, this great country and this world end up being restricted as well. We as the people and citizens in this country and around the world are not happy with this unpleasant situation at all, but at the same time, we become satisfied with it, and accept this undesirable condition as an end, and just because we as the people have been educated to accept that the world and people cannot change, and accept such failure as a way of life. As the Haitian proverb goes, "*se la vie qui kon sa*" or "that is the way life is." As a result, we become discouraged and hopeless by not even trying to find better ways out, and by not even raising our ambitions and our ways of living higher than those who came before these last two generations. At the same time, those school leaders and professors really think that they are doing a great job for the people, for the world by teaching us as modern people and students to control and restrict one another from being developed, and never

167

realize that such a teaching method is deplorable and inefficient for us as modern people because the majority of us in this country and around the world would never grow. If we as the people cannot grow, this country and the world cannot grow, either. The majority of subjects that they continue to teach in school have expired for the modern world. Instead of giving their students and us as citizens a modern point of view and better direction to see and find the right path, so the leaders and their graduates can lead the people that they are serving efficiently, they do the contrary by embittering and mis-educating us. Consequently, the leaders and graduates end up perceiving and seeing the majority of people and countries that they were supposed to lead and serve as outcasts and enemies for life, and make themselves appear to these people as their outcasts and enemies, too. Therefore, the world never really goes forward no matter how hard these leaders have tried, and no matter how much money they have spent, mainly because the trifles, stumbling blocks, and disorganizations they have drilled into these leaders' and people's minds are preventing them from coming together and joining one another to develop the world for the people.

Many of the professors they had in their schools have led them and the citizens to believe that they can be great leaders for this nation and to the world merely by the fact that they are well situated, or came from a noble family, or have a certain status or gender, or went to a certain school. As a result of this fatal misleading, the majority of people in this country and around the world end up believing that the most distinguished persons for leadership positions are those who have a JD or an MBA, or came from places where they never have any contact with the common American and the masses at all, and have never experienced any moment in those countries that are considered to be great enemies of theirs and this country. Since the students who were about to become leaders of this nation and the world were not required to create any strong constructive programs to uplift the weak people, communities, and countries while they were in college or graduate school, as a result, many of these leaders can only struggle for the little things which are going to uplift the social level, race, class, and gender that they are from, but not the communities, states, this country, and the rest of the world where the majority of people live. In fact, after many of them have finished their political terms, the communities, states, and countries which they were representing and serving end up having more social and economic problems. For example, all their graduates emerge as captains of a sinking boat; they are trying to stop the boat from sinking deeper in the water while they have not been trained at all for such a task. As a result, every captain that has been put in charge of keeping the boat afloat for the passengers has failed to stop the boat from sinking and has failed to give the passengers any better hope; each captain leaves the boat lower in the water for the next captain.

The same analogy applies to this country and world leaders. Due to the lack of quality training and education the leaders have received, they are unable to really save the people and the world from sinking deeper in this mire. Each leader leaves more of a mess for the next incompetent leader to deal with, while the people, this country, and the rest of the world are suffering and dying. For instance, the people, communities, genders, races, religions, sexual orientations, communities and countries that used to be weak actually become weaker and weaker. While these poor people have great potential, vision strengths, and ideal to better themselves, their communities, states, this country, and the rest of the world, the great professors, school officials, leaders, and citizens in this country and around the world must educate their graduates to cooperate with one another and the citizens which they are representing, so that this task which seems impossible to achieve can become possible to accomplish. We as the people, school officials, leaders, citizens, and countries have to know the most essential thing to improving ourselves, this country, and the rest of the world is great cooperation. For example, any family that does not have a strong cooperation among themselves and appreciation for one another will never grow. Therefore, the leaders of this country and the world must set a world structure so that every country's leaders and citizens can be taught to cooperate because the entire planet is suffering high cost of living and a lack of quality natural resources and minerals. All countries in the world are suffering the same insecurity, high crime rates, disease rates, deficits, and economic debasement, and if they do not join one another for this struggle, it will be way worse for the generations to come. Since all countries and citizens in the world are suffering the same undesirable conditions, the only result of this nonsense is for school officials and experts in this country and around the world to cooperate and work together to stop this crisis. The best experts, teachers, leaders, and professors have to update their teaching methods for the modern world, so the people who want to be educated and trained to fight this crusade can be no longer stopped by nonsense requirements which have no bearing at all on the social and economic problems that we as people are facing. All the school admissions requirements are not helping the solution. If they were, why do properties, war, terrorism, poverty, high crime, disease, welfare, and incarcerations keep increasing on a daily basis? There can no longer be among every race, community, and country, the puerile contest that has existed since the beginning of time. It's a social and economic matter for this country, other countries, and the rest of the world.

Therefore, everyone in the world has to make an effort to achieve a solution.

If the leaders of the most powerful countries in the past had cooperated so they could create a method to benefit all races, genders, social classes, religions, and countries, they would never have lost their empire and power in modern times. The leaders in this country and around the world cannot let school admissions become competitions because the development of this country and the world depends only on a great educational system. If Oxford and Cambridge were serving all people, social classes, religions, and genders in England and citizens of countries around the world, they would never have lost their educational number one status in the modern world. The same thing goes for the schools in ancient times such as the Sorbonne and many more. Not passing laws and policies so all citizens in this country and the world can get a quality education will always put this country at great risk socially and economically because having two systems will always result in failure: one would be up and the other would be down; one pulls in, the other pulls out. By having so much competition, the world has to fail because school officials are more concerned with competition among themselves than with the welfare of this country and the world. As a result of this mess, neither this country nor the world would ever grow. If the majority of citizens do not grow, this country and the world itself would never grow. The educational system was created to uplift and better humanity, not to have the most important system in this country and the world to be overcrowded with men and women who have more interest in making a profit. And to undo what others in the past have done rather than to uplift and better humanity will always tear this country and the world apart. Letting such men and women with such mentality and vision control the most important system in this country and in the world only cripples this country and the world even more. Because the bright men and women that they are going to educate are only there for puerile contest, they would educate their graduates to only plunge into law, politics, business, medicine, education, and more spheres only for competition, not for the common good, not to better this country and the world. If they were preparing, educating, and training these bright students to better the world, the social and economic problems such as crime, high illiteracy rates, high debts, welfare, prison overcrowding, discrimination, poverty, racism, sexism, war, terrorism, and immigration would be diminishing, not increasing.

The more lawyers we have in the modern world, the more racism, police brutality, discrimination, and injustice that blacks, Hispanics, Asians, illegal immigrants, homosexuals, females, Middle Easterners, and many other citizens will suffer. Not because these lawyers could not be better servants for these people, but because they were not trained at all to confront and solve these social problems. They were mainly trained to become crooks and ambulance chasers. The more business graduates these schools produce, the more economic debasement this country and the world will suffer. The professors did not train their students cooperate with one another so they can better and develop the poor communities, the poor states, and the poor countries economically so this country and the world can grow economically. They mainly train their students to compete with one another, increasing the interest rates and the high cost of living, so the people in the poor communities can close their businesses and their banks, so they can take over their communities and enslave them economically and socially. They teach the economy students to make property loan interest rates high so they cannot have good-looking property or improve the look of their communities, states, and countries. These people's communities, states, and countries are unattractive and distasteful because they have no business for themselves. The people that they are enslaving themselves for probably never have experienced a moment in those communities, states, and countries. They mainly teach their graduates to become the modern slave masters, after they enslave their own fellow Americans, such as blacks, Hispanics, Asians, females, others, and this country economically. They teach them to exploit the citizens of other countries, mostly those in poor countries, put those citizens out of business on their own lands, take their business away from them, and exploit them for cheaper labor so they can grow richer, as the previous slave masters used to do in Africa and other poor countries in the old days. Since these poor people end up having nothing to live on and cannot live on their lands, they end up leaving their lands and immigrating to rich countries. Afterwards, these narrow-minded and foolish Ivy League professors have some nerve for blaming the poor for immigrating to this country and other wealthy countries, while they teach their foolish graduates to exploit them for natural resources and other things. Why do these racist, biased, prejudiced, and narrow-minded professors not teach their graduates to exploit the Europeans for natural resources and for cheap labor? The ancient ones used to exploit the same races, countries, and continents. Those in the modern world are doing the same thing to the same people and continents, and they have some nerve to label their graduates as educators. The old slave masters had weapons; the modern ones have degrees. In the end, both are doing the same thing to poor people, and the narrow-minded congressmen do not say anything about it. No wonder this country has so many enemies. These narrow-minded and foolish Congressmen and women who just voted to waste trillions of taxpayers' dollars for a wall on the Mexican border and reinforce the immigration laws have to know that these things won't do any good unless they refine their so-called foreign policy. Poor people from other countries do not come here because of Hollywood or your T.V. shows. They immigrated to this country because the so-called foreign policy and education only benefit Europe, China, and Japan.

All the powerless people's communities, this country, and the world end up being so handicapped and crippled economically because these bright kids were taught to turn business to a competition, instead of a way to better humanity. As a result, modern people are still working harder and harder. Most of them cannot even take two weeks' vacation because everything is way too expensive. These schools officials turn social science programs into a contest too. They only allow a small percentage to be educated, and give a bunch of government tests that have no bearing on why people really commit crimes, why the crime rate is out of control, why children are having two or three babies, and why our politicians and leaders are so corrupt and unintelligent. They turn education into a contest and a luxury, while kids are in the streets committing crimes, and while people, communities, and while the citizens of other countries hate and are willing to kill one another merely based on what people in the past have done, stated, and written. These professors taught their students to control the political sphere while the people who could be great leaders for their communities, states, this country, and the rest of the world are restricted from getting in. They are educating to control the medical field while people who have the interest and passion to better their neighborhoods, communities, states, this country, and the rest of the world medically, and while millions of our brothers, children, and sisters, are dying due to lack of knowledge of medicine.

In order for this great country and this great world to stop sinking in this nasty mud, the school systems have to be filled with great leaders and humanitarians who can educate children to work for the common good, and not for war and competition. Consequently, the majority of people who live in urban communities, this country, and many poor countries have no business enterprise worth anything. The bright students cannot only be taught for personal empowerment, they have to be taught to work for the empowerment of this country and the rest of the world. Teaching students to be selfish will always backfire greatly on this country economically and socially. In reality, for the citizens to do well, the leaders of their countries have to do their part first. The professors have to modernize their teaching method sufficiently so this country and the leaders of other countries can find peace among themselves and become great leaders for us as the people. If the professors really educated the students to work toward world peace and to expand all natural resources and minerals, and to teach the leaders and citizens of poor countries how to use their money properly, they would only produce good results for this country and the world. The future world experts should be taught to work toward world social and economic improvement. The future experts have to learn to direct their attentions mostly to the problems of this country and the world. If professors could teach and train these students to lead and develop this country and the world, instead of controlling and oppressing it, they would accomplish something great for us, this country, the rest of the world, and humanity. The leaders would lead the people in this country and around the world to solve the problems, which previous leaders have tried to accomplish, but were unable. We as the citizens will not advance any further in life if the leaders of this country and the world continue to waste their energy to fight over power and wealth, while the world has enough for all of us to live on and be happy with. The world leaders have to direct their attention mainly to lead the world and the citizens in it. The leaders are not altogether to blame because they have been mainly trained and educated to control the world, not to develop it. If future leaders continue to be taught in such a way, they will find themselves in World War III, instead of the development of this country and the world.

No other leaders and citizens of a country or continent can accomplish this world peace movement and uplifting programs. The leaders of the world have to be trained properly for such a task. All of us are world citizens or leaders; we cannot keep learning to despise and hate one another in the modern world, and our leaders cannot continue to use the taxpayers' money and the resources in the world to oppress and cripple the world, instead of developing it. Leaders and citizens have to be trained and educated not to abuse their power toward their fellow citizens in this country and around the world because they are serving both of them. They have to be trained as leaders if the decisions that they are about to make will rebound in the long run on the people in their communities, their states, this country, and the rest of the world that they are serving, or if the decision would be harmful for their communities, states, this country, and the world, or if they are only benefiting just one side. Having such an approach or belief will always be a failure for this country. Leaders have to be trained as leaders to see farther ahead than the average citizen. If they cannot, they should not even run for public office or represent citizens who are seeking good leadership.

The leaders should be trained in a sense to be great visionaries and accomplishers so they can solve the people's problems, not just give citizens hope, give nice speeches, and raise money for their parties or pockets. The citizens have to be trained and educated in a sense not to vote for or elect talkative people because history also shows talkative people often are not great visionaries and accomplishers. People who accomplish great things and improve the world do not talk too much. Their great accomplishments and actions speak for them. The citizens do not have to ask what candidates have done for their communities, their sates, this country, and humanity. If they do not know or can't remember what their candidates have done for them as an average citizen, he or she is not a good fit for that public office. She or he is not a great leader; a person who just comes to extract votes or other political gains from the people cannot come out of nowhere to run for office because being a leader or politician is not a joke or fun game. Many of them have been misled by viewing public office as a place to gain political power, control, and to be highly respected, mainly due to the fact they have not been trained and educated in how to serve us as the people sufficiently. They have not been properly educated and trained that leading the people is the heaviest burden on earth because the people have a need for us, this country, and the rest of the world to function well. We as the people are not like a car; to use us and leave us when they feel like it, and if our needs cannot be met or supported by them, the country and the world would never be able to function either. Our needs are to decrease education tuitions, create more jobs, get rid of high living costs, insecurity and medical cost, lower the crime rate, poverty, and immigration problems because they are out of control; and look for peace in each community, state, country, and continent, so the blood of innocent people, our brothers, and our sisters can stop being shed.

In fact, the leaders have to start gaining training

by helping the kids and the people in their communities or states to reach peace among themselves without using any violence. If we as people cannot find peace or solutions in our own communities, how can they establish peace in this country and the world? If our leaders cannot provide us as people what we need to function properly, how can they expect the world to function as it is supposed to? In order for a community, state, country, and the world to function well, the leaders have to be competent and well-trained with more modern philosophy courses, so they can love and respect all races, genders, sexual orientations, religions, social classes, and citizens of other countries as a whole, and they also have to do humanitarian projects. They need to learn to cooperate with one another, work together as a team to find ways out of these undesirable conditions, work out constructive programs among themselves to find the light of these modern circumstances, and to teach people who do know how to make an honest living in this country and around the world how to do so. Again, the world cannot go forward if its leaders have not been properly trained to teach us as citizens how to respect, tolerate, and work together as brothers and sisters. By leading people in such a way, we will be able to contribute to the modern world. We as citizens cannot have an interest in the advancement of our country and world if we do not have great leaders to lead and serve us.

The modern leaders and citizens have to learn to gain vision of the modern world by conducting themselves and thinking differently from those men in the past because they are not them, and they are certainly living in a different time and world. The past had so much suffering, pain, and war, not because the leaders in the past were naturally bad people, but because their attitude, behavior, and approach were bad. They were not willing to cooperate with each other for the general welfare of all; they were not willing to work with different races, genders, sexual orientations, social classes, people of other religions, and other countries. Not working together would leave no hope for advancement and no progress for them. As long as the leaders are not willing to develop a modern world peace movement they will never be able to respect, admire, and learn from one another, and they can never get to the point that they would be able to take orders, assignments, and ideas from one another, and settle a matter among themselves without bloodshed.

We as modern citizens cannot say that we cannot take orders or work under a certain person or leader because of their race, religion, sexual orientation, religious beliefs, social status, or the school they went to. Having such a stupid excuse for not placing the right men and women in responsible positions because of their race, gender, sexual orientation, social class, religion, background, or country of origin would always end in disaster for the people, this country, and the rest of the world. The leaders and the citizens cannot be taught to be concerned or afraid whether a person of a certain gender, race, sexual orientation, and religious beliefs will get elected. They just have to be taught to be concerned with which one can get the job done or run things smoothly. And in order for the world to run well, its citizens and leaders have to learn to follow procedure and proposals from the one who is in charge of this country and the world, as long as the leaders are competent, cultivated, unbiased, and fair, regardless if the leader is white, black, female, Middle Eastern, homosexual, Asian, or anything else. If a certain group of citizens or certain countries intentionally ignores the leader's orders and proposals, merely because of a silly criteria or ego, the task cannot be done, and the people cannot be well served either. Also, when leaders despise and mistreat a certain community, race, gender, and country, the work can never be done either. In the end, the people, this country, and the rest of the world would end up suffering.

Teaching us the contrary about great leadership would keep the world from progressing and advancing. This ideology of refusing a person of a certain race, gender, social class, or religion as the leader of a country or the world has been borrowed from the ancient ones in the past. For example, the idea that men cannot take orders from females because men are better, smatter, and stronger is totally absurd and ridiculous. The same thing goes for a certain race, sexual orientation, social class, religious beliefs, and other silly criteria. Subordinating certain races, communities, genders, religions, leaders and countries would always cause conflict among us as the people of this country and the world. Therefore, one side would always be treated better and superior, and would fight, or even kill, to keep the system that way, hurting us, the country, and the rest of the world. And, the other side that has been treated unfairly and kept in the mud would always retaliate. As a result, no individual or country would ever really flourish. When one takes a step, the other one moves backwards. The consequence is that war, hatred, sexism, racism, bias, and prejudice would always have to exist. And no leaders would put down their weapons or stop terrorist attacks until they saw the system was working for everybody and every side. Let's just assume the present so-called terrorists put their guns down or stopped terrorist attacks. It would not mean the next generation would do the same thing. A generation might accept or ignore a certain thing or action from a different group of people or country, but it does not mean the next one will do the same thing. It took over ten generations to abolish slavery. The same thing as in this country, the oppressed race, gender, social class, sexual orientation, and religion will never stop fighting until they really see that the system is working for every single one of them. Otherwise, the same struggle and problem will go on and on until the system changes for everybody. These things have been in this country and around the world since the beginning of time, and also have these causes. So many untrained so-called experts have stated that people are born racist or biased or part of our culture. These people—with MAs and PhDs—never realized and thought that maybe these social problems are occurring due to a lack of modernized and quality education. All these things are not good or healthy for us and this country indeed because the world would have to keep sinking deeper and deeper to a point that poverty, crime, and immigration would really be out of control.

For example, when mob members are fighting among themselves, the wise men or mob leaders have to sit down together to settle matters among themselves peacefully and quietly. If the conflict occurs between them because one of them goes into the other one's territory to make money and take their customers, the one that crosses the line has to step back, or if one disrespects the other, he has to stop. If they sit down and cannot resolve the matter among themselves, one from another state or country gets involved in the matter. A mob leader who is unbiased has them work out a solution among themselves because if they keep fighting among themselves the jobs could not get done efficiently. If the job cannot get done, none of them would make money. Supposedly, these people who have been deemed the worst kind on the planet can find peace among themselves. The world leaders and the other countries that should be greater visionaries and leaders still cannot find peace among themselves. Until they find peace among themselves, nothing can get done properly, and the people will never be able to get out of these undesirable conditions. The leaders of the world leaders should get together to work out a plan that would work for every country and every single citizen in the world so each country can grow economically, socially, and peacefully, and the war issues can disappear for good.

In fact, the European leaders have cooperated and formed a sort of union among themselves so the money in all European countries has the same value. They respect all their countries' leaders around them, and allow Europeans to travel in European countries easily. Since this form of agreement has been established, wars have disappeared in Europe. In fact, England had trouble becoming a part of this program because the other European countries saw that England or Great Britain wanted to control the world, and was more concerned with wealth and power than peace. Europe is doing better than any continent economically and socially because none of the European countries cause any other country in the world immigration problems. Therefore, the world leaders must implement the European system to better the world so immigration, war, terrorism, racism, poverty, and disease problems can stop for good. The leaders of the world and all countries have to come together for a world development and peace program for the general interest and common good. All leaders want the same thing for their lands and their citizens. All of them want peace and safety for their citizens. They want their countries to grow economically, medically, and socially. They want respect and fairness from their fellow leaders and their fellow leaders want the same things too. They want to be treated as men and women, not as children. But in order for this masterful leadership to be established for the world's interest and people, leaders have to start treating each other as brother and sisters, instead of enemies, outcasts, murderers, and terrorists. If world leaders passed a world law for the world interest, it has to be preceded, followed, and respected by all leaders. The law has to be respected and followed as long as it is in the interest of them and humanity, not just a certain country or continent.

World leaders have to refine foreign policy in a way so each country leader has to respect the other's lands, no matter how big or small they are. If the world leader asks every leader that occupies another country's land to leave that particular land or territory as soon as possible, such a request has to be respected. If the world leader asks any country leader that holds hostages, soldiers, or so-called terrorists to release them because they are not criminals, they are fighting for injustice against their lands, such a request has to be followed. If the world leader asks the leaders of every country or group to bury the hatchet and make peace instead of making or purchasing nuclear weapons, such a request has to respected and followed. And if the world leader asks the leaders of countries and groups that already have nuclear weapons to disable or get rid of them somehow, such a request has to be followed. If all the leaders of the world make peace and respect each other's territory, there would be no need for us to continue killing each other. If the world leader asks the leaders of other countries to produce and sell their products on their own lands, instead of exploiting others for cheap labor or other things, and sell them around the world so the citizens in poor countries can grow economically, such a request has to respected and followed. By modernizing foreign policy in such a way, peace, harmony, and success would be the result, and citizens around the world would be able to work on their land, live happily, and stop causing others immigration, social, and economic problems.

The world has seven continents: each continent has certain weather, economic and natural resources. Therefore, world leaders and experts cannot be trained to crowd in one or a few countries and perform a world task. The school system should differentiate the program between the experts in this country and the world. Government officials have to pass laws for world experts to develop modern world programs. The scholars in the world's leading institutions write many documents for every aspect and every country in the world, while they never had even a moment's experience in these countries. They base their whole argument on what the documentaries that CNN, FOX, BET, and others have said about a country and continent. These professors do not realize that in order to have expertise in a certain country or continent, they have to see what caused the problems and know how to fix them. All of them have stated that the citizens of these countries are doing poorly socially and economically because they are poor and uneducated. But not one of them builds any quality school programs to teach them how to rebuild their countries socially, economically, medically, and technologically. Not one of them sees how they can develop any constructive programs to better their country and continent so they can stop causing immigration and high cost of living in other countries. If every single country in the world was providing natural resources and minerals, food, property, oil, and gas would never cost that much in the modern world. If all continents were making their own cars, bikes, computers, medicines, computer games, planes, boats, and other electronic equipment, the world would never have such economic debasement and deficits in the modern world. If the leaders of countries around the world assisted each other in the economic and social struggle, they would not hate and kill each other that much in the modern world. Furthermore, they would not depend on this country for every little thing they need, or call the U.S.A for everything. The leaders of the world have to know that this country cannot fix or support the world socially and economically by itself. Therefore, they have to set a world structure to have world experts teach people in other countries how to improve themselves and be independent. The people in these countries already have land and brains, they just need us to help them develop their intelligence to better this country, the rest of the world, and humanity.

The biggest and wealthiest countries on each continent have to learn and educate its citizens as a way to protect themselves and the little ones, not to control or oppress them, but to assist them when they have a major problem, to be like a big brother or sister to them. If all the leaders on a continent work together as brothers and sisters, and support each other as they are supposed to, then when one of them has a crisis, the others would assist. With such an approach, the world leader would not have to be called for any miniature thing. This country as the world leader would only step in when there was a major catastrophe. The world leader has to form a world structure so the world can be fully developed because without a great structure, the world will always fail. For example, all successful corporations have a great structure for success; otherwise, they would not be successful. A warm country or continent that produces products that a cold one cannot produces for themselves and some extra for the cold countries. They sell the products to them at a good price because they depend on them, too. The ones that have cold weather do the same thing. We all are brothers and sisters, so why do we have to be selfish with one another? Hatred, war, immigration, and other problems would just disappear. When a continent has a catastrophe, the countries on that continent give what they can and help out how they can.

If the leaders of the world work out a program like that together, the leader of the world would not have to support or assist them because they would be as independent, well-situated, and well organized as them. Many criticize poor countries for not helping others in a crisis, but how can the poor countries give something if they do not have anything? For example, can a homeless person give anything? When the people in a poor country see their next-door neighbors have a catastrophe, they feel ashamed due to the fact that they cannot give anything. For example, many kids like to help their parents out when they are sick. They do not want their parents to depend mainly on the government for support. It really hurts them to call the government for help when their parents are sick because these officials would ask so many questions and do so little. But they still call the government anyway, not because they want to, but because they have to. Many countries, and especially the poor countries, do not help other countries when they are in trouble, or affected by some catastrophe, not because they don't want to, but because they can't. If the world had a great structure, no one would want to leave his or her country of origin. Since this country is the world leader, this country has to provide programs run by world experts for every single aspect. If anybody wants to go into such programs, they have to be expected to go to such a country and find solutions when they are having and facing a crisis. For example, a doctor might be tired, but if there is a tragedy, he or she has to stay on his or her feet to help sick people who need medical treatment, even if she or he has to be drugged. Racism and sexism cannot exist in the modern world, and certainly college tuition has to be controlled by government officials because these undesirable problems have to go away, and the educational system is the only system that can help solve all these problems.

Educators and teachers have to welcome or look for people who want to be trained and educated to develop themselves, their communities, states, this country, the poor countries, and the rest of the world. Some professors think this task is impossible to achieve. That is fine, they can be taught and trained by those who can make this impossible task become possible. But if they refuse to do their job, which is teaching the people and facing teaching challenges, they have to be dismissed or demoted, and let real teachers who have an interest and desire to better society, this country, and the rest of the world step forward. Such a narrow-minded mentality and attitude got us in this mess; many ancient people thought a heavy piece of metal could not fly. We have planes that are flying, and have other planes inside of them while flying. Many ancient people also thought a heavy piece of metal could not float on water, and we have big metal boats. Professors and teachers who think this task cannot be achieved and refuse to be trained so all the citizens in this country and around the world can make history by accomplishing the greatest task ever, have to be released from their positions or demoted because if they do not have vision, they cannot train the bright kids and citizens to gain vision of the modern world. Many people thought females had to stay behind in the kitchen or behind the door, while females are now dominant and leading the modern world. We can keep choosing educators who refuse to teach or think that they need a lot of money to teach. Many great philosophers used to educate people under a tree, or in a village. Many people who started medicine did not even know too much about education, but they still started a great science. Lazy, incompetent, and narrow-minded school officials would always go for money rather than teaching people who want to learn and train. More than twenty million kids are becoming criminals due to the lack of education, more than a hundred million at the present time are about to die due to a lack of medical education and training, over two hundred million are dying due to poverty, and over fifty million Americans are on welfare and in jail due to a lack of education while their minds are working and while they can do for themselves, this country, and the rest of the world.

Disadvantaged people are breaking international law to immigrate to this country and elsewhere, while the world leading experts refuse to teach them how to use their lands and money properly so they can stop immigrating to this country and to other countries. The deficit of this country and the world is increasing drastically, while these people hold and treat education as a luxury. While the economy of this country is going down, immigration and terrorist attacks are increasing drastically, and when other bubbles collapse, the same professors or critics write many books, or go to the media to blame the leaders of this country and around the world for destroying this country and the world, while they are the ones who did not educate and train these leaders properly. The people who intentionally deceive the citizens in this country and around the world to lose their foresight and their common sense should be the ones to blame, not the enforcers. These failures are not inherent, they are taught and trained; therefore, the professors' and the teachers' points of view or the educational system must be changed first before world leaders and citizens can construct a world uplifting program to bring all the citizens of this country and the world out of the wilderness. Nothing good can be expected from this country if the educational leaders or officials are more concerned with money or prestigious status rather than educating the citizens in this country and around the world.

They force the majority of blacks, Hispanics, Asians, Middle Easterners, and others to psychologically become criminals, get stuck in the welfare and criminal justice systems, and to be abused and mistreated by the justice and all other systems in this country, simply because the majority of them cannot afford college. The prominent school officials clearly show that they have no good message for the masses, this country, and the rest of the world's citizens. If the citizens in the richest countries cannot afford those outrageous tuitions, how could the citizens of other countries, and what hope is there for us and future generations? Those school officials' examples and attitudes drag this great country and this great world down, and the fact that the leaders of this country and the world do not step in this crusade is even more depressing. Evidently, they have little or no interest and desire to enlighten and educate the multitude. The only interests they seem to have are to make their institutions bigger and fancier, not this country and certainly not the world. The most important thing to uplift this country and the world has a ridiculous and luxury price tag on it, and these professors wonder why everything is so messy, and why the world is getting worse. This educational system brings this country and the world backward towards economic and social slavery because education is not used to improve this country and the world. It is only used for personal gain; since education is not used to better this country or society, leaders cannot expect the weak races, genders, social classes, communities, states, this country, and the world to advance in a sphere. The world cannot go forward when school officials who should have led them efficiently have chosen to go backward, and this is exactly what school officials are doing. Most of them stay in the office or on their campus giving many worn-out theories about why the world is failing economically and socially. If the majority of the children—who will become the future of tomorrow—are restricted in getting a quality education, it is a fact that the future of this country and the world will have to be

189

worse than now unless they change their attitude towards education. They have not tried to gain vision of the modern world by bringing lights and hopes to the masses, poor communities, poor countries, and the rest of the world. These professors, experts, and school officials stay far from the masses, the illegal immigrants, and the people of poor countries that really desperately need them, but give plenty of ridiculous explanations and theories about why these communities, this state, this country, and the world is failing. A free lesson for them: the reason that they are failing and becoming criminals is due to a lack of education, simple as that. All these people, communities, this country, and the poor countries are failing because these professors have not yet figured out their duties. Their main duty is to educate, train, and prepare people and leaders to uplift themselves, their communities, this country, the poor countries, and the rest of the world socially and economically.

It is an injustice to this country's citizens to overcharge for taxes while the property prices, taxes, high cost of living, tuitions, illiteracy, immigration, terrorism, medical costs, soldiers' deaths, and oil price problems are increasing drastically, and larger numbers of citizens in this country and around the world cannot help in this awful situation because the school officials use education selfishly. These professors do not realize that the majority of citizens in this country and around the world have been restricted and held down, and naturally descend to the lower level of poverty and delinquency. The education system is not altogether the problem, but the people who are in charge of it are the problem because they improperly control and manage it.

The fact is that blacks, Hispanics, Asians, Middle Easterners, illegal immigrants, people in poor countries, and other people in this country and the world are going to be trained and educated somehow. But the main question is: which type of education, training and direction are they going to receive? Since school officials have manipulated the educational system to keep the quality education from them, these kids are not able to have a great direction, mental discipline, and great leadership in life. As a result, they are only going to have another education and training, which is going to be problematic and untoward to society. This is street and unproductive education; such education would lead them to be handicapped and crippled for life. Therefore, they are more likely to become criminal and get stuck in the criminal and welfare system instead of being productive for themselves and their country. Once they get caught up in one of these crippling systems they become handicapped for life because when they have a criminal record, they become slaves of the state and this country for good. The police officers have rights to terrorize, abuse, and violate all their civil rights, and they presume guilt for anything, instead of innocence. They cannot vote, they cannot get a job or college assistance, become a part of the justice system, or leave the state or country without telling their masters, who are the probation or parole officers. The state may take their kids away from them; nearly all their natural rights have been taken away from them. This is an outrage, despicable, and unethical for many reasons. These people's natural rights are not granted by government officials or politicians or judges; these people were born with these rights. For example, if a person proposes marriage to another, they give each other a wedding ring. If things do not work out between them as they were expecting, it is really up to them to give their rings back to each other. Neither a judge nor a state official can force them to give back the wedding ring. The same thing should apply to the citizens in this country, especially in a democratic country. There should be a sort of way for the inmates to be able to take their rights back because everybody makes mistakes, and besides the judge, the state, or politicians did not give them such rights; these people were born with them. Secondly, these kids did not intentionally choose these corrupt lives. School officials and many leaders should be the ones to blame because they have manipulated the educational system so these bright kids can be corrupt from infancy until old age. Thirdly, they have restricted and held these kids down naturally to the lower level of delinquency. Fourthly, this country and the world are the ones that are going to suffer, not the school officials. The school officials are making huge money, getting big salaries and bonuses that the taxpayers are paying for, even when they are not getting any good results. They get invited to fancy parties to be treated like Socrates, and kiss the asses of upper class people; besides, most of the school officials and leaders are corrupt themselves.

In order for this country and the world to advance socially and economically, the school officials, professors, and teachers have to do their parts first. They have to educate every race, gender, social class, and sexual orientation adequately so they do not see life as only a competition. And the public officials and the citizens have to be well educated and trained so they won't vote or elect or give the wrong men and women the important positions in this country and around the world. They should train and educate us as citizens of this country and the world not to think that a man or a woman is qualified to be our leader because of the school they went to, the social class they came from, the religion that they are practicing, their gender, sexual orientation, their background, or their country of origin. We as people must be taught, educated, and trained in a way to dismiss all these criteria as silly; things such as color, gender, sexual orientation, social class, religion, country of origin, and the school one goes to. The school the leader went to has nothing to do with the person's leadership. The person can never be a great leader to such a community, country, and the world if his or her heart and soul is not with all the people that he or she is serving because the greatest things in life can be attained only by wise and unbiased leadership. For example, a family that has six children cannot grow if the parents only invest or have interest in a child or two while ignoring the others. The children that they have invested and had more interest in are the only ones who are going to succeed and flourish in life, not because they are the only children in that family who could flourish, but because they are the only ones that the parents cared for, worked for, and invested in. As a result, such a family would never advance, and at the same time, the two children are going to believe that they are smarter, better, and the only ones who can think and uplift the family, while they would never be able to support the family and others sufficiently by themselves. And those who have been neglected are going to dislike and despise their parents because they have only supported a couple of them. This family would end up having constant fights, feeling hatred toward one another, and disliking one another; therefore, they would never go forward unless they resolved their problems, and the family would probably never grow for generation after generation either.

Unfortunately, that is what happens to this great country and to this great world. This country and the world leaders who came before the modern time only invested in and educated one race and gender. At the same time, the ancient leaders went to other countries to exploit them for slavery, natural resources, gold, and more. Thus only one race and gender is doing okay, and a couple of countries are doing okay socially and economically. But they naively believe that they can support this country and the whole world by themselves without including the other races, genders, social classes, and other countries in the development of themselves and the world. The only thing that would come out of this misconception, even in the modern world, would be failure for all of us. Since not all races, genders, sexual orientations, religions, social classes, and countries can live happily, none of us will. Some of us are trying to accomplish and the rest of us are going to tear it down. In the long run, no one will make progress, and everybody in this country and in the rest of the world will be sinking. All of us are in the same boat, and the boat is breaking down and sinking deeper. Therefore, all of us have to do our part to keep it above water and to repair it afterwards. The races, genders, and social classes and other people who have been taught that they are the only ones who can fix the problems in this country and the rest of the world have been misled and misinformed. Due to this misleading, everybody in this country and around the world is suffering high cost of living or war, either on the streets, in poor countries, or big countries. All of us end up being unhappy with life and unsafe regardless of whether we live in poor communities, poor countries, or big countries. The debts for everybody are increasing, regardless of whether they are wealthy countries, poor countries, doctors, intellectuals, or menial workers who are working two or three jobs. Due to this misleading we end up working to live, instead of living to work. In the end, no person or country is safe and happy. Therefore, the leaders have to learn to work together to fix the boat; guess what, they are a part of the boat, and the boat is sinking deeper and deeper. Sorry to say, it might take many centuries. If we as modern citizens do not try to repair it together, eventually it will stop sinking somewhere, by just falling apart, and the world will have just disappeared.

Again, this path that we are going down as people

would lead one of us to create more nuclear weapons to exterminate our own brothers and sisters, ourselves, and the entire world. It may take hundreds or even thousands of years, but someone will develop a powerful nuclear weapon that will be able to destroy the whole world. And once it is created, the leader of a country or someone else would use it eventually, and guess what? Everybody in the world will die. For example, Albert Einstein created the first atomic bomb, which was cataclysmic and destructive to the human race, but eventually it was used on Japanese soil, in Hiroshima and over 140,000 people were killed. A few days later, another one was dropped on Nagasaki and over 60,000 women and children were injured and killed. At this moment many countries are still suffering from the same cause; our embassies are being destroyed overseas, our planes and buildings were crushed on 9/11, and many of us were injured, killed, and damaged psychologically due to this cause. Many of our other brothers and sisters were killed and continue to be killed by these ordeals because many of us have been misled to believe that we have to control and oppress other countries and the world instead of helping to develop them. We as modern people have learned from our teachers and professors to restrict and exterminate one another based solely on the beliefs of ancient leaders who died long ago.

Every community, state, and country is a part of the same boat. Why can't we as modern citizens learn to respect, admire, and work with one another to fix this world's problems, so it can start to flourish as it was supposed to? Controlling and oppressing one another would keep us sinking deeper and deeper. No human race, social class, gender, religion, or sexual orientation should be trained and educated in a sense to control, oppress, exploit, and restrict this country's and the rest of the world's citizens because we as people would never be able go forward. The leaders and the citizens have to be trained to love one another and work for self-development, not for wealth and power, in a sense to better this country, the world, and humanity. Wealth and power were here before we as modern citizens came into this world, and they are certainly going to be in this world after we leave it. Therefore, our leaders should be trained to make all people in this country and the other countries that they are serving happy, and to grow for themselves and humanity. If the leaders of the world and the countries have been trained and educated properly, they will help this country and all the rest of countries in the world to grow socially, economically, and intellectually, so we as the modern human race can be stronger to confront humanity's problems.

The science school professors and officials should teach and train their students in a way to make the medicines for diseases and deadly viruses more affordable so everybody would be able to buy them, but instead they teach them the contrary. Magic Johnson has lived with the AIDS virus for a long time, but he is still living. The poor people who have been affected by the viruses a year ago, are already dead and have left their kids and loved ones behind. To these narrow-minded oppressors, only the rich people are entitled to live, to a fair trial, and to a quality education. These pharmaceutical corporations would certainly make more money if they made these medicines and drugs inexpensive for the common people. Wal-Mart became the most successful corporation in the world because their products are extremely inexpensive. Otherwise, they would file for bankruptcy like the previous ones.

Those leading science schools in the world have misled and brainwashed their students to direct their attention to money and wealth instead of humanity's problems. The major science problems that are facing humanity have been completely ignored and dismissed by the main science schools. In fact, not one science school in this country or the world is specialized to confront major problems that all countries, humanity, and all human races are facing on this planet, such as an asteroid collision, black holes, super volcanoes, nuclear war, super-intelligent machines, and more. One of these things can make the whole human race disappear instantly, but there is no special program or school to prepare modern youths to deal with these major threats as they are. These things are major threats to humanity. The dinosaurs did not suddenly die just like that; they died for a reason. Instead of world leaders training and educating properly to help to develop the world sufficiently to deal with these world threats as they are, they are worrying more about controling the world, while the world itself is facing great threats and dangers. If all countries in the world have grown economically and socially, these major threats to the world and humanity would be much better and easier for the world's scientists, including Stephen Hawking, to deal with and overcome. This major issue is a world and humanity matter; therefore, all citizens in the world should assist as they can, but since we do not live as people, those scientists have to face a lack of finance and support to overcome these world threats.

If we were living as people, brothers and sisters, instead of as cavemen and women, we would help each other to grow economically, socially, and intellectually. Therefore, all countries in the world would end up paying world taxes, and such world tax money would be able to finance the world issues, such as to finance the best scientists among us to carry out these world tasks sufficiently. All these things would be better for us and our children. Again, all these problems have causes. Everything in life should not be a competition, because many of us cannot compete. Therefore, it is the job of those who have a special talent and gift to lead and serve those who cannot. Whoever is more talented and gifted among us has to be recruited or voted for. The best and greatest men and women among us for such tasks have to be recruited because we as a human race are in great danger. Those silly and absurd criteria have to be omitted in the modern world; this world needs a great leader, not a controller as those modern schools have trained and educated.

The teachers and professors cannot just choose to teach a certain race, social class, gender, religious believer, and citizens of other countries for this important task; they have to be willing to teach everybody that has an interest and desire to become great leaders. Also, they have to teach the citizens in this country and other countries better so they can vote for the best men and women among them. Again, a leader cannot serve this country if he or she does not have a great heart and soul for all the citizens in this country and around the world, regardless of their skin color, gender, customs, religious beliefs, culture, heritage, and language. By continuing to teach the future leaders the contrary of leadership, they will never become a part of the lives of all citizens in this country and around the world. If they do not become a part of them, how can they help the citizens of this country and the world and its leaders to develop and flourish under these undesirable circumstances? The leaders in this country and around the world can no longer be taught and trained that masterful leadership is all about giving orders, controlling, corrupting, and manipulating all the systems in this country and around the world. The future leaders in certain communities have to be taught in a sense to have a great relationship with all the people who live in that particular community, and also with all the business owners, judges, lawyers, teachers, policemen, school principals, children, adults, and other menial and professional workers in that community. A leader has to be trained to be creative to keep the community safe and flourishing, by seeing what laws need to be modified and what kind of activities he or she has to help the community's citizens to do to raise money so that the schools in that community do not close down or have the staff cut down; what public school campuses he or she has to keep open after regular school hours to create programs for the children in that community so they will be off the streets; what laws or policies he or she has to create to keep the major corporations out of his or her community so the people in that community can grow their business for that area to grow economically. Such a leader has to be creative to see which public schools he or she has to keep open so the common people in that community can know their civil and political rights, and to see if the kids in that community can create a car wash, a catering service, or other food programs to raise money for the community and to keep themselves busy. Who are the citizens in that community who are great leaders to do some voluntary work for the children and the elderly? What strategy does he or she have to approach so the people in that community can have their own homes and have the crime rate go down. Again, if the leader is not taught to be creative, to love, to appreciate, and to have a great relationship with all the citizens in that particular neighborhood, he or she can never improve such a community socially and economically.

The same theory applies to a world leader. If the leader never lived among or close to other religions, races, sexual orientations, social classes, and nationalities, how can such a leader understand and have a great relationship with everybody in this country and around the world? How can that world leader see what the whole country really needs: to have a great relationship and feel comfortable with every citizen, race, religious practitioner, gender, sexual orientation, social class in this country and around the world? And if the world leader does not travel to all the continents in the world, and almost all the countries in the world, how can such a world leader have a great relationship and feel comfortable with all the countries' leaders in the world. Again, this country and the world are sinking mainly because the main leader has not been trained adequately to work together with the leaders and citizens of all communities, states, and countries for the general welfare and the world's interest. If a leader does not live among the citizens, suffer and cry with them, do what they do, live as they live, enjoy what they enjoy, feel what they feel, and think what they think, how can such a servant fully understand and serve the people? How can the public servants of the world work together and feel comfortable with each other, and all the citizens and other leaders in this country and around the world, if they cannot do such things. Moreover, how can this country and the world ever be uplifted? The leaders must be trained and taught in a sense to live among the people, to understand the people's problems, to work with the people and for the people, and to find solutions to the people's problems. Furthermore, the leaders of countries and the world have to learn and be trained in a sense to think with the people and for the people, to feel with the people and for the people, to die with the people and for the people. If the leaders cannot be educated and trained in such a way, nothing good can come out from them or their system. The future leaders have to be taught and trained in a sense to study all the communities, states, this country, and the world sufficiently. By studying them well, the leaders will be able to create modern systems and laws to develop special capacities that will force and help the people to develop themselves, their communities, states, countries, and the rest of the world. And the people have to be taught to elect only the best men and women among themselves, like John F. Kennedy, Jean Jacques Dessalines, Catherine Flon, Nelson Mandela, Capois Lamore, Martin Luther King Jr., Bob Marley, Toussaint L'Ouveture, Carter G. Woodson, Malcolm X, Rosa Parks, Mahatma Gandhi, and many more. Even though the majority of these great leaders have been dead for so long, they are still alive in a sense to the people. They were the greatest leaders for the people in this country and around the world because they were fighting for all people's interest and peace, not just for the whites, blacks, yellows, blues, greens, males or females. Also, they are the best leaders because of their wise and masterful leadership. They loved or love the people that they were or are serving. They were willing to sacrifice everything, including many biased laws and even their own lives for the people. The best and strongest leaders develop and make the weakest people stronger, not weaker.

New Program for the Modern World

The future school officials will have to be educated and trained in a sense to modernize history, literature, philosophy, anthropology, and other social science classes and programs in order for the next black, Hispanic, Asian, Middle Eastern, female, and homosexual generation to know their history, literature, and have a better race relationship and understanding among themselves—and for others to understand them well. The rest of the people from all countries have to study and appreciate their philosophy, literature, heritage, culture, and language along with the ancient philosophers because if they do not educate and train in a sense to create better social science classes or programs, they are still going to resent, despise, look down on, and not appreciate their own while admiring and imitating others. The majority of modern and past textbooks do not mention anything good about the rest of the people, social classes, and religions, except to attack, oppress, exploit, restrict, shame, and condemn them. Many books that the school system is using were written by mostly narrow-minded and biased writers. They wrote in a way that other races, genders, sexual orientations, and people of other countries have not done or accomplished too much in the modern world and for humanity. Every race, gender, sexual orientation, and other groups have to get the same attention in the schoolroom. Keeping the rest of the people out of the school curriculum does them, this country, and the rest of the world more harm than good because they will always be alienated and unappreciated themselves, and they will only have a desire and interest in appreciating and giving their attention to another race, culture, literature, language, and heritage.

Therefore, self- and sexual-consciousness would continue to exist in the future world. Everybody does not learn to appreciate and desire to hear things about themselves, to study and to develop their own people's history, philosophy, literature, and art. Since many biased and incompetent writers have written in a sense of blacks, the Italians, Hispanics, Asians, Middle Easterners, poor people, and others belonging to drudgery, prostitution, menial jobs, crime, and terrorist organizations as their sphere, the next generation of them will toil in the same things to make a living. By not developing and modernizing social science classes, the next generation would continue to believe that they do belong in these lower spheres. At the same time, they would refuse to make any effort whatsoever to change their status in society and in the modern world as the present ones. No race, gender, and sexual orientation can develop socially and economically if they are in a mentally undeveloped state. The school officials and professors who are in conservative fashion by educating and training their students to remain where they are, are not helping the students in this country and around the world to face these social and economics ordeals. Besides, these school officials are getting paid to change and to create new innovations for society and the world, but they still oppose changing the school curriculum so the status of the other races, gender, social classes and sexual orientations can be changed and improved in the modern world. Opposing change is not good for this country and the world. In fact, it was never good because life changes on a daily basis. Many of these professors have stated that people cannot change and the world cannot change. In a sense, they are right because in order for us as people in this country and around the world to change and improve, school officials have to do their parts first by teaching us new things. Again, that is why they were appointed for these positions and get our tax money to do so. If they develop and create modern constructive classes and programs to develop all citizens, communities, states, this country, and the rest of the world socially and economically, the leaders and citizens of all countries will be learning and training how to use their lands properly for growth, and living on their lands peacefully and happily.

Citizens in this country and around the world cannot be forced psychologically to leave their communities, their races, genders, states, and their countries into a world peculiarly their own. Not modernizing the educational system so all the students and citizens can be educated and trained properly to do for themselves and to uplift themselves, their races, genders, communities, states, countries, and this world socially and economically would force them to desert and leave their native lands.

The school officials have to know that the educational system is not working and was never working for all citizens in this country, around the world, and for humanity, because it was never created to benefit the entire human race. The educational system was created initially to only benefit the white male upper class, and to enslave the minds of other races, genders, sexual orientations, social classes, and people of other ethnicities and countries since ancient times. The educational system is not working only for white males, white communities, and white countries due to coincidence. It was intentionally created to work such a way since the beginning of time.

To be more explicit, let's look over the courses and programs offered in the school curriculum. The majority of things that have been written about the white male upper class are superb, brilliant, and outstanding. And what has been written and offered about Hispanics,

Middle Easterners, blacks, Asians, homosexuals, Italians, Irishmen, females, the poor from other countries, and others places them in an inferior and ridiculed status. The previous and the present school officials have made no effort to upgrade the school programs sufficiently so the rest of the citizens in this country and around the world can learn great things and accomplishments about themselves, their countries, literature, history, languages, races, genders, sexual orientations, and their heritages as they do the Egyptians, Romans, Greeks, Hebrews, Englishmen, Teutons, Mongolians, Europeans, and the white American male upper class. The rest of the people have to be insecure about themselves, lack confidence, and be undeveloped mentally, socially, and economically because they have been taught mostly to see their races, cultures, heritages, literature, genders, languages, sexual orientations, and countries as problems to society and humanity. Hispanics, Asians, blacks, Middle Easterners, homosexuals, poor people, females, and others have no options except to only have interest in studying other people's history and status other than their own because they have been neglected for so long and dismissed as nonentities in the school curriculum by conservative school officials and professors. Instead of the rest of the people learning to spend billions of dollars to promote their own literature, philosophy, language, knowledge, heritage, and to become more interested in their own culture and background, they learn to promote and advance the works of others. The white male upper class does not have any interest in studying and developing the rest of the people's social science classes and programs or trying to imitate them. So why on earth do the rest of the people have to spend most of their time and money studying to imitate them? Ignoring and dismissing the history, languages, genders, races, literature, philosophy, culture, and heritage of the rest of the people in this country and around the world clearly illustrates that they are unimportant and insignificant human beings, and that there is nothing in their past, culture, heritage, and literature that is notable and worth studying.

Homosexuals, blacks, Indians, Hispanics, females, Asians, Middle Easterners, poor people from other countries, and middle and lower white male social classes are as human as the ancient philosophers and the white male upper class. There is nothing more shameful and appalling found in the rest of the people's communities, races, genders, sexual orientations, and countries than what is found in the white male upper class and the ancient philosophers. Every race, gender, social class, and people of other countries have their ups and downs, and all of us as citizens have contributed to the progress of the world and humanity, so why is it that the rest of the people have been and continue to be dismissed as insignificant persons in the modern world's school curriculum by the narrow-minded conservative school officials? Continuing to drill into the rest of the children's and citizen's minds that their races, genders, sexual orientations, social classes, and countries have not done anything significant since the beginning of time and in the modern world would always make them feel inferior, unimportant, insignificant, insecure, disgraced, shamed, and unconfident about themselves and their heritage, language, sexual orientation, culture, countries of origin, and ancestors. If they feel incompetent and inferior, they will never try to develop their own ideals or thoughts, or attempt to grow or to accomplish anything so they can be noticeable and independent. In order for the powerless people in this country and around the world to develop and flourish well in life, they have to have self-assurance, confidence, believe in themselves, and feel sure of themselves. But how can they have them, if there are not modern classes and programs for them;

psychologically, they have to be handicapped and enslaved mentally, because their minds and thinking are controlled, oppressed, and limited by others.

By not helping and guiding the rest of the modern citizens to develop their own thoughts and ideas, they can never grow, and the white male upper class does not have to worry about them becoming their competitors in the professional spheres, and standing up against them when they try to humiliate and control them. The white male upper class would not have to worry about blacks, Hispanics, females, Asians, homosexuals, Middle Easterners, and others growing their communities and countries economically and socially because they already mis-educated and brainwashed them to believe that theirs can never grow, and they cannot depend on themselves, and they cannot work together to leave the drudgery, welfare, poverty, and criminal life behind for good. If the professors and school officials left that conservative lifestyle and created modern social science courses and programs, the rest of the people would produce as many or more philosophers, thinkers, and others professionals as the ancients and the white male upper class; and they would accomplish as much good as them, or more and better than them. As the poor people in this country and around the world grew, they would aspire to have as much equality and justice for them as for the white male upper class. As long as the rest of the people only learn about others' philosophy, literature, languages, heritage, and culture, they will always feel inferior and insecure, and detest themselves, their races, genders, sexual orientations, communities, heritages, cultures, languages, and backgrounds. And they will always continue to depend on the whites and the government to uplift them, and citizens in poor countries will continue to possess the same fatal dependency on this country and other wealthy countries around the world as well. And they will also continue to admire and perceive the white male upper class as Socrates, masterminds, Plato, the ancient Greeks, Hebrews, geniuses, and more while they are just imitators. The mentality and intelligence of the leaders and citizens of this country and the rest of the world will not change if the prominent school officials are not replaced or demoted. And if the prominent school officials do not replace or modify the educational system, the rest of the powerless people in this country will be annihilated just as the American Indians in the past.

By not teaching and educating the rest of the people and the citizens of poor countries to feel as good and confident about themselves as the white male upper class, and to learn to plan to do for themselves as the white male upper class, the rest of the modern citizens and the citizens of poor countries will always be docile and tractable to the white male upper class. For example, in ancient times, the white male upper class used to tell the Irish, Italians, females, blacks, and others that they were inferior, unintelligent, slaves, and sub-human. Therefore, they had to stay out of public and other prominent spheres. Unfortunately, a large number of them admitted such things as the truth without questioning them, and placed themselves and their children in the lower and inferior status without being told to do so. In the modern world, these so-called professors, educators, scholars, experts, and geniuses continue to do and teach the rest of the people the same ridiculous things, including the Harvard University president. A large number of us still accept these worn-out theories and ideas.

Sorry to say, the majority of people's minds are still controlled and enslaved in the modern world. Again, men like Lawrence H. Summers have lost vision of and touch with the modern world for so long, and should have never taught in the modern world. The only reason things remain the same way as before is because school officials and leaders like Lawrence H. Summers enslave and control the rest of the people's minds, instead of developing and serving them. Allowing wiseacres like Lawrence H. Summers to be in charge and lead the most important systems and agencies in this country and around the world is a huge mistake indeed. The ancient conservative narrow-minded people or modern narrow-minded and biased men and women like Lawrence H. Summers have stated or written: "the rest of the people, races, genders, religions, and citizens of other countries have to learn to do and provide for themselves, and to find their own way out of these undesirable conditions." But how can we? Nearly all the systems and the agencies in this country and around the world have been since beginning of time—and continue to be—manipulated, monopolized, and corrupt by them, and our minds continue to be controlled and enslaved by them. Instead of them being great educators, leaders and lawmakers to develop the rest of the people so the world can finally grow, they proudly duplicate and borrow the old biased ones' ideology, that had initially developed such systems and theories to enslave, restrict, and oppress the weak ones in the past.

Many of these conservative school officials, leaders, and lawmakers are still sending their recruiters to the poor communities, states, and other countries to observe the rest of the people in action, as the ancient ones used to do, so they can recruit and bribe the brightest minds among the lowly people's communities, states, and countries to always remain powerful, while the rest of the world is getting weaker and weaker. These school officials have to update their programs in the modern world so the rest of the next generation will be well-thinking men and women, and will be learning how to deal wisely with the conditions they will find themselves in, rather than asking for help or depending on or taking orders from the white male upper class, which does not know anything about them and does not have any interest whatsoever in knowing anything about or developing them, except to continue taking advantage of them and keeping them in the darker position.

The old worn-out theories and false tradition that the white male upper class is smarter, superior, and better than females, blacks, Asians, homosexuals, Middle Easterners, poor people, and others has to disappear. And those ridiculous, absurd, and worn-out theories that this is a white man's world and that the world belongs to them have to vanish as well. Such theories cause this country to be at war every couple of years, and also cause the majority of the people in this world to want this country to collapse and lose its world leadership status. The conservative and liberal school officials have to reconstruct the whole educational system so the worn-out and expired courses and programs that have been offered in the modern world are upgraded and refined for the next generation. And the future leader of this country has to serve, educate, and lead the lowly people, races, communities, genders, sexual orientations, religions, and the poor in other countries efficiently, so this country and the world can finally re-flourish as they were meant to. The future students should not be charged high tuitions as before and in the modern world. The school officials can find trillions and billions of taxpayers' dollars to spend on their schools' design and architecture, so their schools can look more attractive than the people, this country, and the world that they were supposed to make look gorgeous and eye-catching. The school officials should invest the taxpayers' money to develop and educate the youth because they are the future and hope of this country and the world. They should refine and reconstruct the educational system as a strong and

211

productive system to uplift and prepare the future students and leaders to better serve and lead the lowly children and people in this country and around the world adequately, so they will not have to imitate, duplicate, or try to live like Socrates.

Furthermore, the school officials should improve the education system so the privileged and fortunate students and people would learn to develop and uplift the weak ones rather than exploiting, oppressing, enslaving, restricting, and exterminating them, all while still being perceived and regarded as the geniuses, heroes, great leaders, and lovers of all mankind. The conservative and the liberal school officials have to develop modern classes and programs so the future blacks, Hispanics, Asians, Middle Easterners, homosexuals, females, the poor, and other students will not spend most their time and money on advanced works of Shakespeare, Chaucer, and other Anglos. They should spend most of their time studying and being trained in a way to develop and direct their attention mostly to the myths, legends, and traditions of their own ancestors, folklore, and people; also, to their own poets, thinkers, philosophers, and proverbs, and to the development of their own philosophers for the modern and future world. The future business students in this country and around the world should not spend most of their time studying about Wall Street or how to make the white male upper class richer. They should spend most of their time studying their own genders, races, sexual orientations, communities, states, this country, and their own countries well so they will be able to develop them economically, to grow rich, and to learn to depend on themselves. The rest of the future medical students should not spend most of their time studying how to extract more money from poor people, and make the insurance and pharmaceutical companies richer. They should spend most of their time learning and educating in a sense to find cures and make medicines that they will make available and affordable to the lowly races, genders, the elderly, children, and citizens in their communities, states, this country, poor countries, and the rest of the world. The future leaders of this country and around the world should not be taught and trained to remain conservative and waste trillions and trillions of taxpayers' money in advanced nuclear weapons to hurt one another, destroy humanity in unnecessary wars, agencies, and in biased laws. They should spend most of their time learning and studying how to direct their attention to build a great relationship among themselves, and reach a world peace movement and development so the problems of immigration, hatred, terrorism, and war can be solved so the innocent children and citizens in this country and around the world won't have to continue to be killed for unnecessary reasons. The future students and citizens should not spend time learning and studying the worn-out theories that they are naturally born to hate, despise, and demean each other's language, heritage, religion, customs, culture, countries, manners, and backgrounds. They should spend most of their time studying modern philosophy and anthropology courses and programs to appreciate, admire, care for, respect, and tolerate one another's differences in a peaceful manner. The future businessmen and women should not spend most of their time learning the corrupt ways to exploit the poor communities, races, social classes, genders, states, this country, and the poor countries for cheap labor, so this soil can have more hatred and enemies. They should spend most of their time studying social responsibilities and world responsibilities, and to pay and treat their employees fairly and to respect each other's community, territory, country, or continent so the others can grow rich and be independent as well; so the natural resources and minerals for other communities, states, this country, and other countries can be expanded hugely; and so the high cost of living, property prices, immigration, and lack of natural resources and minerals can finally decrease in this country and around the world for good. The rest of the people and students should spend little or none of their time learning the worn-out theories and false traditions of ancient philosophers, sociologists, criminologists, psychologists, and anthropologists to find solutions to the problems in the modern world. They should spend most of their time studying and directing their attention to their own backgrounds from the point of view of anthropology and history, so they can develop their own modern sociology theory, research, and studies to advance their people, race, gender, community, state, this country, the poor countries and the rest of the world in the social sphere in life. Sociologists and criminologists should not spend their time learning how to waste trillions in taxpayers' money on worn-out theories to punish non-violent inmates severely, or to turn them into career criminals, or psychologically lead them to use everything around them or what they find in jail or in prison as weapons, including their bodies, spit, and urine to infect other inmates or the correction establishment staff. They should spend most of their time studying modern ways and methods to develop better constructive social science classes and programs to keep the non-violent inmates busy by learning and doing productive things, so they won't have to waste their time in their cells learning and thinking to develop criminal minds to hurt and to kill each other or the correction officers, or to become nightmares and predators in their society and this country upon their release. The future leaders of the communities, states, this country, and the world should not spend any time studying and learning to serve and protect only one race, gender, sexual orientation, and social class sufficiently. They should spend more or all of their time studying to serve and protect all citizens in this country and around the world sufficiently. The future leaders and attorneys should not spend too much time studying other sneaky ways and loopholes to keep manipulating the system so that poor cities and communities can continue to be overcrowded and victimized by the liquor and gun industries. They should spend most of their time studying and learning modern laws and social science classes to protect and serve all races, genders, social classes, communities, states, citizens, this country, and the rest of the world sufficiently so the gun industry should be liable for causing so much damage in this country and around the world. The political science and laws students should spend no time studying to protect and defend the worn-out and biased laws that help the lowly communities' citizens, races, and countries acquire guns and liquor to kill and to exterminate one another. They should spend more time studying new ways and systems to better protect and serve the people, so guns and liquor won't fall into the hands of kids or the wrong person. The leaders of the world should not spend any time continuing to study the biased and worn-out theories and foreign policies that provide and assist the leaders and citizens of other countries in acquiring guns, nuclear weapons, and other resources to aid them in exterminating their fellow citizens, men and women, and the citizens that they were supposed to serve. They should spend more time studying modern world philosophy, leadership, and foreign policies and theories to make leaders that have problems with those of other countries settle their matters in a peaceful manner and work together for the general welfare. The citizens and leaders of this country and the world should not spend any time studying and learning to say "God bless their country or America," or look for their country's or

America's dream. They should spend more time studying and learning to achieve the dreams of their country and the rest of the world, and to say God bless their country and the rest of the world. The poor people in other countries and the rest of the citizens should spend no time learning and studying how to violate international law to immigrate to this country and to other countries. They should spend more time studying and training to appreciate and to develop their own lands socially and economically, and to live on them abundantly. The future leaders and businessmen and women should not spend any of their time studying and learning how to take all the jobs overseas for cheap labor so the poor communities, states, and this country's citizens who patronize their business would live without jobs, to the point of turning to breaking the law as an occupation, or for the corporations and businesses in poor countries having to file for bankruptcy or close their doors.

The future leaders of the world, business professionals, and lawmakers should not spend any time learning how to serve crooked corporate CEOs or allow their country and people that they were supposed to serve and lead be crippled or lose their status. They should spend most of their time learning and studying how to pass modern world laws or foreign policies so each country's leaders can stay on their lands to establish most of their businesses there. That way, each country and continent can grow their economy, so they will not cause or victimize, through immigration, another social and economic crisis. The future leaders of this country and the world United Nations should spend no time studying worn-out foreign policies that have their soldiers and policemen and women occupy and control other lands and countries for good. These future leaders should spend most of their time learning and studying modern foreign policy methods to send the best and noble soldiers and policemen to go to train, teach, and prepare the people in poor countries to protect, lead, and serve the rest of their citizens and their countries sufficiently. Furthermore, the United Nations has to recruit world engineering, agriculture, and other experts to teach the poor how to grow, produce, and invest in their lands. After such important tasks have been accomplished and succeeded, these great and righteous soldiers, policemen, and educators have to return to their native lands.

Blacks, Asians, whites, Middle Easterners, homosexuals, and others in this country and around the world should not spend any time studying the worn-out history and religious theories, beliefs, and false traditions to hate, despise, go to war, and exterminate one another. These great men and women should spend more time studying and learning better and modern theories of these subjects, to make peace with, tolerate, respect, and work with one another for the general welfare of their country and the rest of the world. The future social science experts should spend no time studying the old worn-out theories and programs that mislead the rest of the people to think that they cannot develop and flourish, and escape poverty, welfare, and criminal life. They should spend more time studying the modern social science theories and programs to educate and lead the poor children and other citizens to break these unnatural barriers and walls in their lives and to overcome them. The females, blacks, homosexuals, Asians, Hispanics, Middle Easterners, poor people, and others should not spend time studying that they are problems and liabilities for this country, their country, the world, and humanity. They should spend more time studying and learning how to be influential in science and other professional spheres, and to occupy the same professional grounds as others. Also, they should spend time to break the slave mentality and to believe that they are as good, smart, and intelligent as the white male upper class, and that they certainly possess what it takes to be influential and dominant in the professional spheres in life. The future leaders of this country should not spend any time learning to waste trillions of taxpayers' hard-earned money on unnecessary government policies and laws to keep restricting the rest of the people from developing and to remain in the lower order of society. They should spend most of their time studying and learning the modern ways and methods to direct their attention to the masses in this country and around the world wisely and intelligently, before they get wider and cause more immigration problems. The future school officials, leaders, and citizens should not spend any time studying and learning to remain old-fashioned by voting and requesting unnecessary wars and invading others when they have problems or are being victimized. They have to spend most of their time learning to see and understand what has caused the problems and to settle them peacefully, so more soldiers and innocent people won't have to kill or be killed, and more kids won't have to grow up orphans or with single parents; and they should learn to stop voting and demanding wars or to attack others before they see themselves and their countries tangled up in a World War III.

The school officials should not spend any more time making up unfounded reasons for increasing the GPA requirements and college tuitions. They should spend most of their time learning and studying modern ways to lower the GPA requirements and college tuition drastically, and to develop modern and better productive classes and programs to uplift, advance, and develop the lowly students, communities, states, this country, and the rest of the world's students' minds and intelligence because they are not selling them a mind or brain, they are just playing a part in their development. The future leaders and citizens in this country and around the world should not spend any more time learning, studying, and admiring the conservative fashion, such as refusing to interact and work together with other races, genders, social classes, religions, countries, sexual orientations, and people of other continents. They should spend all their time learning and developing the modern social science programs and classes so they and their students can interact, respect, admire, and work with one another; visit one another's countries, learn one another's languages, appreciate one another's cultures, customs, religions, and backgrounds, and to agree to vote for a world peace movement and development.

For example, in the movie "Remember the Titans" with Denzel Washington, different races and ethnicities of kids become stronger to win a high school football championship and to become winners in life as well. But the only way to accomplish such a great task is by learning and respecting each other's backgrounds, and learning how to put their differences aside in a peaceful manner. After they have learned how to respect each other properly, and forget all the negative things others have said about them, they end up working together as a team and winning the majority of the games and the championship, and become great friends with each other at the end. Again, the only way we as people can overcome the problems of immigration, sexism, racism, terrorism, poverty, and high cost of living sufficiently and find peace among ourselves in this country and in the rest of the world, is if the school officials and leaders teach and educate us properly to see each other as brothers and sisters; and also teach and train all races, genders, social classes, religious practitioners, sexual orientations, and people around the world to respect and tolerate one another, and to work together for the general welfare, not for self-interest, nor a race, nor a gender, nor a country, nor a continent.

So far, the best system that exists in the modern world is the European system. The entire continent has systems and policies to benefit and serve all citizens and countries in the European continent sufficiently. The future world leaders should spend most of their time learning and studying their method and how to expand on it; they can start by creating international laws and policies to create special days for all the world leaders to get together, see what causes them to hate each other so much, and find the best solutions to deal with problems as they are. If a certain country's businesses have to leave other lands, so be it. If a certain country has to stop dumping waste and other chemical dirt in some country's water or anywhere else, so be it. If a certain country has to leave with what they have and build on it, so be it. If the leaders of some countries ask for other countries' soldiers and wiseacre businessmen and women to leave their lands as soon as possible, so be it. Each leader or group has to be heard and their wish should be heard freely and followed through, without trying to bribe the countries' politicians and other leaders because in the long run, it would backfire greatly on this soil and the rest of the world as well. We as Americans have a large number of soldiers die in Iraq on a daily basis, and the Iraqis have their innocent children, citizens, and soldiers die as well, all while the oppressor Iraqis and Americans are making huge profit off military weapons. How can these oppressors sleep at night and still call themselves true Iraqis or patriotic Americans? Neither the Republican nor the Democratic party knows what to do or how to approach these matters wisely and intelligently, but all of them want to control the House and Congress. Both political parties have their main agendas on the Iraq war, as this country, Haiti, Africa, Asia, and other lands are safe and doing well. The world leader and the leaders of other countries have to know that the world itself is doing poorly and is unsafe, and the best way to approach these matters is to refine this country's and other countries' foreign policy and pass modern laws and policies so wiseacre school officials and professors in this country and other countries can teach their graduates and leaders to step out of other people's countries, and be satisfied with what they have on their own lands. That way, others can grow themselves, and innocent Americans' and other peoples' blood can stop being shed. Also, immigration and other social and economic problems can finally stop for good. After each country's or group's leaders in the world have stated that they have acted in such a way and done such a thing, a modern world program will develop to better the entire world and humanity. Such a meeting has to be televised and broadcast worldwide so all the world's citizens can see it and start working and planning for general welfare, instead of killing each other and the world. Again, each country's leader, Prime minister, or President has to be free to speak out about any injustices against them, their country, and their people. Each leader and citizen has to admit their faults and failure, and accept criticism. Then, each of them has to give their word to pass modern laws and foreign policies to have great relationships with one another and to respect each other's point of view, lands, and others greatly. No grudges, resentment, and retaliations can be allowed to emerge from their citizens, nor from the leaders, nor from those so-called allies. Every person and leader will be making peace and agreeing to respect each other's territory, culture, customs, businesses, language, and heritage, and each country's and religion's leaders will agree to take advice and procedure from each other and the world leader, as long as it is in the world's best interest. They would have to learn and study to work together as people for the common good, general welfare, and humanity.

Subsequently to this world agreement and union, all leaders and citizens in the world have to applaud and congratulate each other for changing and bettering the world for themselves, their people, country, continent, and humanity. And all of them have to congratulate and thank each other for reaching the new "Independence day of the world" for their people. They heal their gallant wounded, injured soldiers and honor the dead ones for fighting and defending their country.

The future movie writers, reporters, and other writers have to learn not to spend any more time remaining conservatives by writing modern biased books, movies, articles, newspapers, and other scripts to encourage us as modern citizens to hate, attack, kill, oppress, and demean each other. In fact, they should spend most of their time studying the modern and better social science classes and methods to know their responsibilities and jobs as modern writers and leaders sufficiently, to write better and modern plays, scripts, stories, or books to help encourage and congratulate the modern leaders and citizens to bring peace and harmony between them, and to the lives of the people in this country and around the world for future generations. Furthermore, they should learn to overcome the hatred, racism, sexism, bias, and discrimination problems among us, and to become better citizens and have a promising world for the next generation. For instance, no writers in the modern world should ever attempt to write a movie or book like "Birth of a Nation" because this type of movie and work is despicable, unacceptable, and an outrage in the present time. We as people in this country and in the world would be better to each other if we had received a better and proper education, guidance, and leadership from our school officials and other leaders.

By developing more modern and better social classes and programs for the rest of the people, the next generation will have more and better literature, philosophy, other social science, business, and medical books available to them, and their lives will be touched like the ancient philosophers and the white male upper class. They will have books, classes, and programs based on their own accurate history, background, literature, language, customs, art, philosophy, education, medicine, religion, and economic imperialism. They will have their own textbooks, and other books about the "Modernization and Civilization of Hispanics, Asians, Blacks, Middle Easterners, Females, Homosexuals, the Poor, White Middle and Lower Class in America or in Europe or South America, or in Africa, in Asia and in Europe, and in Other Continents." Their own art, culture, heritage, philosophy, economics, medical, and political books will be as noticeable, respected, and influential as the others as well. The economic, social, and medical classes and programs or textbooks will be based on their own development; they will be referred to and titled as "The Development of Their Own Communities, History, Races, Genders, Sexual Orientations, Countries, and Religions." Again, in order for the rest of the people to develop and grow, they have to develop from what they are; by creating better classes and programs for them as a part of the curricula in this country and around the world, their communities, this country, poor countries, and the rest of the world will grow stronger and become richer and more loveable. Instead of the conservative and liberal school officials and professors keeping the biased classes and programs out of the modern school curriculum, they continue to use the same biased and expired books to teach the rest of the people to despise, demean, and to fight among themselves so they can never grow, and to perceive those who are the cause of the problems, such as Socrates, as righteous men and women. Instead of the other professors and school officials teaching these bright kids and citizens to vote and cast out these biased and expired professors, school officials, and leaders that continue to enslave, insult, and make the rest of their fellow classmates and citizens in this country and around the world feel inferior, incapable, outcasts, criminals, incompetent, worthless, and useless, the rest of the professors teach the powerless and confused people to respect and believe these narrow-minded, biased, racist, and prejudiced professors because they have a bunch of papers—called a degree or certification—in the modern world. Education is not on a piece of paper, it's in the brain and mind. Having a bunch of papers does not mean a person is well educated, smart, and intelligent. It merely means such a person has been trained to memorize certain theories and formats.

Instead of not teaching the rest of the people and the poor in other countries to not be content and satisfied with what the white upper class males or the rich countries set aside and handle for them, they teach them to greatly appreciate them and ask for more, while the development and wealth of a country is derived from the production of the country itself. Instead of developing better and constructive programs to teach the modern citizens and students to vote the biased school officials, leaders, and lawmakers out of the systems of their country and their world peacefully, they teach them to accept an apology, or that such a leader is too powerful to be removed or released from such a position while the power of any organization or any leader is derived from the people. These school officials do not realize that in order for the rest of the citizens in this country and around the world to be secure about themselves and their backgrounds, and be able to flourish, they as educators and teachers have to be educated and taught in a sense to appreciate and love themselves, their cultures, backgrounds, and languages. By teaching them to admire and imitate the ancient oppressors, nothing good would come out of it because they would end up handicapping and crippling even more. Also, it would make them despise what they have and who they are. Every race, gender, and social class has contributed to the progress and development of the human race and the world. Every race, gender, sexual orientation, and citizen has their own history. The weak people know so much about the ancient Greeks, Romans, Hebrews, Socrates, Plato, the Englishmen, the white male American upper class, and other European history, language, heritage, and proverbs, while they know little or nothing about the development and the civilization of their own.

In fact, the majority of so-called educated black leaders never read the book "Travel in Africa," and never heard of the Tarikh Es-Sudan, or knew that the ancient Africans of the interior started, and even eventually became, a big part of the development of science. The only thing these so-called educated black leaders, including Condoleezza Rice, know is what the white upper class knows. Since the white upper class says these things have no importance, as far as these so-called educated black leaders are concerned, it has to be true. These so-called black educated leaders know so much about European, Chinese, Japanese, Middle Eastern and other region's poets, leaders, and history, but little or nothing about great Africa, Jamaica, and Haiti's emperors, arts, and culture. They know all the educational theories from Egyptians down to Socrates, but they still refuse to embrace and become great parts and assets of their communities, culture, and the citizens of their ancestors' continent for the future ones. And since the great black books, educational theories, knowledge, and lessons did not figure in the courses that they pursued in these so-called great schools of thought, why should they do any research of their own to study real facts? Nearly all these so-called leaders and educated people are merely imitators and wannabes, and blacks in this country and around the world are right for calling them Uncle Toms, sellouts, and house slaves. How can they serve humanity and the world sufficiently if they cannot serve, lead, and protect their own kinds, or the places that their ancestors, parents, and they themselves are from? These followers keep fighting for political power and equality, while their race is only slightly lifted above poverty in this country and around the world. A free lesson for those so-called great black leaders and educators: you and the rest of the black race can never have much influence in the political and other influential systems in this country and around the world, if the race as a whole is doing extremely poor in the academic, business, medical, technology, and other professional spheres in this country and around the world. In order for you and the rest of your race to be respected and treated equally in society and the rest of the world, they need to have a system that is supporting and protecting the black race and others, instead of the oppressors. No wonder why Bill O'Reilly and other white male upper class people love and invite them to their party that much.

All the things that their great leaders have left for them as heritage such as jazz, freedom, and others, have either been dismissed, despised, or turned over to the oppressors. The majority of those black so-called great leaders and scholars do not even know or have any interest to know that the ancient Africans developed their own science theory to create poisons for arrowheads, to extract metals from nature, and to refine them for development of the industrial and minerals of art. The ancient Africans provided the Egyptians the product of the mixtures for the chemical method of Egyptian embalming. Furthermore, they also brought their wares and ideas to influence the history of Greece and

Carthage, and the ancient Africans were the first to domesticate sheep, goats, cows and pigs, and they were also the first ones to develop the idea of trial by jury, and produced the first instruments and helped the world in the discovery of iron.

Furthermore, in 1858 James Douglas became the governor of British Columbia. Alexandre Dumas (1802-1870) still remains one the best poets in history and wrote many plays and novels such as *The Count of Monte Cristo*, and co-wrote *The Three Musketeers*. "In 1909, explorer Matthew Henson co-discovers the North Pole. Elijah McCoy's (1843-1929) Ontario name and invention started the phrase 'the real McCoy.' McCoy invented the lubricating cup or the drip cup."
(http://www.islandnet.com/~bcbhas/achieve.htm)

Frederick McKinley Jones (1892-1961) "was born in Cincinnati, Ohio. An experienced mechanic, he invented a self-starting gas engine and a series of devices for movie projectors. More importantly, he invented the first automatic refrigeration system for long-haul trucks (1935). Jones was awarded more than 40 patents in the field of refrigeration."
(http://www.factmonster.com/ipka/A0878300.html)

Dr. Daniel Hale Williams "founded the Provident Hospital in Chicago in 1891, and he performed the first successful open heart surgery in 1893."
(http://www.infoplease.com/spot/bhmscientists1.html)

"1880-1884 Lewis H. Latimer invented the first electric light with a carbon filament."
(http://www.islandnet.com/~bcbhas/achieve.htm)

"Granville T. Woods (1856-1910) invented a telegraph that allowed moving trains to communicate with other trains and train stations."
(http://www.hutchnews.com/Nie/Black%20History%20Month.pdf)

"In 1853, Mary Anne Shadd," who was an excellent

teacher, became "the editor of the (Canada west) Provincial Freeman newspaper. In 1859 Abraham D. Shadd was elected to Raleigh County, Ontario (Canada West) town council. In 1861 Anderson Ruffin Abbott becomes the first Canadian born black graduate of a medical college (University of Toronto). In 1951 Addie Aylestock becomes a minister - perhaps the first black woman in Canada to gain this distinction. In 1957 Ed Searles becomes one of British Columbia's first black lawyers. In 1958 Willie O'Rea becomes the first black to play hockey in the NHL. In 1964 Lincoln Alexander becomes Canada's first Black Member of Parliament. In 1994 Emery Barnes becomes the first Black British Columbia Speaker of the BC Legislature. In 1995 Justice Selwyn Romilly is the first black to be appointed to the British Columbia Supreme Court." (http://www.islandnet.com/~bcbhas/achieve.htm)

Furthermore, they should teach black students about other great black leaders such as Nelson Mandela, Bob Marley, and Jean Jacques Dessalines, who helped Haiti to become the first black independent country in the world in 1804, and that the greatest and tallest pyramid was built by the king Zoser, the history of Cleopatra VII (69-30 B.C), and more. In fact, nearly all those so-called great black educators or leaders have to read *Don't Blame the Blacks Because Slavery Systems Still Exist* by Jean Ricardy Georges to fully enlighten or free their enslaved minds. That way, they can properly learn how to lead and free the great black race instead of continuing to blame them in the modern world, especially phony leaders like Bill Cosby and others.

Also, the rest of the people have to study about their own culture so they won't have to imitate, be ashamed of and feel insecure about themselves and their countries. If scientists can find out that dinosaurs used to live and occupied the Earth millions of years ago, modern school officials and experts can find out about the students and the people in the past to really teach the powerless people in this country and around the world properly and sufficiently.

This is a modern time; therefore, every race, gender, social class, and sexual orientation in this country and around the world has to know their own past so they can develop their own modern thoughts and ideas about the nature of the universe, politics, humanity, freedom, life, and necessities. Why should the rest of the citizens have to try to live, speak, and act like Socrates and others or assimilate their culture, heritage, custom while they can hardly understand them, and were oppressed and exploited by them? Again, these lowly people could never relate to them. Besides, these poor people had and continue to have great leaders and philosophers who were wiser than Socrates and others. The only reason their great leaders and philosophers were and continue to be dismissed and regarded as nonentities in the modern world is because those narrow-minded conservative school officials have brainwashed them, instead of educating them. Being American is to love, unite, elevate, distinguish, and respect themselves and others to a higher level, regardless what our differences might be.

Again, education does not benefit all races, genders, social classes, and the entire human race, nor covers all countries' philosophy, literature, and art, mainly because these bright students and citizens have only been taught to advance, develop, influence, and contribute to others, instead of themselves. Every race and gender in this country and around the world has its own art, beliefs, thoughts, history, literature, customs, and culture. Why is all the attention directed to one side, and why have the outstanding contributions been made only to the ancient ones and the European arts and heritage? Blacks, Hispanics, Asians, homosexuals,

Middle Easterners, and females in music, film, poetry, and sports have made great contributions to America and to the world. The rest of the modern students have to learn facts about themselves, their cultures, history, and literature, so when they go out in life, they will not have to feel inferior or imitate others as the modern ones do. And why should they assimilate the heritage, culture, and customs of others or imitate them, when they have the best men and women among them, and when they are wise and intelligent enough to produce better than them? Socrates and the other ancient philosophers have done right and wrong things, as have the leaders and philosophers of every other race, gender, and countries around the world. Evidently, the main reason that the rest of the people in this country and around the world have not produced as many or more modern philosophers as the ancient ones is mainly due to the fact that they have never been taught and trained properly to become thinkers and philosophers for themselves, their own people, and their lands. Most things that these students have learned and studied about anthropology, history, and other social science programs at school are what others have done in the past, and then they go out in life to imitate and duplicate them. As long as these school officials, professors, and leaders want to remain in a conservative fashion, they have to expect the rest of the citizens in this country and around the world to only have a desire to copy and contribute to other people's and countries' philosophy, art, literature, languages, and wealth, and for them to continue to be left out in the educational system and in world progress. In order for modern discovery and invention to be done and accomplished in the rest of the people's culture, philosophy, literature, and art, the world school officials have to stop teaching the rest of the students and the people to duplicate, contribute to, and advance other people's heritage, literature, culture, history, and work as their primary duty and goal upon their graduation. The school officials have to develop better constructive social science classes or programs so the rest of the students do not have to graduate from conservatories as they have been doing since they were allowed in schoolrooms.

Another reason that the rest of the people do not develop as much or more as others, and continue to go backward toward serfdom as before, is because the brightest and the best among them have been trained, taught, and educated in a sense to join the oppressors, and to regard the rest of the people who are doing the best they could to leave the uncomfortable predicament that they are in, or their descendants, as lazy, inferior, criminals, and despicable persons. Therefore, by brainwashing and keeping the brightest ones among them in the dark, they would always have no vision, interest, or understanding to see that their responsibilities and duties, as the fortunate graduates and educators, are to go to teach the lowly ones what they have been taught, so those who got stuck in the dust can be prepared and trained to find their way out. The school officials have to realize that every race, gender, community, nationalities, sexual orientation, and religious believer has their own kind graduated from the top leading schools and institutions in this country and around the world, but they are still unable to advance in the professional world. The main reason for that is because what they have learned and taught is not solid and strong enough for them to reach and pull out those who have been neglected and forcibly pushed aside to a higher level. Most of what they have learned and taught in school or in the classrooms is to admire, imitate, advance, and enrich those whom they see from afar, those who they cannot relate to, and those who have demeaned, despised, oppressed, restricted, exploited, and enslaved them, their ancestors, communities, races, sexual orientations, genders, and their compatriots socially and economically since the beginning of time.

The school officials must bear in mind the reason that the rest of people and countries have continued to get weaker and be left in the mud is because those who have a chance to be educated and trained among them have been trained adequately only to advance and enrich another community, race, gender, social class, country, and continent, instead of their own. And in order to uplift them and this country in the economic and social sphere, school officials and leaders have to do a thorough scientific study of Hispanics, Asians, blacks, females, Middle Easterners, homosexuals, and others, and develop in them the interest, desire, and power to do for themselves, their families, communities, this country, and their native countries. Also, the world leading institutions and experts have to develop modern world programs and studies from each country and continent to develop in their own countries and continents the interest, ambition, aspiration, desire, and power to do only for themselves and their lands. Again, not all teachers, school officials, experts, and leaders are incompetent, ignorant, dishonest, and corrupt; the great ones simply have not been prepared, trained, and taught properly their responsibilities and duties to the world. In fact, many of these school officials, leaders, and teachers believe that they are doing the disadvantaged races, genders, sexual orientations, communities, this country, poor countries, the rest of the world, and humanity a great favor by remaining conservative and enslaving their minds. These school leaders have not realized in order to uplift the world they have to know more than what the biased and narrow-minded school officials, professors, writers, and reporters have written about these students and the people that they are serving and leading. For instance, when a community, race, social class, and a certain country are overcrowded with more menial workers, poverty, disease, illiterate people, criminals, troubled and pregnant teens than professionals, such a community, state, country, and continent is not in such an undesirable condition because the youths and citizens are pro-violence, disease, illiterate, welfare, poverty, and the criminal life and love to remain in the inferior status, but because of the failures of their school officials, the community leaders and experts, their states' leaders, experts and lawmakers, this country's leaders, experts and lawmakers, and the world leaders, lawmakers, and experts as well. For example, if a family has four children, but only one is doing well, the fault for failing is not that of the other three children; it is the parents' fault, indeed. Perhaps the parents have paid attention mostly to one child; love, work, appreciate, care, and support mostly for one of them. What the parents have invested in the family is what they are going to get back in return; the other kids fail probably because they feel despondent, left out, treated or labeled as inferior, losers, and outcasts. They were probably abused mentally, physically, and verbally, and not appreciated and noticed for what they have done by their parents, who only see what these kids have not done. Many parents naively think these things do not matter when they are raising kids or a family, or cause kids to fail and be disadvantaged in life. The fact is they do matter, and by ignoring them they are kidding themselves and hurting their family.

The majority of sociologists, psychologists, criminologists, and other social science experts do not emphasize and write more modern books and theories to educate the public better. Then these professionals still wonder why kids are fighting among themselves so much, why crime, teen pregnancy, and delinquency are increasing so much, instead of decreasing. Let's just assume the other three children had major problems to flourish; if they did, the parents could modify their parental methods, create better rules, spend more time with them, send them into better after-school programs and other productive activities, or the parents could ask for help elsewhere, such as T.V. shows, and invest the little that they have in all four of them. When the majority of children and people are doing poorly in a certain community, state, country, and the world, it is not the children's fault nor that of other people; the fault lies with the school officials, lawmakers, leaders, business, social science, and medical leaders, and religious leaders because they are the ones who can create, and are in charge of the systems and the citizens. If they are incompetent, biased, prejudiced, pro-war, wiseacres, selfish, conservatives, and inconsiderate the problems have to get worse for the next generation, indeed. And nothing good has been accomplished for the next generation, except to have larger numbers of persons imitating, duplicating, and doing what others have been doing. Bad parents equal bad children and bad leadership equals failure, shortcoming, letdown, and disappointment; it's as simple as that. The people, and the children in this country and around the world cannot do well in life if they do not have great leaders and school officials to lead and to educate them properly. Otherwise, leaders and parents would not exist and be needed. If a parent wants to party, fight, neglect their children, and think only about money, cars, clothes, and other silly things, her or his family would never grow. They may have money, but not grow, like this country. We have the most wealth in the world, and we are still growing. And this is why most of the richest people usually divorce more than twice; they care, sacrifice, dream, and think only of having more money, not to improve and better their families. The same thing goes for leaders; they wish to remain conservative, while the majority of people that they are serving and leading are dying and suffering from war, poverty, jails, and disease, year after year, generation after generation, and century after century.

What happened before will continue to happen now and in the future as well; the same outcome as before will keep occurring each year. Those who were rich will become richer, and those who were poor will become poorer, and the deficits of this land and the rest of the world will continue to get worse and worse, until we as Americans lose our...

Our leaders have to spend more time studying and learning how to serve and lead the citizens better because the only reason that they exist and were voted for is to lead the people: no more, no less. The majority of people are failing in this country and around the world because they are missing something, and for them to find what they are missing, or find the light which they have been looking for since day one, school officials have to teach and prepare leaders better, regardless if their graduates are planning to join the republican or liberal political party. They have to teach the present students and citizens to become great school officials, leaders, lawmakers, and humanitarians to pull each other and the world out of this darkness and lead the future generations down the right path, so they can find the way and remain in the light which those who came before them never saw or experienced.

For example, if a late model car is not working, obviously it is because it is missing something or something is not working as it is supposed to, not because that car was made to work in such a way. Therefore, the owner has to hire a modern mechanic to study the car and to fix the problems. But if the owner hires an old car model mechanic, such a mechanic would be unable to fix the problem. However, the mechanic is going to talk and act as if she or he knew how to fix the problem because the mechanic has to get paid. Rarely, the owner would find an honest mechanic that would say to him or her that his or her experience and expertise cannot solve the problems or are not sufficient to fix late model cars. The same theory goes for the majority of experts, teachers, school officials, lawmakers, and religious leaders; they know that we as the people were not supposed to live and act in such a way to each other, and they also know that they cannot serve and help the lowly people, communities, states, races, genders, religions, homosexuals, and the citizens of the world sufficiently with their social and economic problems. But at the same time, they have to act and speak as if they could serve and better the problems of modern citizens just to get the positions or salary that they want or to get elected in public office. The weak people, races, communities, genders, this country, and the rest of the world's citizens have not failed in their struggle; the school officials, leaders, and lawmakers have failed them and continue to fail them even in the modern world. The leaders know the majority of citizens and children in this country and around the world have failed and remained in the lower order of the society due to lack of education, and the economy. So why do they not lower school tuitions and the entrance requirements, and invest the taxpayers' money in the people rather than protecting and keeping worn-out theories and laws alive. School leaders must know and learn that in a different time, problems require different approaches, studies, laws, and methods to confront and to overcome them. Again, as long as school officials and the leaders of communities, states, this country, and the world don't realize that we as taxpayers are paying to better our social and economic situations, and want to remain lazy by copying off the old ones, instead of developing something new for us as taxpayers and employing something of their own, the ills

236

affecting us, this country, and the rest of the world have to keep growing bigger and bigger because the disease won't go away in a conservative fashion; otherwise, it would be long gone by now.

As long as school officials, who label themselves as Republicans or Democrats, liberal or conservative, refuse to modernize the educational system to study the history, language, manners, and customs of all the children and people in this country and approach them intelligently and wisely, they can never connect with them. If they cannot connect to all people and all students in this country that they are serving, they can never understand them. If they cannot understand them, they can never reach them. If they cannot reach them, these people and these communities can never flourish and grow from what they are. If they cannot help them to grow and flourish, forget it! The world can never, ever go forward. Again, we as the people have to grow first; then this country would be able to move forward. The same thing goes for the world's leading universities and institutions: as long as the professors and experts of the world remain conservative, instead of world educators and teachers, they will always refuse to upgrade and advance the world teaching method, and this country and other wealthy countries will always see and experience the same immigration, resentment, hatred, wars, and other world problems towards their countries. Again, schools like Harvard, Yale, MIT, Stanford, Princeton, Penn, Brown, Columbia, Dartmouth, Chicago, Oxford, Cambridge, Sorbonne, and McGill, and many more universities have no right to refuse to modernize their teaching method and their programs to work together for the general welfare. They have to do their jobs as world educators and experts; if they are world universities and they refuse to expand their programs to advance and better the lowly countries that are a part of the world, then what good are they to this great world?

If they feel that these world tasks and responsibilities are too much for them to handle, they can ask for help; but if they refuse it mainly because of their egos, they have to lower their ranks at world universities and let other schools and institutions that can serve and better the world step forward and do what they think is impossible to achieve and to accomplish. Children, mothers, the elderly, and other people are dying; the world is suffering, crippled, and sinking into the mire. Any institutions and experts that love to teach, and are willing to change history and the world, should come forward. Teachers and professors that have what it takes to make the citizens of poor countries grow to better themselves and to stop breaking international laws so they can sneak into other countries without authorization, must step forward. Again, this job requires the most considerate humanitarians and brightest men and women among us. Instead of school officials demeaning females and others, and wasting taxpayers' money on worn-out theories, they can use the taxpayers' money wisely and intelligently by expanding and creating world programs for the weak people and countries around the world. Instead of them drilling into the minds of children and other citizens what they have borrowed from the old and biased writers, they should develop more and better programs and classes to teach, train, and prepare the world experts sufficiently for their tasks, responsibilities, and duties, so they can go to poor countries and teach and prepare their leaders, school officials, and citizens that are otherwise poorly circumstanced how to advance. Teach and train these poor people to establish and better their school system, teach them how to grow their lands socially and economically and to live on them peacefully and happily. The world-leading universities have to develop new and better programs to study their history, language, culture, heritage, manners, and customs adequately, and teach them to develop from what they are sufficiently rather than imitating and duplicating others.

The world experts and educators have to be taught and trained in a sense that the majority of these people have never had the chance to educate, develop, and flourish themselves. Therefore, in order for these professors and teachers to help these poor people succeed in this world's important tasks and movement, they have to be kind, great teachers, understandable, and have great patience for these people to grow; and they must teach these poor people how to respect, appreciate, and understand each other, their country, and the world so they can unite to rebuild their lands together for themselves and the general welfare. The world experts have to learn and teach people in poor countries what they are today, what approaches they have to take, their strengths and weaknesses, and how to use and produce what they have for themselves and for the citizens of other lands. Teach the leaders of these poor countries the proper ways to gain control of their lands and the suitable way to lead their citizens, and how to produce and protect their lands so the exploiters and oppressors cannot continue to exploit them for cheap labor, and other things, or take and use their natural resources and minerals for their interest. Train and teach them the proper way to get rid of race- and self-consciousness that they have had since day one about their culture, heritage, and background. Also, teach the proper way for them to think, plan, and develop for themselves and their lands, such as their own banks, credit cards, art, poetry, businesses, natural foods, schools, and more, instead of killing and slaughtering each other and other citizens as an occupation. Teach modern and better philosophy and anthropology classes and programs so they will respect, tolerate and work for the interest of their lands and the world, instead of the oppressors' and exploiters' interests. Enlighten and train these poor people how to use their wasted lands properly, how to plant them, and to develop their latent power so they will grow and flourish in the medical, technology, social, and economic sphere, instead of making exploiters bigger and richer while their countries are reduced to nothing. Teach these poor people the right way to use their intelligence and their lands so they can depend on themselves rather than on other countries. Afterward, they will grow socially and economically to pay world taxes for their, the world's, and humanity's interest. So when their country, continent, and brothers and sisters are hit with a natural catastrophe, they would have support from the world to help them get back on their feet because they are paying world taxes and supporting the world scientists financially. The people of poor countries have to be taught the proper way to settle matters on their lands peacefully, or to seek help elsewhere or from the world leaders when they need it. That way, they won't have to use force or get weapons from oppressors and world destructors or the arms industry to destroy one another, their own lands, and humanity. These poor people have to be taught and trained in a sense to respect and take orders from their leaders and the world leaders, and to have a good relationship with one another. However, if their leaders are exploiting and using them, instead of serving and leading them, they have to ask the world leader for a new election to vote them out of office peacefully. They have to really learn and be taught properly about their duties, responsibilities, and tasks, and those of their leaders, and the leaders of the world leader; they have to learn and to be taught to vote for the best men and women among them. They should spend most of their time studying leaders that can relate to them, understand them, care for them, and be willing to sacrifice everything to serve and develop them. They have to know these things before they study and adore others that they cannot relate to, and who were never working for their interest and welfare. They have to be taught to admire, respect, love, and take orders from their country, continent, and world leaders as long as it benefits their lands, citizens, the world, and humanity. They have to learn to give equal attention, admiration, and respect to the leaders who gave their lives for them and for their freedom like other world leaders who gave their lives to benefit and better the world and humanity, such as John F. Kennedy, Jean Jacques Dessalines, Bob Marley, Nelson Mandela, Martin Luther King Jr., and many more.

The future world experts, school officials, and other leaders have to be taught and trained in a sense to be more humane, kind, patient, compassionate, considerate, and thoughtful than the previous and the modern ones. They have to be educated and trained that the world was not meant to be as it is, and that the weak people in this country and around the world did not intentionally choose these awful situations that they are in. Why would they? Their conditions and ways of living are disagreeable, despicable, undesirable, and inhumane. The main reason that a large number of weak people around the world end up living in such a way is because their former colony leaders that used to occupy and colonize their native countries in the past totally wiped them out, by taking millions of them as slaves, their precious gold, diamonds, and the goods they had in their countries, including their minds, intelligence, confidence, pride, and other great important valuable monuments they had on their lands before the ancient leaders or oppressors finally decided to give them their lands back. For instance, after a revolution, their countries were totally destroyed, even though they became physically free. They were still handicapped mentally and intellectually because they came out of slavery or another type of oppression system where they were prohibited from receiving any type of education and productive training. Therefore, these honest and great warriors, combatants, and freed-men and women knew nothing additional about their situations and how to grow out of the miseries and systems that were placed upon them, their people, and their lands. These countries of these poor warriors and freed-men had no outlet but to go down, where they did not plan and intend to go. The freed-men and women had received no support from their previous oppressors or the slave masters, except to continue to pay them money for the physical freedom they had gained, and for the destruction, and pain they had caused them, their children, their people, and their lands.

Furthermore, these poor warriors, leaders, and freed-men and women found nothing on their lands and in their minds that enabled them to find their way out of their difficulties. These lowly countries and their citizens would never have been so handicapped socially and economically in the first place, or ended up in such an awful and inhuman condition in the modern world if the ancient world leaders, school officials, and educators had provided them some assistance, such as training and educating them as they should have been, instead of demeaning, enslaving, oppressing and controlling them, as large numbers of people are still doing to them in the modern world. These lowly freed-men and women fought and gave their lives to become independent and to take charge of themselves and their lands. But due to the lack of preparation, training, and education they had received from the previous world leaders, they were unprepared and unable to lead and teach their citizens how to gain ground in the basic things of life. Since these oppressed and exploited people were not prepared and trained sufficiently to think, plan, act, and produce for themselves and their lands sufficiently after gaining their physical freedom, unfortunately they became economically, socially, and mentally enslaved, but not because they did not have what it took to develop and be as influential in life as others.

For example, parents or guardians who abuse their kids instead of protecting and developing them, usually have their kids revolt against them or run away. Therefore, the kids are not getting sufficient preparation, education, and discipline to become successful in life. Children who do not receive any early quality education, nor training, nor discipline normally grow sour in life, not because such a kid was born to be unproductive and bitter in life, but because of the kid's circumstances. The same analysis should apply for these poor countries and continents, and the warriors and leaders who got the rest of them through the physical combat and revolution for freedom. They were great and sincere fighters, warriors, and leaders. However, they had more physical strength and enthusiasm to protect and lead them to physical freedom than actual knowledge and education to teach and lead them to develop their minds, themselves, and their lands sufficiently. These countries' leaders were great and did the best they could to enlighten and train their people to develop and to become independent in all spheres so the oppressors would never be able to control and enslave them again. Unfortunately, the little education and training these brave warriors were teaching their fellow freemen and women copied from the method of teaching of their former masters and oppressors. And since these theories and education were made only to develop and advance the oppressors, other Europeans, and to enslave them, these brave and courageous men and women had to fail socially and economically. As a result of the lack of education and training these great heroes and heroines had, they could not teach the others how to develop socially and to create business opportunities on their land so they could grow rich and their lands as well; but again, this was not because they did not have the same intelligence, wisdom, knowledge, and abilities as those who did, but because these courageous and brave men and women had a knowledge of anthropology, history, philosophy, medicine, art, math, success, and other things that were unfortunately copied from the old European, narrow-minded, self-centered, and prejudiced white males who were educated and graduated mostly from Oxford, Cambridge, and Sorbonne.

In fact, these racist, biased, prejudiced, and narrow-minded educators and school officials were content to see that these poor freemen and women had shortcomings in the economic and social sphere, especially when they saw the poor people were slaughtering one another for amusement, and had an economic debasement that reached to the point of starvation. These biased and untrained educators, leaders, and kings wrote and stated in many documents that the freed-men and women in these countries were doing these things to themselves and to their lands because they could not think or be as reasonable as whites. At the same time, these narrow-minded and prejudiced readers, writers, leaders, educators, and kings who labeled themselves as kind, passionate, philosophical, wise, and righteous were oppressing, exploiting, and murdering innocent people for world power and wealth, as their imitators in the modern world are doing. These so-called philosophers and leaders failed to see that it was not the poor people's fault for doing these things to themselves and their lands, and being unable to move farther from the influences of the life and mentality of slavery. It was their fault for psychologically forcing these weak people to take these awful positions and fail in the social and economic spheres.

The future world university experts and school officials have to develop better modern educational methods to give the people in poor countries a new point of view on education. These important tasks require the best modern world experts, school officials, and educators among us, not those who label these oppressors, murders, thieves, and exploiters as great philosophers and thinkers. If they were that great, their countries would never have lost their world leadership status, and not those who think that it is impossible for the people in poor countries to learn and succeed as the old ones did. And certainly not those who still think and believe that the ancient prejudiced and vicious philosophers and leaders were right and just for behaving and treating the ancestors of those people in such a way. This world task and responsibility requires leaders who can draw out from within these people the power to plan, act, and elevate themselves and their lands to a higher status. The conservative and liberal school officials must be awakened to really educate the students and the people about the modern accurate psychology and philosophy of education. These school officials have to develop modern programs to find out why these people are doing poorly in society, and what old bad ideas and attitudes that they have adapted from their pasts, which still prevent them from advancing in life. They have to create modern social science classes to see these poor people as future assets of the world, rather than as liabilities and problems. They have to develop great philosophy, history, and anthropology classes and programs to make all students and people appreciate one another, and not take school or education for granted, because it is the most important thing they need in life. They should create new interesting and productive classes and programs, so they can feel connected and related to them, and have great desire, interest, and enthusiasm for learning and developing rather than making them drift away and feel inferior, incompetent, out of the system, or uncomfortable in the educational and other professional spheres.

The school officials have to teach the poor citizens, races, genders, sexual orientations, and social classes to use their money wisely, and to oppose the incompetent and unintelligent government officials that give the corporations tax breaks. In fact, they should write to their congressmen and women and ask them to take a portion of the corporation tax money and invest it wisely in those schools that have been or are about to be closed, and in those Americans who have been left behind. Take another portion to invest in more advanced programs in accredited colleges, technical schools, and institutions, because if the tax money were diverted to more practical use, the people who were liabilities would become assets for the future of this country. By preparing and teaching these people to become assets, they would become creators and thinkers for themselves and their races, communities, sexual orientations, genders, this country, and the rest of the world. If they are trained and taught to become great thinkers, this country and the world will have great achievements and accomplishments tomorrow. Millions of bright people are on welfare, in jails or prisons, breaking the law as an occupation, immigrating to this country, and becoming huge liabilities for the taxpayers and this country's government chiefly because what they have received either from the school system or the government is not strong enough for them to succeed and grow out of these problems. Due to the inefficiency of the support these children and citizens have received from the school officials, untrained lawmakers, and leaders, they have been unable to produce and do creditable jobs and work for themselves and their families, communities, states, this country, their native countries, and humanity.

Developing and creating better constructive programs to advance them socially, economically, and intellectually would also advance this country and the world in the same aspects as well. If these people received great support and leadership from school officials, lawmakers, and other leaders, they would regain their loss of ground, and they would not seem impossible as many untrained educators and professionals have said. Also, the leaders of poor countries would not have their citizens breaking international laws to immigrate to this country and to other lands. In fact, these poor citizens would get rid of this fatal dependency on the government, the taxpayers, and the wealthy countries that they have had since day one. They would no longer be restricted to menial jobs, drudgery, and prostitution as they have been for so long. In fact, they would grow out of these things. With proper unification and organization, leaders and lawmakers would make arrangements among themselves to serve and lead the people efficiently, such as to keeping the public schools open after school hours, and on the weekends so the weak people who do not have skills can be trained. The people who did not graduate from high school can be prepared to get their GED, and the people who do not speak or write the English language can be taught instead of being criticized by narrow-minded reporters and leaders. By leading this country in such a way, the people of poor communities would learn how to become frugal, creative, and bright instead of them wasting their money on cars, consumer electronics, clothes, video games, and other silly things. They would learn how to save and spend their money wisely to give them, their children, family, community, state, and this country a better direction in life. Most of them would own a house instead of being exploited by wiseacre landlords. By them owning property, they would be more concerned about keeping the streets, community, and state safe and promising. With the quality education they would receive from the state, they would respect and help each other more, and be able to create jobs for themselves and their community. They would know when to start a family and the proper ways to be great parents to their children, and how to approach their kids properly when it comes to sex, alcohol, drugs, weapons, and respect for authority. The people in poor communities would know the proper ways to love, support, care for, and protect their kids, families, and neighbors; and teach their kids how to avoid conflicts, respect others, authority, and laws, and stay away from the dreadful activities and products. By investing corporation tax money wisely and intelligently, a large amount of productive programs would be established. Then, fewer people would be on welfare and in the criminal system. In order for these weak people to grow out of these ordeals, tax money has to be used wisely and intelligently, and school officials have to leave these conservative fashions. Again, all the problems in this country have causes. Cutting these corporations a break and remaining conservative will always do only bad for this great world. Such methods and systems have to go in the modern world. Continuing to keep these people in the dark is keeping the world in the dark; the poor communities need to grow so this country can grow.

The people in weak communities have to learn to think and train to do this country good instead of harming it. They have to train to create their own restaurants, banks, grocery stores, food industry, sneakers, clothes, and others. The major corporations have the poor citizens of India, Haiti, China, Mexico, and other countries making pairs of sneakers, jeans, suits, and other things for a few dollars and sell them for hundreds and more dollars in the poor communities in this country and around the world. Since the average American cannot even afford them, these corporations are not serving this country and the world. They are exploiting us as people to make their pockets heavier, just as the ancient Egyptians, Greeks, and others used to do. Again, the majority of the people in this country and around the world are held down to the lowest order of society because they are economically enslaved by those so-called leaders and gifted people, while they are just imitators of the previous oppressors. The people of poor communities have to learn to make their own products and sell them among themselves. There is no brand solution for their salvation, except for them to learn how to act, support, and plan for themselves. Millions of parents cannot afford clothes, and many kids are making minimum wage, selling drugs, and breaking the law to buy clothes made by Nike, Reebok, Jordan, Puff Daddy, and the products of other major retail companies. These CEOs have not done a thing to help the massive communities to develop, while the masses spend trillions a month in their corporations. In fact, when they give charity to them, they have their CPAs write it off on their tax return. How many schools and hospitals have they established for their customers' kids? Not one. And what do these narrow-minded lawmakers do to stop the CEOs of these corporations from taking all the jobs in this country overseas? Nothing. How much money did those CEOs make last year? Millions. How much were their bonuses? Millions. How many politicians and other leaders are on their payrolls? Way too many. These CEOs use their fatal psychological expertise to brainwash and enslave these weak people's minds so they think and believe that they need their products to look attractive and be strong, and the powerless people do not have any interest in building and patronizing a business in their community and state. All these things occur due to the lack of modern quality education. By educating the weak people better, they would learn to create, appreciate, and support their own community and state enterprises and schools before others that are far away or that have hardly experienced a moment in their community or state. By teaching and educating them in such a way, they would end up having better businesses in their communities, which means better natural resources and minerals, foods, hospitals, medicine, banks, restaurants, and industries in their communities. Therefore, the rates welfare, crime, drugs, and prostitution in the communities of these poor races, genders, and others would be decreased drastically, as well as this country and the world. As a result, the property tax, high cost of living, illiteracy rates, and others would diminish as well. They would not have to work two or three jobs to afford the basic things in life, and slave for people who do not live among them in their communities and states. In the end, the war on the middle class, this country, poor countries, and the rest of the world would eventually stop, which would result in promise for this country and the rest of world, instead of a small percentage of stock holders, CEOs, VPs, and others.

Again, the weak people here and in other countries cannot learn to duplicate others in order to develop they have to learn to develop from what they are and where they are. Poor people cannot continue to learn and copy other people from far away in order for them to develop because others are otherwise circumstanced. By trying to imitate and duplicate the people who have already established themselves and have a great business, the weak people's communities and businesses would always fail because they would not be strong enough to compete with the others, and since they are duplicating and imitating others, instead of developing something new, they cannot give customers anything new and better. As a result of the lack of modern business classes, one street or community would have many of the same type enterprise. All of them would struggle for an existence in competing for the patronage of the neighborhood or community. Eventually, one or more of them would have to close or file for bankruptcy. And the one to close or file chapter eleven will be the imitator because they did not provide the customers with something new that was strong enough to compete with the originator. This sort of shortsightedness has been obvious in the clothing industry by the weak races. One was created by artists and athletes, and then, nearly all of the artists that make it huge in the music industry end up imitating the first one. Eventually, they close or file for bankruptcy because the race, the neighborhood, and the community do not need that many clothing and sneaker lines. If they developed something new by creating better products that were more fashionable, affordable, or help the communities, race, country, gender, or continent socially and economically, eventually, they would probably put the originators out of business. It takes a smarter person to push a smart one aside. Pricing their products as high as the originators, or higher, ignores the community social responsibilities and would not help them. Businesses succeed as long as they have customers, as long as they can give something new to please and satisfy the public. Since these weak people, communities, and countries were taught and trained by conservative men and women, they would not be able to gain vision of the modern world. Since they have not gained vision of the modern world, the graduates in their communities could not develop modern programs for them to develop something new to give their races, genders, sexual orientations, communities, native countries, and the world a better status. Every race and country has its own tasteful meals. They could start by introducing them to the world as something new. Again, teaching these people here and in other countries to imitate people from afar that they cannot relate to keeps them crippled and handicapped more, instead of flourishing. Bill Gates, Jay Z, John D. Rockefeller, Larry Flynt, Oprah Winfrey, Donald Trump, Wyclef Jean, and many others did not become the wealthy people in the modern world by imitating and duplicating each other. Therefore, the modern school officials have to leave that conservative fashion and stop teaching the weak people to imitate and duplicate those who have been dead for so long, or those that they cannot relate to, and only see from afar. Wal-Mart is booming in this country and around the world because it created a method to develop from what it is and where it is, such as giving the world something new, which are inexpensive quality products. The doors of opportunity for the weak races, communities, and countries are wide open; these conservative school officials have to develop modern programs so these people can be educated and trained in a sense to develop from what they are. By learning and training to create opportunities for themselves, their communities, their states, and their countries, they will be booming on their lands like others in this land, instead of imitating and duplicating them.

Again, the school officials and professors who choose to remain conservative or traditional can never really teach modern students the right way because they are teaching modern students and people to keep pace with the development of the material things in modern life. It is not because many of these professors and school officials are incompetent, biased, or narrow-minded, but because they are opposed to change, newness, and freshness. As stated before, a mechanic that only has knowledge and education for an old car can never repair a late model car. These important tasks can only be accomplished by professors who favor change, regardless if they are part a conservative or liberal party. If these professors remain conservative, the weak people, communities, races, genders, sexual orientations, and poor people will never receive quality education and training, or have the proper attitude, education, and training towards success, life, and development. And all the classes and programs in school would continue to identify with and benefit the same race, sexual orientation, and gender as in ancient times. The world or the people do not change mainly because the school officials refuse to let the dead remain dead. Remaining conservative or duplicating the dead ones makes these problems get bigger and bigger. Frankly, conservative professors made education look like religion; it does not change at all. The school officials must study the past to better the future, not to bring us closer to the past. Therefore, since the educational system never improved, the same problems that existed in this country and in the world hundreds of years ago unfortunately still remain; and the races, communities, genders, sexual orientations, and countries that were weak a hundred years ago remain the same, or are getting worse. Again, in order for the weak people, communities, and countries to become strong and dominant and to change their conditions and their status in society and in the world, school officials have to do their parts first. The educational system has be changed from teaching the weak people and students to not spend most of their time in schools and to be satisfied in their lower status, to working together to advance in the professional sphere in life. It must change from we as people to accepting war, immigration, poverty, high cost of living, hatred, racism, sexism, and other social and economic problems as final and just; to overcoming them.

Every second and every day, new opportunities emerge. If the weak people do not learn how to focus on and take advantage of them, others will continue to take them. And the lowly people will always be oppressed and left out in the mud, and continue to say "life is not fair," or "why us?" or "why does the same race, gender, and social class always get the opportunities, and become stronger and richer?" Therefore, the weak people should not learn to wait for the oppressors and exploiters to give them employment. In fact, the main reason they got left in the mire is because they have only learned to depend on others, while the others are just looking for more loopholes to use them and make profit off them by any means necessary. The school officials have to develop modern programs to teach the weak people, communities, and countries to get back on the right track that they have been pushed off for hundreds and even thousands of years. And the only way for them to find the right path is to learn to act, develop, produce, invest, and patronize their own businesses, lands, races, and countries, instead of depreciating and despising them. Furthermore, students in the weak communities, races, genders, and countries have to be proactive and have visions as great businessmen and women, by learning to create their own quality, nice, and fashionable clothing lines with cotton and wool, develop their own agriculture, shoes, purses, clothes, sneakers, and other industries in their own communities, and sell them there. Again, their communities and countries would gradually grow and become influential in business and other spheres. And teach them how to pass modern laws to prohibit people who are not from their states, countries, and continents from establishing their empire there. Instead of criticizing the poor people for wasting their money on silly objects such as cars, clothes, shoes, purses, technology, jewelry, and making others who do not live among them richer, teach the weak people how to invest their money wisely and intelligently in their communities, countries, and continents so they and theirs can grow rich as well. If the people of each race, country, and continent were taught to support and invest in themselves, each would have grown socially and economically by now, and such a thing as the richest men and women would never have existed in the modern world, as the ancient kings used to be. If each had their own products known and introduced in the markets of their own country and continent only, they would produce more jobs, banks, corporations, and enterprises of their own. Millions of people in this country and around the world would not have to be on welfare, be in the criminal system, cause or suffer from immigration problems, high cost of living, or high property tax, have their jobs go overseas, and exterminate each other as an occupation. The weak people, races, genders, social classes, communities, and countries cannot become strong if the educational system refuses to work out a better and modern system to uplift them from where they are and what they are. The poor people of the world have to be taught to stop asking others for loans with high interest when they can create their own banks with low rates for themselves and their lands.

They have to be taught to stop depending on the lousy public defenders to represent them and learn how to do their own legal research, or establish their own law firms in their communities to represent them and their businesses in legal matters. The law and political science professors and school officials have to stop being conservatives as well. They have to develop new programs and teaching methods to serve the weak people efficiently because they continue to be victimized by the same vicious legal system in this country and around the world, merely due to the lack of modern legal support, knowledge, training, and education. The majority of these legal and political professors and school officials, who are getting paid to develop better legal and political constructive programs to serve and lead all of the citizens, choose to remain conservative, just as prominent church officials do. These professors and school officials must develop modern law and political classes and programs for their students to really serve the poor people in this country and around the world instead of teaching them to keep protecting and defending the biased, racist, and prejudiced legal system, which cripples the world. In order for millions of kids to stay off the streets, for millions of people to stay off welfare and out of the criminal justice system, and for the poor in other countries to flourish and stand strong, they have to learn their civil and political rights so they can protect themselves and vote for the right men and women. These people have been victimized, oppressed, and restricted because of the prejudice against them and their communities, sexual orientations, religions, social classes, genders, and countries. Nearly all members of the white male upper class know their civil and political rights. Therefore, the deprived and poor people in this country have to study the civil and political rights of their lands as well; not to practice the law, but to study them so they can protect themselves, their communities, and states, and become strong. These school officials and professors produce more lawyers in the modern world than in the old days. However, the majority of them have trained and studied for the wrong reasons, which are for selfish purposes to be a part of the elite class, and to figure conspicuously in society. Millions of people are still victimized by prejudice, bias, and racism in the modern world. More millions of innocent people are still facing long prison time, life without parole, death row, and deportation, or are labeled as terrorists and confess to crimes which they did not commit while they are totally innocent. Millions of parents still have their kids snatched away from them by government officials for the wrong reason. Millions of American youths still get stuck in segregated or poor schools merely because of their skin color; millions of innocent people still get abused, mistreated, humiliated, tortured, and put under surveillance by biased, incompetent, and racist government officials; millions of American jobs go overseas and the majority of gigantic corporations still exploit and oppress the poor for cheap labor and other natural resources and minerals. Again, we have millions of attorneys who have been taught and trained in the modern world for the wrong reasons.

The majority of lawyers have not been trained and educated for the right king at all. In fact, they were trained and educated in a conservative lifestyle, to protect and keep the same old biased laws in the modern world so the deprived races, genders, sexual orientations, communities, and poor people can continue to remain in the lower order of the society. Again, these major failures exist in the modern world, not because the lowly races, genders, sexual orientations, social classes, and poor countries have failed, but because these conservative school officials and professors have failed them by teaching and training their graduates to remain conservative. The majority of these law and political science school officials oppose inventiveness and novelty. Therefore, they cannot prepare their students to confront and overcome the ordeals that the rest of the world has been facing since day one. Since these professors and school officials have continued to fail the people, unfortunately, this crisis that we as modern people are facing has to get worse, instead of getting better. They are teaching and encouraging their students to remain conservative by keeping homosexuals, blacks, Hispanics, naturalized citizens, Asians, Middle Easterners, and females out of politics and other powerful systems in their own country and world. Instead of teaching their students to develop something new so this country and the world can recover, these professors are teaching and training their students to defend and protect the biased system so nothing can be changed. If a thing cannot change, the world cannot change; if the world cannot change, this country can never improve.

The world is in such a mire because the majority of the ancient leaders and citizens were not educated and bright enough to teach everybody to appreciate, enjoy, respect, and admire one another's villages, cities, countries, and continents. Their lack of knowledge and common sense continues to cause our downfall, shortcomings, and blindness in the new world. For instance, let's just assume for one second that all of us were of the same race and sexual orientation, had the same goal, interests, vision, appearance, height, gender, weight, and social status, spoke the same language, had the same characteristics, features, customs, culture, and heritage, ate the same food, and wrote and listened to the same music, and all countries in the world had the same weather, the same everything. Would this country, the world, and we as the people be better off? Of course not; therefore, everything is this way for a reason; we as people have to learn to appreciate, respect, and work with one another. In fact, no other country can be a better leader for the world, except this country, which is the United States, not because we are Americans or the wealthiest country in the world, but because this country has more diversity, different ethnicities, cultures, languages, customs, and heritage than any other country in the world. Therefore, we as Americans just have to update all the systems in this country with better and modern classes, programs, and laws to serve and lead the world sufficiently.

The medical school officials and professors have to modernize their method of teaching by training and teaching all races, genders, sexual orientations, and social classes better. As before, most of them still remain conservative, including the president of Harvard University. These school officials cannot admit that mostly the white male upper class is in their science programs, and have medical and others science programs tuitions so high. They have to modernize their programs and admissions requirements, and expand the science schools in this country and around the world so people who have an interest in pursuing a career in medicine and in other science spheres can be taught and trained to overcome the medical catastrophe in the poor communities, this country, the poor countries, and the rest of the world. By developing and expanding the medical and other science programs, the high cost of medical care, debt, and medical malpractice would gradually disappear because there would be more passionate and caring doctors to better and enhance the medical sphere. Also, more and better medicines would be found to eradicate deadly and untreatable disease. Moreover, by creating better medical and other science programs, people who want to serve and better society and humanity medically would crowd into the sphere, rather than those who only want to make their pockets heavier. More of the citizens of the next generation would be found in science fields, instead of in the welfare and criminal system. With a better approach to medicine and science, the world will never lack medical or other science professionals. To accomplish this great task, school officials have do their parts first by creating masterful science leadership. Inefficient medical and science systems create higher medical costs, more manifestation of diseases, germs, and bad health, and the loss of poor people's lives worldwide. Many great conservative professors and officials are trying to accomplish this important task because they actually believe that they are doing society and the world a great favor by only accepting their own race, social class, and gender in the science schools. But they never realize that the people that they are following control and use medicine and other science spheres for selfish purposes, the destruction of humanity, instead of saving and bettering it. The passionate school officials have to step in and develop a better way to call attention to the health problems of all human races because unsanitary conditions of the weak people here and in other countries mean the loss of health and lives for people everywhere. They have to develop ways to carry on new programs to see which communities and countries they need to start going to and providing affordable medical care for the poor people who have been neglected and overcharged for so long by the conservative school officials, professors, and medical providers. A better medical system to teach all modern students and citizens the proper ways to give adequate medical attention to the world means great prosperity for them. These conservative professors and school officials do not realize that keeping the majority of the people in this country and around the world out of the medical and other science systems will always impede the progress of medicine. It will also cause understaffing, which results in more millions of future innocent children, elderly, and citizens suffering and dying. The people in this country and around the world have to know that the race, gender, and social class that were crowded in the medicine sphere hundreds of years ago are still the same ones in the modern world, only because the modern science professors and school officials, including the Harvard president, still believe and use the same worn-out theories and false traditions that the ancient professors and scholars stated and wrote, such as that only upper class white males have the intelligence for science and other prominent spheres. Since they continue to admire and duplicate the dead and incompetent writers and so-called philosophers, we as modern children and citizens have to suffer and die.

The political science and law school officials and professors really have to do their parts first. In order to lift up the world, they have to start by creating new programs and courses. They cannot remain conservative and teach their students to remain conservative. They have to teach students—who are about to become leaders—to pass better, modern laws, bills, and foreign policy so everybody can do for themselves to grow socially and politically. They have to teach and train all races, genders, sexual orientations, and religious practitioners to know enough about the government systems in their communities, states, and this country. Teach the weak people the proper ways to be a part of the political system, instead of remaining unnoticed in state and national politics. If these professors and leaders oppose any novelty and change, things will never get better for the people, country, and world that they are serving. They have to teach and train their graduates to think of the best modern laws and policies to pass so this country and the world can improve socially and economically. Things remain as before in the modern world because many kids who are interested in becoming modern leaders are taught to keep things as they have been for the past century, instead of improving them. As before, the race, communities, sexual orientation, social class, and gender that was benefiting from all the systems continue to benefit and get richer in the modern world. Not because they are smarter, or are the only Americans in this country, but because the old system was created to only benefit and protect their side and interest, not Asians, Hispanics, blacks, females, Middle Easterners, and certainly not homosexuals and the poor countries. Teaching their students to remain conservative, or to serve and protect the same side, is not in the interest of this country and the world.

The poor and oppressed citizens should not blame the conservative/Republican party, leaders, and fanatics for keeping, restricting, and oppressing blacks, Asians, Middle Easterners, homosexuals, females, naturalized citizens, and people of poor countries because the modern school officials still continue to brainwash, mislead, misinform, and mis-educate them so they can keep things as they were hundreds and even thousands of years ago. To be more explicit, the races, genders, sexual orientations, religions, and countries that used to be enslaved, exploited, and oppressed in the past are still going through the same crisis. Again, these despicable things are still occurring in the modern world mainly because these leaders and people have been misinformed and brainwashed, instead of being educated. If they were not taught and trained properly to leave the conservative lifestyle and system, the odd old ways and systems still have to remain in our country and world. Again, these situations are not going away on their own. We as people have to be educated and trained to reject these atypical things so future generations will not have to face hatred, prejudice, sexism, racism, discrimination, war, slavery, poverty, disease, costly living, and other injustices as we and our predecessors have experienced. These conservative people and leaders were not naturally born biased, racist, sexist, greedy, and selfish exploiters and oppressors; they were taught and trained to be that way by the modern and previous prominent reporters, school officials, professors, and leaders.

The weak people who were taught in classrooms or by the biased reporters to isolate themselves, or were forcedly pushed aside from national and international politics in the past have to learn to plunge into these spheres. And the conservative leaders and people who were mis-educated and misinformed that they have the natural right to push others aside and keep them out of the prominent systems and agencies by any means necessary, as those in the past did, have to reread modern books, and be reeducated from the modern educational system to refine their brain and intelligence because the world has to start going forward.

The next generation should be taught and trained to use their votes, funds, and tax money wisely, rather than giving them away to people with little or no vision or common sense. Why should we remain conservative? Our buildings and embassies are bombed in this country and overseas, and large numbers of people and soldiers from this country are dying on a daily basis. The costs of tuition, living, poverty, welfare, disease, and medical care are outrageous; ninety five percent of our jobs or products that we can produce are made overseas. The countries and citizens that we were supposed to lead and serve want us to disappear, our world leadership status is in jeopardy, and our professional rates are declining drastically. Our American flag is being burned on a daily basis by Americans and citizens in other countries, and the majority of our jobs go overseas while citizens in this country cannot get jobs, are unsafe, and kill each other for money. Our tax money is wasted, our schools are closing down and our country is deterring other people that can provide and produce on their lands and for themselves. It does not take a genius to see the old systems are not working for us as modern citizens. Again, the main reason that these things occur in the modern world is because we have been taught and trained to keep things as they are, and accept them as final and just instead of finding our way out of them. The future generations must to be taught and trained to vote for the best men and women among us, the ones that can bring all people, races, communities, states, and countries into harmony and concerted action for a new world, regardless of their skin color, sexual orientation, gender, religion, social class, or other silly criteria, men and women who can provide weak students and citizens what they need to develop and flourish; to elect leaders who are not going to use politics for their own agenda, or their race, gender, and social class; leaders who will use their ability, capacity, and intelligence to better and strengthen the world as a whole.

The school officials and professors have to create modern programs to teach blacks, Asians, Hispanics, Middle Easterners, females, homosexuals, naturalized citizens and other Americans how to become great figures in national politics, rather than being a tool for ignorant politicians to use because the rest of the people in this country can no longer be ignored as citizens, taxpayers, or real Americans, and still let the majority of Congress members or the political parties be only upper class white males, while they are as American as they are, and brighter than them. The rest of the people have to be taught and trained that if they refuse to be a figure in national politics, they deserve to be ignored and disfranchised. The rest of the citizens have to learn new methods so they won't have to send letters and go knock at the doors of political parties, which do not have interest in changing and bettering their conditions. The professors and school officials have to create new and sufficient programs so all students and citizens know that the real meaning and purpose of politics is to serve, protect, and lead all the people in this country and around the world sufficiently; not a certain race, gender, social class, sexual orientation, and religion. And that the real meaning of world leadership is to lead and serve the world efficiently, not to serve a certain country or continent, and certainly not to have any allies in any form because having allies will always backfire on this country eventually; they have to know and learn the many countries that had or have wars with this country; the citizens of other countries that want to exterminate us as Americans, or are a great threat to us or this land mainly because our previous and some modern leaders have either supported other countries to attack them or taught and helped them attack other countries.

Modern political science and law students and citizens have to learn that the real science of government is deeply rooted; not mainly to tax the citizens, lock them up, humiliate, control, and pity them, but to lead, develop, and protect them, which it was created and intended to do. Therefore, people, races, communities, states, and countries that are slightly lifted above poverty have to be served and led well to develop and flourish so they won't have to depend on the government or this country for basic things which they need and can provide for themselves. The development of the world is profoundly rooted in its economic foundation. Therefore, by restricting and oppressing them to remain slightly lifted above poverty keeps the world where it will be harder for them to go forward. Therefore, the law and political science school officials and professors cannot keep teaching the future leaders to remain conservative; they have to teach the future leaders to create new productive programs to uplift the people that have been viciously pushed out of the systems since day one. If they develop new programs for all races, genders, and homosexuals, they will become more desirable everywhere. By them becoming enviable, they will change from inferiors, threats, and liabilities to assets for future taxpayers, their communities, races, genders, sexual orientations, states, this country and their native countries. They would become great men, women and great leaders, not just common people. In fact, they would give themselves and these places something new to develop, rather than terrorizing, and being burdens for their countries and the world.

The next generation of poor people will produce something new and magnificent, rather than thinking and believing that the world or the government owe them something. For example, John F. Kennedy, who was one of the best presidents this country ever had, said, "Ask not what your country can do for you, ask what you can do for your country." By developing new and better laws, political classes, and programs, the future powerful leaders of this country and the world will never devote most of their time to remaining conservative or to secure political offices for their gender, race, agenda, and social class. They would devote all their time solely to the development of something of enduring value for all citizens. The leaders would learn that they have to be great citizens first in order to be great leaders and serve all people efficiently. They would learn to sacrifice everything for the people that they are leading and serving, rather than defending and protecting the inadequate and biased systems that are deteriorating their country and the rest of the world. The future leaders have to study and learn better modern philosophy, law, and political classes and programs so they will not see and treat any race, gender, sexual orientation, social class, or country's leader and citizens as enemies, outcasts, and inferior. And they should learn not to see political campaigns and elections as a competition to empower and protect themselves, their race, social class, gender, and interest, instead of the people, this country, and the rest of the world. They have to teach that—regardless of which political party they are from—their main job as leaders and public servants is to serve and deliver the people, this country, and the world from these dilemmas. By modernizing the teaching method, the leaders will be better educated, trained, prepared, and modernized to lead and take better care of the modern and future citizens. As a result, this great country and world will ascend and recover from the revelry in an impossible utopia.

The future leaders of this country and the world have to be taught and trained to respond to the citizens' call as a matter of duty; they have to love all citizens, sexual orientations, social classes, and citizens of the world. Future leaders and citizens have to be trained and educated to use their liberal mindedness to create new constructive laws and programs, so they can bring the elements together for the common good rather than keeping them old-fashioned. In order for the future leaders to grow the weak people, races, genders, sexual orientations, social classes, countries, and the rest of the world socially and economically, they have to be taught to turn those, who many untrained and unwise people and leaders have labeled and perceived as inferior, into great achievers, accomplishers, and assets. It is an insult indeed, for females, blacks, Hispanics, Asians, Middle Easterners, homosexuals, and the poor in other countries, and others to be discredited and demeaned by the narrow-minded school officials as incapable competitors in the professional battle of life. Again, these people and the poor in other countries have failed because their leaders, school officials, and leaders have spent most of their time criticizing, demeaning, insulting, oppressing, and enslaving them mentally instead of modernizing and decreasing their tuition so the weak ones could study and train to develop their confidence to flourish from what they are. The weak people, races, genders, and others have not done and provided too much for themselves and their lands, because they have never been taught how to do so. Those professors and school officials have to upgrade the programs so the rest of the people can learn the proper ways to do for themselves, their communities, states, and continents. They will grow to depend on and govern themselves, their communities, states, and their countries, rather than letting others who despise, exploit, and oppress them govern them.

The rest of the people here and in other countries are outraged, because they find themselves and their manhood and womanhood insulted, compromised, abused, and humiliated for amusement. They have to be educated and trained to be radical, rather than allowing people who do not have any interest whatsoever in changing and bettering their conditions to manipulate and use them, their communities, races, genders, sexual orientations, and their countries as a means to an end. Those who pretend to have an interest and desire to serve and lead them are not going to do either, like the ones before. When they had no further use for these weak people, they would continue to increase their taxes and retirement age, close the schools down in their communities, and decrease the funds for their schools and other productive programs for their children.

Type of Systems Required for Future Generations

The majority of citizens in the world have an attitude of contempt toward their own people, races, heritage, countries, and continents because in their own universities and those around the world, they are taught to admire and support other countries and continents socially and financially, and to despise their own. In fact, in the world universities only a few courses offer the history of the black, Hispanic, Asian, Middle Eastern and other people's countries and continents. In the world universities, the citizens of those countries and continents are studied only as problems and dismissed as sub-human. Not one of the world university experts or presidents thinks like a World University; they should offer additional courses, programs, and training on the philosophy, history, sociology, and anthropology of peoples of black, Asian, Hispanic, and Middle Eastern countries and continents. Most of these connoisseurs, who are supposedly world experts, know nothing good about the present conditions of the majority of world citizens because they were taught to not waste their time that way. Also, they went to be educated in a world educational system, which continues to see and dismiss the black, Hispanic, Asian, Middle Eastern, and the people of other countries and continents as inferior. Most of the textbooks that these world universities are using and most courses these world students are taking pretty much teach them that the citizens of white countries and continents are smarter, superior, and better than the black, Asian, Hispanic, Middle Eastern, and people of other countries and continents. In fact, most of the scholars and experts of world universities write and place the majority of citizens in a place where they must be convinced of their inferiority. By the time these world university students complete their degrees and requirements, practically all of them are uneducated towards these peoples, and have nothing sufficient to uplift the world citizens, except the European and a couple of Asian countries. Therefore, almost all of the graduates of world universities become worthless in the development of the black, Asian, Middle Eastern, and Hispanic countries and continents. After spending half their lives studying in the world university, these graduates still cannot give something new to these black, Hispanic, Middle Eastern, and other countries and continents except what their predecessors did: dismiss, demean, criticize, oppress, and exploit the people of these disadvantaged countries and continents.

The majority of theories and traditions they have been taught in the world universities have been worn-out and expired for so long that these modern world graduates are unable to give the citizens of poor countries and continents what their predecessors have wanted since day one, like teaching them how to make a living and be self-reliant on their own lands, so they can become a constructive force in the development of their countries and continents. These so-called scholars at world universities and institutions are great threats, dangers, and destructive in the lives of the citizens of these oppressed countries and continents instead of a deliverance for them. They have never become a practical force to help and lead these people to come up with a sufficient program and solution to better their lives, countries, and continents. They just continue to brainwash them to make the same oppressors and exploiters richer and more powerful. It is depressing indeed. The presidents, school officials, and professors of world universities do not realize that they are the ones who are crippling the world by teaching and preparing their students to benefit and work only for one side. Preparing their graduates to drill into the minds the students and citizens of poor countries and continents that they are still inferior and incapable of improving the undesirable conditions in their countries and continents has made these poor people too hopeless and weak to overcome their awful situations. In fact, this sort of educational system is a modern way of destruction to this country, their countries, and humanity, indeed.

This sort of world educational system is a new sort of "mind enslaving" in the modern world because it kills the Hispanic, Middle Eastern, Asian, black, and other countries' and continents' citizen's aspirations, desires, ambitions, dreams, goals, and aims from developing, and dooms them to more vagabondage and crime. This sort of education is much more important to deal with than the anti-immigration, slavery, hatred, war, racism, exterminating, and other movements because these sorts of things would not exist in the modern world if they did not start in the world university schoolroom, and were not printed in the books that the world university students and citizens study. Since all the world universities, offices and campuses are located in the white countries, and since all the widely known scholars have been trained to remain in the white communities, countries, and continents only, those so-called world experts end up having no real world expertise, and no time, enthusiasm, or interest to deal with the economic, social, and medical problems which concern and are killing the black, Asian, Hispanic, Middle Eastern, and the citizens of other countries and continents.

All the classes and programs these world universities have offered, like languages, literature, religion, philosophy, history, mathematics, science, social science, medicine, and economics, have a good purpose mainly for the white communities, countries, and continents, as in ancient times. Again, due to loss of vision of the modern world, history keeps repeating itself. Nearly all the classes and programs that the world universities have offered in the modern world for blacks, Asians, Hispanics, Middle Easterners, and other countries and continents are a complete waste of time, just like the ancient ones. The main reason these awful social and economic problems are getting worse is because the presidents and experts of world universities have not yet learned properly and efficiently how to develop their own ideas, thoughts, and intelligence to really educate and train these poor people to develop themselves and their lands from what and where they are. Almost everything that these world universities, school officials, and professors are using, and almost every thought they are applying to the people of these countries and continents has been borrowed from the ancient philosophers, Egyptians, Romans, Greeks, Teutons, Aristotle, Socrates, Plato, and others.

In schools of business, medical science, theology, social science, economics, and other subjects, these world university students are taught an interpretation of leadership worked out by those who have justified their favoritism, prejudice, bias, and poor leadership as rights, just to enslave, oppress, murder, restrict, and exterminate others. Deriving their sense of right from that sort of teaching and leaders, the graduates of such world institutions can have no better message, training, and ideology to grip and better the unfortunate countries' and continent' citizens who have been ill-trained to serve and lead. But a few considerate and thoughtful businessmen and women, medical doctors, social scientists, religious and other leaders do the best they can with the little they have received from these schools to better the lives and conditions of people in poor countries and continents. Unfortunately, they are still unable to help these poor people to find the way out of their past and present difficulties because what they were taught in those schools is not solid and sufficient enough to help them teach the people in these countries and continents how to uplift themselves and their lands economically and socially. The only countries they can help and serve are the white countries and continents because these are the only countries that the world universities have really prepared and equipped them to serve and lead. But at the same time, these mis-educated and ill-trained world school officials and presidents naively believe that their untrained and unprepared graduates can really develop and better the world for modern world citizens. At the graduation ceremonies of these world universities, the presidents of their schools tell them to go serve and improve the world while their graduates have not been trained, taught, and prepared at all to better the rest of the world, except those they have been serving already. In fact, these world universities and presidents should have been frank with their graduates and the world upon their graduation by telling them that they have not been trained and educated to better the world, they just have been educated and trained to exploit and oppress the powerless countries and continents. Telling their students to serve and better the rest of the world's citizens from whom they have been estranged, and whom they were taught to despise, demean, enslave, restrict, and oppress has to be nothing but a huge failure for them, this country, and the rest of the world.

These world universities and school professors have to realize that such a task can never be attained by the ancient biased and narrow-minded imitators and followers because the ancient world's university graduates were nothing but antisocial, biased, prejudiced, and unsympathetic towards the black, Hispanic, Asian, Middle Eastern, and the people of other countries and continents. Since their present graduates are the imitators and duplicators of the ancient ones, they have to serve within the interests of a certain country and continent, as before, and restrict themselves in all social and economic matters that concern the black, Asian, Hispanic, Middle Eastern, and other countries and continents.

Therefore, the possible tasks and achievements for these powerless people always seem impossible to accomplish, mainly because the world university graduates were never taught and trained adequately to work out a program for the interests of citizens and countries throughout the world. The greater part of the money that the students from those countries and continents have paid the world universities to teach and prepare them how to better their countries, continents, and the rest of the world for future generations, has unfortunately gone instead into these schools' architecture, design, unnecessary research, studies, and their leaders' six- to seven-figure salaries. And all the education that these poor and hopeless students have received, sorry to say, has put them two steps forward, and ten steps backward. The education they have paid for and received is unable to help them find solutions to deliver their countries and continents from such undesirable problems, and has brought no enjoyment and amusement among them to be happy as brothers and sisters. The presidents and school officials of those world universities have taken these students' money to teach them to imitate and live as the people that their ancestors perceived as monsters, oppressors, and slave masters. Education from such a world educational system has continued to cause the citizens of black, Hispanic, Asian, and Middle Eastern countries and continents to grow more sour because it has led them to become too pessimistic to become a constructive force for themselves, their countries, and their continents. As a result of this one-sided educational system, the majority of educated people in the world end up imitating the Europeans and the white Americans, rather than developing something new for bettering and developing themselves and their lands. Sadly for these deprived people, they do not realize that imitating others, instead of developing something new to lift them up in life, continues to lead them to huge failure. Even in the modern world, these lowly people still wonder if God has forgotten about them or if they have what it takes to develop socially and economically. Due to the lack of support, confidence, intelligence, guidance, and wisdom these vulnerable people have continued to receive from the worn-out philosophy and other anthropology theory classes from the world universities' so-called experts, scholars, school officials, and the media, they still think of themselves and their lands as unworthy of consideration. Since blacks, Asians, Hispanics, Middle Easterners, and others have continued to receive no respect from the majority of the people of white countries and continents, their leaders, and their media in the modern world, they still possess the same fatal dependency, lack of self-confidence, insecurity, and self-consciousness that the majority of their ancestors had in the past. Therefore, they do not even endeavor to develop their own gigantic businesses, banks, industries, Hollywood, cars, foods, clothes, pharmaceuticals, school systems, or technological equipment in their own countries and continents so their citizens could have jobs, and be busy doing something productive for their countries and their continents, instead of despising and killing each other.

Since the majority of the presidents and experts in world universities are useless and worthless to the rest of the world's development, they fail to assume their responsibilities as world university scholars and experts to notice that the majority of the world's citizens are the victims of their conservative educational system. The traditional education that the rest of the world's citizens still receive in the modern world merely gives information about the past to these poor people rather than teaching them adequately the proper ways to confront and solve the problems that their lands and continents have been facing since day one. At the same time, these scholars and experts at world universities do not realize that by not providing the world citizens a better educational system to find productive things to do, they are going to employ themselves in unproductive things. For example, if a parent puts four kids in a room without giving them something productive to do, the kids are going to find unproductive things to do without being told, such as being annoying and picking fights with one another. Therefore, if all these presidents and experts at world universities—who are supposedly more intelligent and smarter than the average person—cannot foresee that if the world leaders do not have something productive to do as brothers and sisters, they would end up doing something unproductive and unpromising for themselves and their lands, such as annoying, picking on, demeaning, and fighting with one another; if the presidents and school officials of world universities cannot foresee such a simple thing, how good and smart are they, and what good are they doing for the world?

For example, if a family has four kids, and all of them fight with each other constantly, the parents have to sit down with them and have them talk it out. Often, brothers and sisters fight with one another because one is touching the other one's property, or one tries to control or get in the other one's affairs too much, or one is too greedy and selfish, taking the other's food and money, or one is irresponsible and careless, or one is too annoying, or one is too territorial. Regardless of what the problems are, they can find solutions as long as the parents care and know how to address the problems astutely and intelligently. If the parents do not intervene as soon as possible to put a stop to the nonsense, one is going to hurt, exploit, abuse, and take advantage of the others. Therefore, that family will never grow because their problems do not get resolved. The parents have to step in on the matter as impartial and unbiased mediators; their jobs are to help them to cooperate, help, and learn how to fix their problems so they can work together, respect each other, and tolerate one another, regardless if they like it or not, or if they want it or not. However, if the parents do the contrary by taking and protecting one side, such parents would make the problem worse for the kids, for themselves, and for their family as well. The parents' main job is to get their kids reunited peacefully by any means necessary. If the parents cannot have them settle the matter among themselves and become a family again, they have to go see a family therapist to help them find the problems, no matter how long it's going to take or how much money it is going cost for each session. They have to see the therapist as long as it takes and follow the therapist's orders; the parents should not care or place wealth and power above their family's interest. Otherwise, their kids would end up like the majority of Hollywood stars, rich but stupid and messing up; the kids would become useless and worthless for themselves and their family. Like the majority of athletes and so-called leaders of this great nation and the world; in fact, the majority of Hollywood people are not even qualified to be a decent babysitter. Such family's kids would grow up to be ruthless and egotistic towards one another; therefore, such a family would never grow, and they would have social and economic problems for life. But if the parents do the contrary, which is the right thing, by sacrificing and placing their children and family above all, their family will grow socially and economically, and become independent.

Clearly, under the current world university educational system, which produced our world leadership in politics, business, social science, medicine, and other spheres, we as people continue to go backward toward more destruction. All country and world leaders have the same common interest and want to reach for the same common goals for their people, countries, continents, and humanity, which are to cause the problems of high cost of living, poverty, disease, unemployment, crime, and immigration to disappear or decrease drastically. However, these wonderful dreams and tasks can never be attained for the present population and future generations as long as the presidents and school officials of world universities do not develop another sort of leadership with a different liberal world educational system, so we as modern leaders and citizens can start to develop and produce, instead of continuing to be busy demeaning and exterminating each other and humanity. Since we as modern world citizens and leaders have never been educated and taught well to develop for ourselves and our world, we had to fail. Not because were are natural-born oppressors, exploiters, and losers, but because the world school officials and we as the people end up following and imitating the ancient biased, prejudiced, sexist, racist, and oppressive systems and methods, which have blinded us from seeing the vision of a better world for future generations, and prevent us as modern citizens from admiring, respecting, tolerating, and working together with one another for the world's citizens and general interest.

So, in order for the world to change from going backward and start going forward, the world universities and experts have to be properly awakened before it's too late. They have to know that this country and the rest of the wealthiest countries can never really go forward if the majority of citizens in the world want to immigrate to, or despise, or depend on this country for social and financial support. Therefore, they have to modify the educational system and the foreign policy so the wiseacre businessmen and women can stop exploiting the others for cheap labor and natural resources. The majority of the citizens in this country suffers from such an approach, and are in major debt for overseas products, while the poor and other people are generating more hatred and resentment towards this soil and us as Americans. The world university experts and scholars have to learn that the proverb that says "there is no place like home" does not only apply for Americans or Europeans; it applies to the rest of the citizens in the world as well. The citizens in this country and Europe have no reason whatsoever to blame illegal immigrants for coming to this country or causing major social and economic problems because nearly all CEOs and VPs of corporations and industries in this country and other European countries oppress and exploit the poor in their own lands for cheap labor and resources. To be more explicit, the Americans and the Europeans should go in their closets, food cabinets, garages, and their workplace to see that over ninety percent of the products that they use on a daily basis are made by these people. They push them and their businesses aside in their own countries. How would they feel if other people were doing these things to them? These narrow-mined, biased, and racist CEOs, VPs, stockholders, leaders, and reporters are making trillions off these poor people, but they never realize that these things will backfire on the world in the long run. A few hundred years ago, the previous oppressors went to Africa and enslaved millions of helpless Africans to build this country. The previous slaves, and we as modern freed-men cannot even get our reparations from government officials, or from the people that our ancestors made rich in the modern world. Brown University and others were built by slaves; what percentage of blacks are accepted or work at Brown University and in their medical school in the modern world? Less than ten percent. But the worst thing is that blacks are still blamed for destroying this country, and forcibly pushed aside in all the prominent systems, even though they are the ones who practically built this country. And now, these narrow-minded, racist, biased, and incompetent professors, leaders and reporters blame those weak people for coming over. Why they do not have their products made in Germany, France, Italy and other countries? In fact, we end up in huge debt for buying European and Asian products. All of these ill-trained and ill-taught leaders and reporters are saying that illegal immigrants are taking their jobs and causing a war on the middle class. These poor people would never have come to this country or gone to other countries to cause social and economic problems if a large number of people and leaders in this country and other European countries did not exploit them, take their country's wealth, and cause a war on their middle class or country first. All these narrow-minded people and leaders always try to emerge as victims and mankind since day one, while they are the ones who cause such crises in the world and for themselves in the first place.

These prominent imbecile newscasters and other leaders are talking and writing about war or problems on the middle class. What about the war on blacks, females, CEOs, homosexuals, and the Native Americans who cannot even build their own casino or other prominent business in Rhode Island when they are the owners of the land? Furthermore, what about the war on Middle Easterners, Hispanics, Asians, and other communities and countries. Are they not Americans? Are they not a part of this country and the rest of the world? Who do these narrow-minded, biased, prejudiced, and racist reporters and leaders think created and control the sex or porn, video games like Madden, Halo, Warcraft, and others; hip hop, nuclear weapons, guns, obnoxious movies or TV shows, drugs, liquor, and other ferocious products and industries in this country and around the world? Where do they think these confused and brainwashed people from poor communities and countries learn how to hate, and find the weapons, drugs, and other obnoxious products and ideas to kill each other when they are not united? Who do these despotic men and women think are misusing and misappropriating the educational system; the prominent lawmakers make it impossible for poor people to either get a quality education or develop and live in their communities and lands happily. Since the school of thought these narrow-minded people went to did not prepare and educate them properly in how to develop a mind of their own to think and to handle their affairs wisely, they have to blame somebody as the previous ones blamed the slaves. Again things remain the same because they became the products of the previous oppressors. At the same time these so-called best reporters and leaders do not realize that criticizing and demeaning the majority of people would do this country more harm than good in the long run. Again, this great nation and the rest of the world can never go forward as long as these narrow-minded people are the ones who are in control of the newscasts and other prominent systems. Sorry, indeed, for their fans, as the old proverb goes, you can fool some people sometimes, but not all the time.

Those prominent reporters, professors, school officials, world leaders, and the rest of the white male upper class need to become angry with themselves and their peers for not serving and leading well, rather than blaming the poor people, blacks, Asians, Hispanics, Middle Easterners, females, homosexuals, and others for bringing the world where it is. This great country is all but lost because it is failing from within and from without. For instance, thirty percent of this country's population is doing menial work as cashiers, waitresses, drivers, etc.; twenty percent or more are addicted to porn, sex, violence, alcohol, gambling, drugs, food, violent and obnoxious video games, movies, or T.V. shows. Sixty percent or higher are hating, despising, fighting, or exterminating each other because of race, gender, sexual orientation, religion, culture, customs, ethnicity, and social class. Fifty percent or more are unable to receive a quality education or afford higher education or training; ten percent or more are either on welfare, in jail, on probation, on parole, or in some type of criminal system; fifty percent or more of us are in major debt; forty percent or more of us are either divorced, about to be, in therapy, or married more than twice; fifty percent or more are either unable to get quality medical care or are in high debt for medical care; seventy percent or more deadly or fatal virus cures or medications are controlled for selfish purposes, while the people are suffering and dying; sixty percent or more are either overweight or suffer obesity, or are having major surgery for silly things; five percent or more are either in Hollywood, sports, or any sort of entertainment business sphere; sixty percent or more higher education students are in school for law, business, finance, science, computers, history, psychology, or English; five percent or more of the population are either at war with countries overseas, or placed in overseas military bases; ninety percent or more of this country's industries are either closed, or brought overseas; eighty or more percent of politicians, religious officials, and other types of leaders are either fighting among themselves, for their political party, or for contributions, religious, their own, or corporations' interests rather than for the people; five percent of the white male upper class is manipulating all the systems in this country and around the world to oppress, exploit, and control the people, this country, and the rest of the world for selfish purposes; and ninety percent of overseas citizens either hate us, burn our flags or embassies, kill U.S. soldiers, want us as Americans to disappear from this planet, or cause us major immigration or terrorist problems. Therefore, there are more inefficiencies and negatives than positives. We as the people and this country are going backwards while the conservative reporters, leaders, and school officials are doing nothing good to overcome these ordeals, except to stimulate our going in that direction. For example, if a family has five kids, and four of them are suffering major addictions or any other type of social problems, that family will never grow until the parents change nearly all the approaches and aims.

Any great previous world ruler, in order for them to collapse, had to fail from within first, and then from without. We as modern people are going down blind alleys; the school officials, the leaders, and the ill-trained reporters are doing nothing good; they just teach us how to admire the Hebrews, Greeks, Egyptians, Socrates, Romans, Teutons, and Aristotle more than teaching us how to respect and admire our fellow Mexican, homosexual, black, Asian, Middle Easterner, Muslim, and Hispanic brothers and sisters. They teach us more how to spend more trillions on military equipment and biased laws, rather than reaching for peace and creating programs to uplift the rest of the world. They teach us as people how to hate and demean each other, and waste money more rapidly on silly cars, jewelry, and technology, rather than how to invest wisely and intelligently in our communities, states, this country, and around the world. They teach us how to exploit, oppress, restrict, criticize, and insult the people overseas more than teach us how to help them to overcome their social and economic problems on their lands. They teach us more how to admire and worship them and their graduates like Socrates and to pay them millions, rather than teach us how to create for ourselves and lower the high cost of living. They teach us how to plunge into the technology, business, science, and legal spheres more than teaching how to create, invest, and support our own agriculture, clothes, shoes, electronics, cars, and other industries. They teach us how to accept our inflation, war, other social and economic problems as final and just in this country and around the world, rather than teaching us how to overcome them. They teach us how to blame and hold confused people for driving under the influence or pulling a trigger rather than teaching us how to hold their peers and friends, who are making and protecting such products, accountable. Again, as long as the educational system is controlled by conservative people, they will always treat it as a conservative religion, and we will not be able to make opportunities for ourselves, our country, and the rest of the world to solve these major problems because we will always be learning the same fatal fateful lessons, theories, and traditions as the previous ones.

The present leaders who are in charge of the world educational system never attempted to develop any method of their own to make the world a better place. They just continue to copy the narrow-minded, greedy, selfish, biased, racist, sexist, and exploitive people of the past that had no interest in and enthusiasm for developing the world for the people. Therefore, teaching the present leaders of the world to duplicate the wrong ones has led the present leaders to mistake the tasks and duties before them as previous countries, world experts, scholars, and leaders have done. This inadequate educational system has led the undertakings of the world's connoisseurs and experts toward social and economic uplift of this country and Europe rather than the entire world. The aims of the present experts and leaders of the world are like those of the narrow-minded people before: to become more powerful and to control the world economically and socially, rather than actually assisting the school officials and leaders in other countries to develop their lands for their citizens and the world's citizens. The outcome is the same as before: little or no thought is given to the social and economic problems of poor black, Hispanic, Asian, Middle Eastern, and other countries and continents. The traditional narrow-minded conservative scholars and experts did not take the citizens of poor countries and continents into consideration, except to belittle, oppress, enslave, and control them. They have led the former students who were about to become experts and leaders of this country, other countries, and the world to become the imitators and duplicators of the ancient oppressors who called themselves philosophers and leaders. Therefore, the countries and continents that were likewise eliminated, exploited, and oppressed in the past have continued to be victimized and oppressed more in modern times. Since the students who were about to become future experts and leaders of their countries and the world had not trained and studied properly at all for these important tasks and responsibilities, they ended up doing what others have done in the past, which is to be inefficient. Not because they did not have what it takes to be great leaders, but due to the fact that they had not trained at all to develop their country and the rest of the world. Unfortunately, by the time the majority of them became prominent journalists, reporters, writers, producers, leaders, CEOs, scholars, physicians, senators, presidents, kings, queens, prime misters, or U.S. senators or presidents, they knew that they had become the most prominent people in their country and in the world. However, few of them could perform their responsibilities and duties to their communities, states, countries, continents, and the rest of the world.

Since the majority of the current world experts and leaders were not really taught and trained properly, they end up being of no great service to their communities, states, countries, and the rest of the world. Therefore, when they see undesirable crises in the poor countries and continents, they do not know how to intervene, reach out to them, or join them to work out a constructive, strong leadership for them so they could rebuild their countries economically and socially. They do the contrary, providing the people of these poor countries and continents with more weapons, liquor, drugs, deadly viruses, and exploit and oppress them for cheap labor. As a result of this corrupt system and foreign policy that they copied from the ancient ones, the people of these poor countries and continents cannot get any better to reorganize their lands for themselves and their people. They cannot rebuild themselves and their lands socially and economically, or rebuild their businesses, hospitals, schools, and universities. These leaders and citizens are the modern slaves for the overseas business oppressors; they end up as restricted as a child in their own countries and continents. Those that are overseas are oppressed, enslaved, and exploited as well, so they cannot grow and develop those who are in their native countries. The overseas and the national ones are restricted to small things in life; at the same time, they become satisfied with these undesirable conditions. Since those who remain in their native lands are oppressed, and the others who are overseas are oppressed and enslaved economically and socially as well, neither of them will ever grow enormously. Since neither of them can flourish, their native countries and continents cannot grow either. The leaders of their native countries and continents cannot become a great constructive force in the development of their countries and continents for their citizens. If these countries and the world experts and leaders were educated in a better modern leadership school system, they would learn and study the proper ways to direct their attention to the social and economic problems of these countries, continents, and the rest of the world. Instead of wasting more trillions of taxpayers' money on immigration reform policy, homeland agencies, wasting their time on the borders, and biased and prejudiced foreign policies, they would invest those hard-earned tax dollars to overcome these problems.

Because these so-called world experts have copied the old methods from what the biased and untrained kings and philosophers stated or wrote hundreds and thousands of years ago, this is a white man's world and the world belongs to them. In addition, these untrained and prejudiced professors and school officials have taught their students to continue to oppress and exploit the poor countries, continents, and the world as if they had a natural right. These incompetent professors never realize that they are teaching their students to cripple the world more simply by not teaching them something new and exceptional. Their previous graduates were about to become experts and leaders of the world; therefore, like any great leader and educator, they have to better the world by helping and teaching the poor people in this country and other countries how to take businesses opportunities in their communities, countries, and continents, rather than letting the wiseacres take them for selfish purposes. And they have to teach the science world experts how to modernize their social, psychology, criminology, science, and medical classes for their countries so they can better their countries and grow rich as well. These so-called distinguished world professors, presidents, school officials, and experts do the contrary. Therefore, the economic debasement that these countries have had is getting much worse, indeed. And the high rate of disease, crime, and illiteracy are way out of control, and getting worse. While these poor people have the same minds to better their awful conditions, due to the inadequate training of world leadership and expertise that their former graduates have received, they have no remedies and solutions to grip or to repair the social and economic problems of poor countries and continents.

When the students of these world experts and leaders finally become so-called experts and leaders of the world, they have no interest in helping and bettering these poor countries and continents so that the lowly and oppressed citizens could live abundantly on their lands. The only people the world experts and leaders seem to be great for are the European countries and a few countries in Asia. When their graduates see the poor countries with such economic debasement and undesirable social problems, they cannot aid them; not because they could not serve them, but because these so-called well-known world professors did not teach them how to address such world problems intelligently and wisely, and did not teach them properly about the true meaning of world leadership. Instead of the so-called notable educators teaching these bright students to be great servants for the world, they equipped them only to serve their countries' allies. Also, they taught the world experts and leaders to only say "God bless America" and look for the American dream, while these graduates were about to become world leaders. How can the world leaders or this country be doing well, if the world is not doing well as a whole? It is like saying a mom is doing well, while all the kids are poor and fighting among themselves. Teaching them to serve one side when they are about to be servants and in charge of the world, will always result in huge failure for them and the rest of the world. They would look for one side's interest instead of that of the entire world; the previous ones lost their leadership mainly for the same reasons. Instead of these professors turning these bright students into great leaders of the world, they are turning them egotistical, self-centered, and selfish like the ancient ones. And they still wonder why other people hate us as Americans and still burn and spit on our American flag, and why everybody wants to fight and exterminate us.

One free lesson for those who label themselves and their colleagues as distinguished world professors and experts: people who have interest in becoming world leaders cannot learn to pick and choose sides. Such a person has to be trained to be completely unbiased and impartial, whether she or he wants to be or not. For example, a thirteen-year-old couple that got pregnant cannot say that they are too young to have a kid or be parents; if they knew that they were too young to have an infant, they should never have started having sex in the first place. Since they intentionally brought the baby into the world, they have to learn to take care of the baby by any means necessary. Therefore, if the world universities refuse to teach the future generation of leaders to say, "God bless America and the rest of the world," they should step down from their duties. And if they refuse to include the rest of the world economy and social problems on their list, they should get a job at these conservative TV or radio stations. The Englishmen, the Frenchmen, and others can say God bless their countries only and look for their countries' dreams only because they are not the world leader, unlike us. We are the leaders of the world, and as long as we lead this great country and this great world, we have to include them in our dreams, goals, and desires, whether we want to or not. And as world experts and leaders, we have to assist them with their social and economic problems, as we do for our nation. Again, this has to be done whether we want to or not because it comes with the job. Therefore, the future world leaders and experts cannot learn and study to pick and choose as the ill-trained previous and modern ones do now; it is not up to us to do what we want to do, it is up to what the position and title requires us to do.

Future generations will have to be taught that the world duty is similar to a CEO's duty for a company. For instance, a CEO's job description for a great company is to be responsible for the entire company; therefore, the CEO has to have masterful leadership in order for the company to always flourish. The CEO would have to help the employees to think outside the box and to recover from failure. The CEO's greatness has to be based on the accomplishments of the company or corporation. The CEO must know what the job should be, and the responsibilities it includes. The CEO is responsible for the success or failure of the company. In fact, all falls on the shoulders of the CEO. The CEO's duties are to know his or her responsibilities and to delegate them well to others. The CEO has to hire the best staff for him or her to accomplish great things for the company. The CEO has to develop great strategies and be a great visionary for the company and the staff; he or she must hire a great management team to help him or her to develop great strategy. The CEO ultimately sets the direction, such as which markets the company needs to enter, what product lines they must develop or improve, what budget needs to be set aside, and what type of employees he or she needs to hire to succeed, or what employees she or he needs to retrain, demote, or fire. The customers must be more important than the CEO's personal interest or belief because without the customers, there would be no company. The CEO must hire, fire, and lead the senior management team well. The CEO must hire great employees and retrain or fire the lousy ones or the non-performers. The CEO must resolve differences or problems among the staff in a peaceful and fair manner, so they can always enjoy working together for the interest of the company. The CEO is the leader; therefore, he or she must set great direction, plans, and examples for the company, and modify them when needed so the company can always go further. With a great CEO and management team, the company will always go further and, the customers and employees will always be happy and productive.

In order for future world experts and leaders to be well prepared to serve future generations, they will have to study better modern courses on world economy, sociology, science and technology. Only teaching and brainwashing youths to imitate, admire, and worship the old dictators and autocrats, men like Alexander the Great, Caesar, Napoleon, other kings, Socrates, and others with fatal political and international foreign policies, will always end up doing more harm than good. These old despots and the old Englishmen murdered, exploited, and oppressed millions of inoffensive men and women for their interest and world power. If they were looking out for people's interest in their country and the rest of the world, including the females and the common men, they would never have lost the world leadership status. When many so-called philosophers, heroes, and leaders were writing about "logic and ethics," they were referring to and writing for themselves, Socrates, and Members of Parliament (MP), certainly not for the English females, peasants, Irishmen, Italians, other Europeans, blacks, Asians, Jewish men, and others citizens in the world. Otherwise, Roger Williams and other Englishmen and women would never have left England in the first place.

Since the old English political system was directed against the interest of its citizens and the rest of world, eventually it collapsed, and they have lost practically all their empire; this means that the world was not created to be owned by any human race or social class. In ancient times, the Roman Empire and many other kings owned white slaves. Eventually those kings lost their leadership and everything else. Also, the old Englishmen, Germans, and Portuguese who owned black slaves and mistreated the Italians, the Irish, women, and others also lost their leadership to this country, which also keeps the world from going forwards socially and economically. Again, no human is supposed to own other humans or the world; such a right of ownership does not exist and has never existed. Furthermore, Adolf Hitler killed millions of innocent Jewish people and tried to have the white Germans occupy most of Europe and the rest of the world. Eventually, Germany lost its empire; in fact, Germany is still paying many countries' reparations, including the United States, at this moment for causing World War II, and not even historians can say for certain what happened to Adolf Hitler and how he disappeared. History clearly shows the world needs a great leader, not owners, and certainly not oppressors. If any human race, gender, or social class still tries to own and control a certain race, country, continent, or group of people negligently and for amusement, as the ignorant oppressors tried before, then the same result will keep emerging as before, such as war and huge economic problems; millions of innocent people would continue to die. The same thing would keep occurring one generation after another, until the whole world collapsed for good; not because we are bad as people, but because we are taught to follow the wrong ones. These professors do not even realize that by successfully imitating the biased and selfish ones, nothing great and new has been accomplished. There has only been a larger number of educated and sincere people doing what the selfish and biased ones have been doing since the beginning of time. Besides, many of the old world leaders and so-called philosophers were not even that bright in the first place. If they were as intelligent and wise as these untrained professors made them appear to be, why have they lost this great world leadership, one time after another? If the citizens of the world loved and appreciated them, their leaders would still be leading this great world. Teaching these bright students to imitate the selfish ones or their poor philosophical methods and political system, instead of teaching them to develop a new great world leadership method of their own, will always result in the same problems as before: hatred, racism, war, enemies, sexism, innocent deaths for power or wealth; greed, and control of the world instead of developing and serving the world citizens as they were supposed to. Instead of teaching these youngsters who want to become leaders of world how to solve conflicts between countries, how to put their differences aside, and place the interest of world citizens above their own, and how to bring all the leaders of the world into harmony and peace with each other, instead of wasting more trillions of taxpayer's money on nuclear weapons and others things to kill and exterminate each other and the world.

Most of these untrained professors are teaching these bright kids—who are about to become leaders—how to keep exploiting and oppressing the poor countries and continents. At the same time, they do not even realize that teaching such a method would keep causing the same immigration problems that this great country has had since the 1800s. Furthermore, they do not realize that holding down the people of these poor countries and continents will worsen the social and economic problems in this country and around the world. Instead of creating new innovations to prepare these young students to lead this handicapped country and world well, they continue to follow the same inadequate system to teach them about trifles.

The professors must develop modern political methods for future generations, instead of utilizing or copying inadequate political methods. Future generations are not only about to become the leaders of the United States and of the world, they are reaching the highest position a man or woman can ever reach in life. Therefore, like any great leader, they should be taught to be wiser and more considerate than the incompetent ones, whether dead or alive. They should be able to develop efficient methods of their own, not copy someone else's philosophy, political system, approach, beliefs, and principles. Future generations will have to learn that philosophy, politics, and religion are unlike mathematics, for example. Two plus two equals four, now and since day one, but philosophy and politics must change every generation and every century because each generation or century has different views, beliefs, and attitudes toward life, nature, and the universe. Therefore, the educational system has to change constantly in order for it to be suitable for the people. Many things were normal and legal in the past, but abnormal and illegal in our times, and what is legal now may not be legal in the future; like slavery, for example. The educational system must be changed to serve the world's citizens well. Miseducating and misleading the bright kids who were to become the world experts and leaders of this generation has led them to be unable to work out a program among themselves to uplift their nations, so the citizens of poor countries can live happily on their lands. Due to this huge failure from the world school officials and presidents, the citizens of poor countries continue to leave their native countries to immigrate to this country and others because they continue to fail industrially, socially, economically, and medically in the modern world. Not because these poor people want to, or are unable to learn, but because their education, which is the most important thing for their improvement, is entirely in the hands of those in the modern world who continue to imitate and duplicate the despotic men who enslaved, raped, exploited, and massacred their ancestors and their lands.

For example, if a company has fifty locations, but ten out of the fifty locations are doing poorly, the CEO of the company must develop modern strategies and methods to help the ten locations that are doing badly to rebuild themselves. But if the CEO doesn't develop any new system to help those stores flourish, and instead criticizes, shames, despises, and humiliates the senior managers who cannot perform well, then such a CEO is not a great leader and example of a CEO, and such an attitude would show that the CEO was not taught, educated, and trained properly to develop something new and great of his or her own. However, if the CEO was properly trained, and was really a creative person, he or she would develop new systems to teach the store managers how to uplift the locations that were not doing well. Perhaps he or she could retrain or release the incompetent managers, and hire or demote. Just criticizing the failing managers without offering them any new solutions to their problems would cause more harm than good. The company would lose more money, and hardworking employees would end up losing hopes and dreams, and they would go look for new employment elsewhere. Furthermore, the senior managers would feel that their struggles to change their conditions were hopeless and end up disliking and resenting the CEO for his or her poor leadership. Not because he or she is a bad person, but because of his or her bad leadership to the company and to them. Bad CEO leadership causes failure and destruction to the company, customers, and employees.

The previous example showed great leadership and terrible leadership. Many leaders of poor countries are great and sincere, but they are unable to sufficiently help and better their countries, which have been socially and economically handicapped for one century after another. Since many of them did not have the right training or skills for such an arduous task, the experts and leaders of world universities have to work out a new program so the leaders and citizens of these countries can raise up to better their conditions. Teaching the school officials in these countries what they would like to know, such as how to provide their people with a quality education so they can teach each other how to earn a living, and take care of their sick citizens. For example, many times employees quit their jobs because they have to not because they want to leave the company which they care for and love. Since everything was going bad in the company, the relationship among senior managers, lower managers, supervisors, and the rest of employees will be awful as well. Therefore, many employees would end up leaving the company that they love not because they want to, but because the company is crushed, and cannot provide them what they need for themselves and their families. If the professors were doing their jobs, instead of misleading these intelligent future world leaders with trifles, they would develop modern world social science, economy, and medical programs, not just for this country, but for the rest of the world as well. Being the most powerful men or women in the world is the biggest title a man or woman can ever reach on earth. At the same time, it also requires world responsibilities, world training, intelligence, and great world leadership. Therefore, the disadvantaged immigrants cannot be blamed for causing immigration problems in this country and other countries. The fault lies with the imitators or narrow-minded professors or instructors who label themselves as distinguished world experts. Experts in what? The only thing these people seem to be experts on is how to impart the ancient information and worn-out theories in the modern world. And since these so-called world experts have continued to mislead the young modern world experts and leaders about the true essence of world leadership, they continue to cause the people of poor countries to keep suffering as before: they lose their roots, pride, confidence, and true identities. They are laughed at, insulted, discriminated against, and they abandon their families, loved ones, culture, and native land. These poor people are mainly restricted to menial jobs overseas, and millions of them have been wrongly killed, exploited, mistreated, raped, labeled, jailed, abused, tortured, shamed, and humiliated by the majority of the citizens of wealthy countries, or the border patrol or immigration officials. Again, not because they want to, but because education, which is the most important thing in the uplifting of the poor people in these countries is entirely in the hands of the duplicators and imitators of those who have enslaved, lynched, raped, exploited, and murdered their descendants.

If those so-called professors and educators were doing their jobs right, instead of demeaning females citizens of other countries, then these heroic people would stay on their lands just like anybody else. The proverb "there is no place like home" applies to people around the world, not just one group, race, nationality, or country. All these immigration problems would diminish drastically if those so-called educators were trying to be real educators by developing modern methods of their own. They naively think paying two hundred thousand dollars or more for a lousy piece of paper and having a high score on a useless government test, or a high GPA, makes them cultivated and wise men and women. They have stated or written that their conservative thinking and leadership would bring us into the light of salvation; and yet, we are all but lost, frightened, and hopeless in the modern world. Besides, the leaders and so-called philosophers that these narrow-minded followers seem to admire, imitate, and worship were not even that wise and knowledgeable about social, political, and world leadership philosophy in the first place because they went from world power in ancient times to no power or prominent status in the modern world.

The program for uplifting modern citizens in this world must be based upon a scientific study of each continent's leader and citizens from within to develop in them the power to do good for themselves, their countries, and their continents instead of controlling them. The world citizens have to know that not all leaders, school officials, and presidents are dishonest men and women. The main reason they are holding the world back is because they have been taught and trained by the previous conservative educational and prominent religious leaders to keep it that way. Due to this training, the modern world and its leaders and citizens are opposed to learning how to refine the systems. Doing so would disturb many laws, policies, and systems in this country and around the world that the long dead regarded as ideal, and we as modern citizens regard as classic. Since conservative people and leaders have such a mentality, they believe that they are doing this country, the rest of the world, and humanity a great favor by holding us as modern citizens and future generations back.

However, when properly awakened, each country's future generations will be able to develop sufficiently in the business, social, and other spheres. Nearly all people in any countries have the capabilities to be great achievers for themselves and their countries. But in order to accomplish this task, the world university professors and school officials who admire the old educational system have to develop another educational system to benefit the entire world as a whole. They have to teach each country's school officials how to train their students properly how to depend solely on themselves and their lands, instead of others people's lands. If they refuse to modernize the world educational system, and believe this task is impossible to achieve, they should either be trained by those who think it can be achieved, resign or be dethroned. With proper unification, organization, and a modern educational system, the future world leaders from the United States and elsewhere can change, lead, and better the world for their future citizens. The present arrangement of all the world universities in America and Europe leaves no chance to emerge from the poverty, high cost of living, disease, crime, immigration, hatred, war, racism, oppression, illiteracy, and employment-stricken world.

In the world, there are seven continents: Asia, Africa, North America, South America, Antarctica, Europe, and Australia/Oceania. Therefore, the presidents and prominent officials of world universities should change from world universities to continent universities. By establishing a main university for each continent in the world, they could teach each country's school officials from that continent how to teach their students and the people that their country and continent are the land of opportunity. Therefore, they have to learn and study to do and plan for themselves, their lands, and their continents. Drill into the minds of these people that they have greater possibilities to become great competitors in the economic and social battle on their own lands than on other lands. The poor people cannot develop because the current world experts and prominent professors have never tried to do the so-called impossible: to teach school officials in poor countries how to plan and do for themselves and their lands. If the experts and presidents of world universities refuse to become radical, they cannot expect war, poverty, immigration, high cost of living, and other social and economic problems to diminish, and they cannot expect the problems of this country and the rest of world to get any better. Again, the radicalism of the world's problems must come from within.

Each continent's main university will teach and train that continent's leaders and citizens how to grow their country socially, economically, technologically, and medically. For instance, the South/North American main university will develop all programs to teach and train school officials in each South/North American country so each one will have their own notable and distinguished experts, scholars, thinkers, and philosophers. The South/North American main university will have to accept mostly professors and leaders who want to serve and teach all races, genders, sexual orientations, social classes, and religious practitioners in South/North America, and to see all future generations of South/North Americans as assets for their countries and continent. The future South/North American university officials have to be unbiased and non-prejudicial in the admissions process. They have to treat all South/North Americans equally and with respect. The majority of students who should be accepted will have to be future school officials who want an educational challenge: to teach kids and people that the modern narrow-minded school officials and professors thought they could never learn and become dominant in the professional spheres. The main South/North American school officials should accept students who want to make education a right, instead of a privilege. Also, people who are passionate about bettering humanity have an interest in becoming the best experts and school officials in their country and continent, and have great enthusiasm to develop their country and continent socially and economically so immigration and other social and economic problems can gradually disappear for good. Each country's school officials from the main university have to be taught to teach all future South/North Americans to find harmony with one another and other world citizens, and to give their country and continent a new status. They have to be trained to have more knowledge and expertise about their country and continent than any other continent in the world, and to have more enthusiasm to develop their country and continent before any other continent. The main university has to teach each South/North American school official to secure men and women of vision to give their students a new point of view of serving, uplifting, and developing their country, continent, and the rest of the world. The main South/North American university should lower tuition fees, and redefine nursery, pre-school, elementary, middle, high school, and higher education as preparation for school officials in South/North American countries to learn and to work out a program to advance mainly their land and continent, then the rest of the world.

The South/North American university experts will have to teach each country's school officials to continue objective subjects like mathematics. However, in the study of language, country school officials have to be taught to speak and write their own native language properly. And they have to study the background of their language before they direct their attention to other languages. Each South/North American country school official has to teach their future generation to embrace and love to speak their native language, and to understand their own linguistic background. Their future students have to study the folklore of their native countries, and develop the philosophy, proverbs, and works of their own writers. For example, in the United

States, each future citizen who plans to become naturalized has to learn how to speak and write the English language properly so they will be able to understand the country's entire system and express themselves sufficiently. Also, in Haiti, future Haitians will have to learn and study how to appreciate, embrace, and understand Creole linguistic history before directing their attention to French and other languages, because the Creole language is one of the greatest heritages their ancestors have left for them.

In the main schools of theology, literature, philosophy, social science, and education of the continent, each country's school officials have to teach that radical reconstruction is required in those programs. Each country's school officials have to learn to omit the false traditions, cultures, customs, and old worn-out theories, such as that God said in the Bible or other religious literature that men are permitted to oppress, abuse, restrict, and kill one another for power, respect, and wealth, or that marriage is only between a man and a woman, or to burn or mistreat homosexuals, females, and others, or to cut a hungry person's hand off, give them ten years in jail, or execute them for stealing to feed themselves and their families. They should also refine the system of thought that misinforms and brainwashes a certain group to think they have a natural right to own, control, exploit, and oppress the whole continent and the rest of the world. Furthermore, the future main continent university has to change the worn-out theories, like that South/North American people can create or follow biased systems and laws to control, occupy, exploit, oppress, enslave, and exterminate others for self-interest, and still be regarded as great leaders, geniuses, and righteous men.

The continents' main universities have to teach each country's school officials the proper way to develop their own history, literature, and race relations courses and programs so future generations will be respected and see themselves as good, intelligent, and noble as their fellow men and women in different countries and continents. Besides, it is an insult indeed for South/North Americans to study and admire philosophers from other continents as geniuses while they have the same minds, and can produce their own philosophical theory and belief about themselves, life, countries, continent, humanity, the universe, nature, and the rest of the world. The South/North American and other continents' main university officials have to work out a program to teach the proper way to study their country's and continent's anthropology and history. Furthermore, in sociology and other social science course and programs, the university experts have to develop sociology as it concerns each country on their own continent before the rest of the world. To teach each country's officials the proper way and approach, they will have to choose to leave the traditional curricula and become dominant and influential in the new philosophy and type of social science.

Each country's officials have to study the proper way to show their country's originality in the artistic sphere, and they also have to teach their country's future generations to be proud, and embrace their heritage in art, music, film, poetry, and sports. Each country's school officials have to learn to draw and create their own art, music, poetry, and film based on their own heritage and ideals, and related mostly to their own culture, background, visions, and country. Each future student will have to learn that their real responsibility is to support, invest, admire, and be supportive of their country's art, sports, music, and film, and to patronize them first just as all other products that they produce economically and socially; then the rest of their continent, then the rest of the world. If they learn to invest most of their money in their native country, their

303

country will always grow and be influential instead of being a great fan of others, or wondering what they are good for. They must also learn to support the rest of their continent financially so their continent will end up having their own Hollywood as well instead of North America only. Each country's future generations will have to learn that they can act as well as others, and do what others have done. If they do not support their own country, but invest and contribute only to others like the modern ones are doing, their lands will always be left out of the art and sports business in the world. Each country's school officials will have to drill into their students' minds that it would be extremely unwise and unpatriotic for them to invest and support the art of other like the previous and the modern ones have done because by investing and supporting only others, instead of themselves, the others will always grow, advance, and grow rich, and their own lands will always remain in the mud; and they will always remain spectators and admirers.

Each continent's main university business and economic school should remove the business administration program. They should offer a couple of business administration courses, but not as a program because such a program does not prepare students to perform real business work. Continent school officials should set modern business classes to train each country's school officials how to prepare their students exclusively in the psychology and economy of their native countries. Future generations will have to learn how to bring jobs back into their country so their citizens can make an honest living and pay more taxes, rather than turning to criminal activity as an occupation. And they have to learn to respect other country's territory in a business sense so they can grow rich. Moreover, each country's business and economics officials have to teach the people in their own country to create and support their own apparel, clothes, shoes, banks, credit cards, food, beverages, sports equipment, and all other necessities of life before supporting any others. All the leaders in the countries of each continent will have to learn to come together so they can create a main continent bank and bank systems for the whole continent, and only for their own continent. Each country from that continent will have to learn how to create and provide countries with their own banks, credit cards, and finance. The citizens of each country will pay between one and three percent in interest; thirty percent of the interest will go in the main continent bank, forty percent will go to the main continent university, and the other thirty percent will go to each country from that continent. The citizens of these countries also need to be taught to ask their leaders and the world leader to pass modern foreign policies so people who are not from their continent can neither invest nor bank with them. Those who have a credit card on that continent will have to pay it off, and leave the country and continent slowly and peacefully. By taking up business opportunities on their own lands, they would grow eventually. Because of their growth, the major social and economic problems of this country and others would disappear gradually as well. Therefore, none in the future will cause or suffer from immigration problems.

Furthermore, each country's school officials will have to be taught well to teach their students to support and spend more of their money on their own country's products and enterprise than on those of the rest of their continent. Each country's future generations will have to learn to invest and work chiefly on their lands, and for their own lands only; not for anyone else. By learning to work and invest mainly in their own countries, eventually they will be independently rich and financially free because their native country will always have plenty of jobs for them, and its citizens won't have to immigrate or depend mainly on others for natural resources. Each country's business and economics officials from the continent's university will have to study many ways to establish a great and huge farm industry on their own soil, to produce their own fruit, rice, and other natural resources and mineral industries instead of worrying about MBAs or being distinguished in the business field. The distinguished businessmen and women of the future will have to be taught to provide jobs for their own country and continent rather than exploiting them for expensive products and cheap labor. The business and economics school officials in each country will have to study and train to develop their minds sufficiently so they can see the wisdom of supporting their native country economically. Each country's business and economic officials from each continent's university have to be taught and trained to teach future generations how to expand natural resources and the production of raw materials for the cold weather countries and continents that cannot produce for themselves. All the citizens around the world depend on food and natural resources from others to live and survive, therefore, they should never control it as the modern and the previous ones did. They should produce more to make them affordable for every country and continent in the world. Each country's school officials should be taught to spend no more than five years in the continent's main university. They should spend most of their lives teaching its citizens how to do the practical work on their lands so they can flourish.

Each country's business school officials should be taught to create their own major food agencies and industries, and to produce and control them for their country's interest, not for their personal interest, or those of their social class, gender, or race. They have to know their main duty as educators is to develop their own resources for their country's citizens to depend exclusively on themselves and their lands. Each country's business and economics school officials have to learn that the success of business is not to pay their managers, stock holders, or CEOs large sums of money, but to make the price affordable for their citizens, and to pay each employee almost the same amount because the enterprise cannot flourish without employees and customers. They also have to learn that a business does not belong to the CEO or the owner; it belongs to the people of the country and it will be the heritage of future generations. They will have to learn that without strong patronage from citizens the business will fail, and without strong business leadership, their country and the continent will fail socially and economically as well. Therefore, each country's school officials have to study the accurate psychology and philosophy of a business: to serve and uplift their country and continent. And the continent's future school officials have to omit the worn-out theories or other things they will never apply in the business program or classes. They have to teach the next generation that by supporting and sacrificing everything for their country and continent, their country will always grow and flourish. Also, the next generation will have something to develop and to go further with. They will never cause social and economic problems in their own country or any other. Each country's future citizens have to know that if an enterprise owner, manager, or CEO is misusing and misappropriating their country's business, or misusing, abusing, or mistreating any employee or customer, or if they are not pleased with the service, they should not stop supporting the business. They just have to ask their leaders to replace the managers or CEO, or refine their approach and product. Future citizens will have to learn that leaving or not supporting their country's business financially would be extremely unwise and cause huge economic failure for them, their country, their continent, and the rest of the world because their social and economic problems would arise again.

The South/North American university officials have to teach each country's school officials to drill into their students' minds from nursery, preschool, elementary, high school, and higher education that their main duty and responsibility as citizens of their country is to invest in and support their country and continent in every aspect, no matter what and where they are. If they do not invest and protect their country's and continent's interest, wiseacres from other countries and continents—who have not studied economics—will come to have them work on their own lands as slaves for petty change, and mislead them that their products are not worth buying so their products can flood their lands and continent. They have to learn that the main reason these ignorant and greedy oppressors make them despise business opportunities among themselves and on their lands is so they can make a huge profit and become richer off their sweat, country, and continent to make theirs bigger and more attractive. Each country's school officials will have to study to bring themselves and their minds into harmony with their fellow citizens and life as they face it, and to respect each other's business territory, no matter what. Each country's business and economics school officials have to learn that the profound way to elevate their native country and continent is by creating more jobs and expanding what the citizens that came before them have left for them as an inheritance. For instance, instead of continuing to let the unemployment rate increase, they should take all their jobs back from overseas, and drastically reduce the salaries of CEOs and vice presidents or presidents. Then, people who are on welfare, in the criminal justice system, and others who are breaking laws as an occupation can finally get jobs. If they refuse to make these changes, people should not support their business and create their own in this country and for us as citizens in this country only. By bringing the overseas jobs back to the country where they belong, all the profit would be made in the country and remain in the country. Also, by paying the future CEOs and VPs what the rest of employees earn, they would always appreciate their hard-earned money and their shares.

Furthermore, the only automobile company that Henry Ford and GM have left for the North Americans is on the edge of bankruptcy, and has laid off thousands of employees and closed many factories. The North American main university officials will have to teach all North Americans to appreciate, invest in, and support the Ford Company and GM products over the European and the Asian automobiles and trucks. By neglecting to support them as the other ones before, they will have to file for chapter eleven like those North American car companies before, and the car prices will have to increase. When the European and the Asian products finally put them out of business for good, the prices of their cars will increase from double to quadruple for future generations. For example, in the seventies and eighties, cars and everything else were inexpensive for us because we were making all our products. Closing all our national industries in favor of those overseas will always backfire on us with higher inflation and other social and economic problems. If the future leaders of North American and other continents learn and study properly how to support and invest their money in their products, their fellow men and women who have been laid off, and factories that have been closed, will be reopened and rehired. More jobs for each country will mean more wealth for each country and the rest of the world.

Many countries in the modern world have offered to buy many of this country's ports, including one of the biggest in Miami because they see that we have already failed from within and without; they already see that we, like any great previous world leader, exercise hindsight rather than foresight. They already know that our school officials have taught us as Americans to despise agriculture and industrial labors; they already know that we go ten steps forward and thirty steps backward. The agriculture and industrial labors that past generations used to admire and appreciate, we in the modern world do not. We are taught and trained more in silly things than the most important and necessary things in life; they already know that without them providing us with food and other products, we will have huge inflation problems. Therefore, teaching our kids and the rest of the world's citizens to despise doing the greatest agriculture and industrial jobs will be a great loss for us and this country. We have over ten million kids in college or high school that are learning mostly worn-out theories, or playing or watching obnoxious video games and T.V. shows, having sex, drinking alcohol, doing drugs, gambling, and learning things they cannot really use in life. But not a third of them can do or build any major agricultural or industrial work for this country. In the end, the educational system is pretty much useless. These officials produce a bunch of graduates who know all the educational law, politics, technology, business, and theories of other spheres; thousands of them are crowded into Wall Street and other public offices. But less than five percent of them can really train and teach citizens properly to create and conduct major food, apparel, and other industries for this country. The citizens of the previous century did not have great technology, or a Ph.D, MBA, BA or BS, but they were living healthier and had a lower cost of living. They were producing for themselves, and did not have teachers from elsewhere to brainwash them. In fact, fast food restaurants even require a diploma in order to get a job. What do these things have to do with flipping a burger or frying French fries? They are charging modern students fifty thousand dollars a year to spend six years of their lives learning how to use mechanical, legal, sociological, and other theories when those that came before them were doing these things with just basic training. Teaching us to despise and mistreat agricultural and other industrial workers will bring this country worse inflation problems than ever, and cause us to always have allies instead of leading the world sufficiently and fairly. This country will always have to depend on others for food or other basic things in life, while we as Americans can learn how to make and produce them for ourselves and our lands with just basic training. And since citizens in the past who were doing these hard jobs were mistreated, despised, exploited, oppressed, underpaid, perceived as menial workers and imbeciles, and were eventually eliminated by the capitalist men instead of being appreciated, helped, and provided with modern scientific methods of farming and industry. These workers pressure their kids to leave the field and to go to those so-called prominent places. Since nearly all the places that were producing all these great works and products have been replaced by plazas, car dealerships, and malls or major buildings for rent, this country has to face inflation, and have other social and economic problems in the modern world. The world leaders have failed in their responsibility and duty so the rest of the world has to fail from within and without as well. Again, the upper class white males have to blame themselves and their professors instead of the poor races, communities, genders, homosexuals, and illegal immigrants because they were taught by these Socrates imitators to exercise their hindsight rather than foresight.

We as the modern world leader have to be proactive and greater than the ones who came before us by not waiting until it's too late to modify our approaches. The economies of other countries are flourishing and their employees are working fewer hours because they have already pushed over ninety percent of North American products out of business. By allowing them to buy any of one of our ports, or to become richer off us, our next generation may have to sell a state or a country from the North American continent. Then, the power of the North Americans will be derived from other continents. They will tell future North American generations what to bring into their own country. Besides, it is an insult for a country to ask to buy a piece of North American lands. While the incompetent North American leaders are wasting a hundred times the amount that they offer to buy weapons for unnecessary war, immigration policy, homeland security, to keep the bright minds on welfare and in the criminal justice system. For example, it's a like a mom asking another mom to sell her kids to her.

Furthermore, the future North American school officials will have to teach the CEOs of Ford and GM to expand their products to the entire North American continent, and to modify their name from Ford Company/GM Company to Ford Company or GM Company to North America. Ford/GM Company North America will make cars, trucks, Jeeps, and government vehicles for each country in North America based on the designs and names each country prefers, so theirs can be unique. For example, if Haiti wants to have their car model called Jean Jacques Dessalines, that name and that request have to be respected and followed. Therefore, the future generations of South/North America will have to learn to buy products mostly from their country and South/North America. If a rich person in the future from South/North America wants to buy three cars, two will be cars from his or her country, and the other one will be from another country from their own continent.

The Ford/GM North American Car Company will have to establish the factory and industry in the country itself. From the profit that the company makes, it will have to give each country a third for their citizens' patronage; thus they can rebuild their roads and their country, which the previous and the present leaders have destroyed due to loss of vision of the modern world. Each future country in North America will have their factory and vehicle dealerships established in the country itself so they will have plenty of jobs for the future generation and be able to rebuild their roads so more cars can be sold. The Ford/GM North American Car Company will be able to sell more cars, refine their products so they can give future generations great quality cars, and have more revenue for the North American continent. The future North Americans have to realize and study that Ford, GM, and other great automobile companies have not failed. The North Americans and the leaders have failed them because they have misled, misinformed, and mis-educated on the duty of citizenship and responsibility to a country, continent, and world. By buying products made in, and supporting their country and the rest of North America, the continent will always grow and flourish. And by helping each continent to develop the same theory, they would grow as well.

Future North American generations will have to be taught and trained to place the products and businesses of their country and continent above those of everybody else, no matter what and where they are. By developing such methods, the Ford/GM North American Car Company will be able to refine their products and the price will be able to decrease drastically, as Henry Ford and others wanted it to. For example, a family cannot grow and flourish if the parents do not invest and support their kids wisely and intelligently. If parents admire and support other families, theirs will never grow, but others will always flourish. Therefore, each continent's main university will have to teach each country's school officials the same theory so their continent can flourish and grow as well. They should only work and sacrifice everything for their native country and continent first, before anywhere else. With such a method, each continent will have their own products, cars, Hollywood, and everything else, and each country will grow economically and socially. With each country growing in the economic and social aspects, they will not even attempt to immigrate anywhere else, call us greedy or selfish, or want to exterminate us, and future generations will not have to waste trillions on weapons, immigration policies, or building a border fence. Since the leaders of all countries will have what they need, the future will enjoy the real American dream, and other citizens will enjoy the dreams of their native countries. They will learn to mainly create and support their own people; to work for , die for, and invest in their own country and continent. And people from other continents that have their cars or other products have to learn to disappear from North America slowly, so they can grow their products and become dominant in the car businesses of the world. The CEOs of foreign car companies will have to learn to bring their car businesses back to their native lands, and then to refine and decrease the price of their products drastically so their citizens can afford them and have plenty of jobs.

The future South/North American school officials will have to learn to support and create their country's and continent's products mainly. With such an educational system they will always grow, and always be able to refine their products for their future generations. Each country and continent will always have jobs and always flourish as much as others. And the false traditions and worn-out theories that products like cars, clothes, technology, watches, jewelry, perfumes, and others from other continents are better or have to be better than South/North American products, or that South/North American institutions, hospitals, pharmaceuticals, clothes, foods, and all other products have to be better than those of Asia, Africa, North America, Antarctica, Europe, and Australia/Oceania and their countries have to be taken out of future books and school curricula because they deny actual facts, refute history, and discredit each of us as intelligent, smart, and capable human beings. The majority of countries and continents in the world have failed because their citizens were never trained and taught adequately to develop themselves, their country, and their continent. The only reason these worn-out theories and false traditions still exist in the modern world is because the old countries and continents that oppressed and exploited the feeble ones in the past, still want only themselves to be rich. Therefore, by teaching them to do for themselves instead of watching others exploit them, they would be able to invest all of their money, energy, wisdom, and resources into their country's and continent's clothes, foods, literature, history, cars, technology, wine, and other things.

Each continent's school officials will have to teach their future superstars to support their country's products first, then the rest of the continent; they will have to learn to be unlike the present clowns in Hollywood. For instance, they are making millions of dollars in North America, but they invest most of their money in other continents' products, such as arts, furniture, jewelry, technology, cars, apparel, purses, restaurants, hotels, and others. Since the South Americans or citizens of other continents were never taught how to become a great superstar and servant to their country and continent, less than two percent of them end up being sensitive, insightful, frugal, supportive, and patriotic. Again, continuing to teach each country's citizens how to invest in and support only others will always increase the high cost of living, movie ticket prices, unemployment, poverty, immigration, and social and economic problems in this country, continent, and the rest of the world. It is also a complete waste of money for North/South Americans to pay millions to modern Hollywood superstars, musicians, athletes, and other entertainment leaders while teachers are making nearly minimum wage, and while many of them do not even support their own country's national cinema, music, sports, and other entertainment; and while millions of North/South American youths cannot eat outside of school because of a lack of financial resources.

The main South/North American university will have to develop new technology programs and courses exclusively for South/North American school officials. Practically all the so-called technology experts from South/North American universities of the present are pretty much worthless in the technological development of the continent. The majority of them were taught that they are geniuses and experts, while most countries in North/South America still experience blackouts. Also, most technology and electronic equipment and products are made in other continents, and all the money for technology and electronic products goes to other continents. All these so-called experts are good only for technology and electronics marketing and promotion in North/South America and around the world. North Americans and others around the world are in major debt for purchasing high-priced technology and electronic equipment even though they have the same brain, mind, capability, ability, and intelligence to produce their own for themselves and their continent at a much more affordable price. The fault is not that of the poor graduates. The so-called experts and the greedy businessmen and women, school officials, and scholars in those spheres are to blame. Unfortunately, North American graduates are mainly educated and trained to repair and sell technology and electronic products of others, and to perceive the makers of those products as geniuses. With proper education and training, they can make their own and become as dominant in the technology and electronics spheres as others.

Those so-called geniuses have never came together to work out a great program to uplift North America and the rest of the world in the technology sphere, except to fill their pockets and control the world like the ancient kings used to. The main South/North American university will have to create a promising technology program for each country to teach how to advance technology in the future world. After graduating from the main South/North American university, students will have to return to their native lands to pass on what they have been taught so future generations can develop their own countries and continents technologically and electronically. They will have to learn how to create industry in their own country to make and name their own televisions, refrigerators, phones, decent video games, cameras, radios, computers, and all other electronic equipment and technology. By developing such a method, each country from South/North America will become a constructive force in the technology of their lands and continent. Therefore, future generations will not have to buy a plasma TV or other electronic products for thousands—as we do now in the modern world—because they would make and support their own products. And, the future Ford/GM North American Car Company will have their own technological equipment in their own country and continent. Again, by creating our own technology and electronic products, the high price for technological equipment, electricity bills, blackouts, and other social and economic technology problems will disappear, and the other continents can do the same things, and respect each other's business territory. Then, each country and continent will grow. In the end, all social and economic problems will be overcome, and the world will be richer; not because we have a Ph.D or an MBA, but because we deal with these situations as they are. A third of the profit will go to each country in South/North America based on population and the amount of purchases, a third will go to pay expenses, including the employees' salaries, and the rest of the profit will go to the main continent university so the education for future generations can be free or inexpensive.

The continent universities have to develop schools of architecture and engineering for each country. In those schools, each country's officials will have to study modern architecture to develop the architecture in their native country and continent in their own way. They have to teach their countrymen and women how to rebuild the houses and roads that others have destroyed due to lack of harmony, cooperation, and love. School officials have to attend architecture programs and courses based only on their own country's design and heritage, and embrace their national architecture and learn to better it, not to imitate or copy architecture from any other country. They should create and design their own banks, hotels, roads, highways, houses, restaurants, and industries, replant trees, leave the animals alone, and take care of them, the plants, the trees, and their water, and protect them so their country will develop infrastructure. And they should connect each country by road and water so future generations will not have to use planes, as we do, when they visit one another's country because many innocent people have died that way.

The main South/North America University will have to develop great writing and journalism programs for each country's school officials to learn and to teach future generations the proper way to write and be unbiased newscasters. School officials must not study to imitate the *Chicago Tribune*, the *New York Times*, CNN, FOX News, ABC, BBC, NBC, the *Wall Street Journal*, the *Washington Post*, and other news services because most of them are biased. They must be taught how to grow and be dominant in journalism and writing with their own style and backgrounds; to develop their own prestigious publishing and news companies; to write, edit, develop, and publish their own textbooks, stories, movies, cartoons, scripts, history, literature, and philosophy based on their own past, heritage, and perception. Students will have to learn to promote and advertise their own country's products, movies, music, and enterprise first, then the rest of the continent. And each country's artists should learn that their main job as an artist is to promote their country's products first, and to set a good example and be great leaders for the youths and citizens who admire, like, and support them. Teach future superstars and athletes to wear and use their own countries' clothes, food, beverages, shoes, sports equipment, cars, and all other products from their country all the time, whether they are in or out of their country. They will have to be taught to embrace and be proud of themselves and the products from their lands, no matter what.

By teaching each country's citizens in such a way, all countries will become dominant in music, movies, sports, and other industries, and make money. The common people will be able to take their kids and loved ones to a game or a live show without paying a large sum of money. Besides, why are modern athletes, actors, and singers getting millions for acting or playing a game, anyway? They are not serving their country, just wasting money on a bunch useless and silly things. Each future superstar will have to learn to support and advertise mainly their country's products. As a result, each country and continent will always have their own products on the market, and no countries and continents will ever be ignored and left out as in the modern world. By developing a new and better educational system for these future artists, they would proudly advertise, use, and promote their country's goods without asking for a large sum of money. And they will refuse to promote drugs, sex, liquor, hateful video games, and other obnoxious products not because they will be better than the modern ones, but because they will be sufficiently enlightened to determine for themselves whether these products, attitudes, and behaviors will help their fans and country or help the oppressors. With this great educational system, future generations will exercise their foresight rather than hindsight.

Since future generations will be taught to exercise their foresight rather than hindsight, the rates of troubled adults and youths, girls going wild, addicts, inmates, welfare, poverty, and violence will drastically diminish, instead of increasing. In the end, the future *bourgeois* and common people will be safer and happier because they will have less tax to pay, spend more time with their families and connect to their kids and friends more, have four to six weeks of vacation a year, and be able to retire at a decent age. Therefore, the rates of divorce, depression, and troubled youth in the future will have to decrease significantly because they will have more time to spend and be connected with their loved ones, parents, friends, and other families. Additionally, the world will be at peace and fun to live in, all countries will have a great relationship with those overseas, and the world will keep flourishing as one. As a result, future generations will be happy and prevail from within and without.

Each continent will have to develop a new medical program for each country. Each country's medical and science students will have to be trained to become school officials and experts for their native country. These medical and other science school officials and experts will have to train students to teach all the citizens in their country who want to pursuit a career in the science field, mainly those who have great aspiration, enthusiasm, and interest to confront the medical crisis that their fellow citizens have been facing since day one. The continent's main university should not look for any loophole to deny any person acceptance in their programs, or set GPA or other useless requirements as main requirements for admission because they are not working. If they were, sixty percent of Americans would never be without any or have poor medical coverage, be obese or physically or mentally handicapped, or end up in nursing homes or die before they are sixty-five years old. Furthermore, there would never be such high numbers of medical malpractice cases, medical professional understaffing, and outrageous medical bills.

Each continent's main university will have to teach and train anybody who has an interest, passion, and desire to help people with medicine or science, instead of people who want to make their pockets heavier, treat the medical field as a luxury, and protect and defend a broken-down conservative medical system. Their admissions requirements should be based chiefly on whether the applicants have a plan for their fellow citizens medically upon their graduation, how far are they willing to go to help and improve medical conditions, what action they are going to take to provide everyone with excellent and affordable medical care, and how they plan, as future medical providers, to provide excellent medical care for all modern citizens who have been neglected medically. Each continent's main university has to teach future medical and science school officials to teach their country's citizens to chiefly help where the medical problems are present. As medical and science experts, they have to build a great relationship, and be glad and willing to share notes and ideas, ask for help when they need it, and work as a team instead of as rivals and competitors. They should be taught to help and serve patients before asking for compensation. Their main job as medical care providers is to solve the specific medical problems that have crippled and killed millions of citizens. Each main continent's university should change the medical teaching method from serving selfish motivations to helping and rescuing the people and humanity as a whole, and developing the power of execution to deal with medical and science matters as people of vision rather than imitating the previous and modern selfish and careless ones. They should not accept people who want to get in the medical field to increase their salary so they can spend it on joyous living and a lavish lifestyle rather than refining medical and science systems. They should teach each country's medical officials to create special equipment, and help others produce it in their own country, to treat ill patients rather than looking at their tongue, taking their pulse, asking them a couple of questions, writing a prescription, and mailing them a huge bill as the incompetent and ill-trained doctors are doing in modern times. The modern countries, world leaders, and school officials have to learn that problems of great importance sometimes take a generation or two to work out. Therefore, for these great tasks to be accomplished, they have to be met with far-reaching plans.

The professors at each continent's main school of medicine and science have to train each country's school officials to teach their citizens the proper way to study the seriousness of their citizens maladies and provide them with excellent medical treatment. School officials have to live up to what they are taught in school and share it with their school officials in their native country and the rest of the world so future generations can build upon their foundation, develop their own experience, and further their training and education. Future students have to learn to treat all people equally because the longevity of their country's citizens will depend mostly upon the medical care they get. The future medical school officials should not spend any time preaching to these kids about the wiseacre doctors who are playing in prestigious country clubs and living a lavish lifestyle from the patients' lives and their salaries. Medical officials must be prohibited from recruiting or bribing medical providers from other countries to come practice medicine on their land, regardless if they are average or excellent in the medical or science sphere. They have to work out a medical and health program to rescue their native country and continent from undesirable medical conditions so children in the future can be healthier, happier, and live longer. School officials have to be taught to establish and refine the clinics and hospitals in their own country as well so they can eradicate disease on their lands, and teach anybody who wants to learn, for free or low cost, how to serve the public. With a new and better science educational system, the number of qualified, kind, and sincere medical providers will increase significantly instead of diminishing, and future generations will be happier, safer, and healthier because they will be treated better and have no debt from medical bills, and government officials will have more reasons to lower taxes.

Also, new, promising citizens will be found, and they will have more assistance to overcome their medical crisis. Then, future generations will never experience the expensive and poor medical service systems we have in the modern world. By teaching them to use medical knowledge wisely and intelligently, their country's status will improve in the medical sphere, and they will believe that they are as capable and smart as others. School officials have to learn to create and develop their own medical program research, major pharmaceutical company, and their own medicine factory and industry in their own country. Their main job is to pay attention to the health of their own country's citizens because unsanitary conditions in their country mean the loss of health and lives for them and future citizens. The continents' schools of medicine have to drill thoughts of helping and rescuing their citizens and humanity into each country official's mind in almost every medical class they enter, and in every medical and science book they study so by the time each country's school officials and experts finish their programs, they will be of great service to their country's citizens, then to the rest of their continent, then to the rest of the world. They will not be biased, selfish, and worthless in the service of the people, as the majority of the present ones are. Between ninety-five and ninety-eight percent of each main university's students will have to be from the continent itself. They will also have to study to direct their attention sufficiently to their citizens, who still indulge in superstitious and religious practices to treat or cure disease. Also, they will have to learn that some citizens practice medicine in such a way mainly due to a lack of medical education and vision of the modern world. But these people want to help their citizens in medicine. Therefore, as medical educators and experts, they will have to provide them with great medical knowledge, education, and techniques. They have to teach them to further their knowledge in medicine and other sciences instead of blaming them for practicing medicine in such a way because if they belittle them instead of enlightening them, it will impede the progress of medicine and will also cause tension on their lands. Each country's school officials will have to have a couple of modern classes on primitive medicine to learn why it was created in the past, and what these people's intentions were towards their village and humanity.

In the countries of South/North America and other continents, many people seldom see a medical professional for a check-up. Therefore, future students will have to learn that it is their job as medical leaders and experts to establish modern clinics and hospitals in these deserted provinces, and to teach the midwives and the herb doctors something new.

Each country's medical school officials and doctors will have to learn mainly about their citizens to find out which diseases their citizens are more at risk for and susceptible to. Then they can develop their own treatments and drugs to eradicate those diseases and begin to examine the diseases that the rest of their fellow citizens in that continent and rest of the world are susceptible to as well. If they find the treatment for another country's citizens, they have to give it out and expand it more so drugs and medical care can be extremely affordable. Also, if they find a treatment for the rest of their continent's citizens or those of the rest of the world, they have to give the treatment theory to the officials of that continent's main university; and they would receive a continent or world Nobel prize for helping them and humanity instead of holding on to the treatment or suppressing it to get richer while their fellow citizens are suffering and dying. These country school officials and experts have to spend no more than five years in the continent school of medicine. They have to spend most of their time and lives doing practical medicine in their own countries rather than studying worn-out medical or other science theories. If the ancient village men and women who created medical science were not even middle school or high school graduates, but developed the little intelligence they had to have their citizens withstand syphilis and tuberculosis well, future generations will be able to study and learn practical medicine in five years or less. Besides, we have a bunch of doctors who spend twelve to fifteen years in medical school or a specialty school, but by the time they graduate, they are in their late thirties, and only extract more money from the citizens and become the slaves of hospitals, pharmaceutical companies, and the insurance companies rather than giving adequate medical attention to the black, Hispanic, Asian, Middle Eastern, white middle class, African, and other communities. Again, no disrespect to them, but the majority of them are worthless to the world and humanity socially and medically, including the narrow-minded and biased Harvard president and those who still protect and worship him.

The continents' schools of medicine have to teach each country's school officials and experts to find and develop quality and affordable remedies for people worldwide who have been afflicted with serious and fatal maladies and viruses so future generations will not succumb to the same viruses and germs. Again, each country's school officials must not spend more than five years in the continent's main school of medicine. However, those who are going to spend another three years have to study to develop their own medical or other science research so they can build their own pharmaceutical companies in their own country and continent. And those wiseacre CEOs and so-called doctors that have placed their medical products, factories, and industries in other countries and continents to sell or to exploit them for cheap labor have to pull their medicines from these countries' and continents' cabinets and markets peacefully. That way, the country's pharmaceutical companies can grow, and future medical providers can grow and be respected in medicine and other science spheres. Each citizen will have to learn to support their country's pharmaceutical products and medicines all the time, no matter what because without their patronage and support, their native country will never grow and become respected in medicine and other science spheres. And they should not sue their future pharmaceutical companies and medical providers for negligence, malpractice, and defects no matter what because if they sue them, they will have no choice but to raise the cost of medical care so they can pay for medical insurance coverage. Each country's citizens will have to learn that unfortunate things happen in life, and the medical providers have to learn and train to do the best they can to serve their country citizens sufficiently with their ability and knowledge. Those pharmaceutical CEOs that pull their medicines and industries out of other countries have to bring them back to their lands to provide their people with jobs, and refine the medicine and reduce the quantity and price drastically so their citizens can afford them easily and receive better medical treatment. The present greedy, selfish, and careless CEOs, stockholders, and doctors have to face the fact that they cannot serve and support the entire world medically by themselves. They have tried for many decades, but it has caused a major medical crisis for the citizens of the world. Therefore, they have to learn to decrease their products' quantity, their price, and their CEO's or VP's high salary drastically, and refine their products so future citizens will live longer and healthier. And furthermore, they must trade in their so-called foreign fancy cars and other lavish products for products made in their countries.

Again, the future CEOs, VPs, or stockholders should not be taught to make millions. They did not develop or invent anything; they will have to drill into their minds that they need to make almost the same as what the rest of the employees are making, and to appreciate them more. Without the other employees or the people, no corporation can function. And without great business leadership, this country cannot function either. Again, businesses belong to a country and the people. Anybody that charges a lot of money for their products should not be supported by any citizen because by supporting these greedy and selfish people's enterprise, the citizens allow themselves to be overcharged, and let the high cost of living in their country keep increasing when these wiseacres feel like it. We as Americans have been despised, perceived and labeled as greedy exploiters and oppressors, or as overweight, unhealthy, or major debtors; high cost of living or American flag burning happens on a daily basis, and citizens overseas want to destroy us or cause more immigration problems for a reason. Everything has a cause, and the main reason is that education has been misused for selfish purposes instead of the greater good since day one, which causes the modern human race to lose vision of the modern world.

No continent's main university should teach people to crowd into any sphere or anyone else's country or continent to make money or abuse, enslave, and control those citizens. If every country's citizens studied and taught to support and do for themselves and their country sufficiently, they would never have high cost of living or cause immigration and other social and economic problems, and others would never suffer from it. And having such high cost of living, discrimination, sexism, crime, poverty, disease, war, demeaning, and controlling clearly shows us that we are not better or smarter than the previous ones. The continents' main universities should undergo systematic training and education for all citizens so future generations will show special aptitude in all professional spheres. The best leaders should not wait for the world's peaceful and development movement to come to them, or to create each continent's main university. If they wait for these narrow-minded and biased conservative school presidents and officials to approve the new world educational system, the majority of the future population will be exterminating each other for fun, and be unknown in the art, science, medical, technology, and other spheres, just like the modern world. They will become mere imitators and admirers and still wonder what they are good for, just like us. North/South America and the rest of the world are not circumscribed by these narrow-minded and biased conservative school officials at these Ivy League schools. Therefore, each country's leaders have to learn and study to become pioneers so the future generations will contribute and be influential and well-recognized in art, science, technology, and other spheres. If every continent and country in the world had their own things, they would depend on themselves, and they would also be recognized and treated as equals. If each continent's main university does not teach country officials to drill into minds of the future how to appreciate what their ancestors have left them and to build upon it, then they will not be educating them. They will be doing what school professors and presidents are doing now, which is teaching them to imitate and live like them and Socrates. People cannot be appreciated and treated equally if they do not learn to bring an equal share to the table. It is a shame indeed, that countries are wasting large sums of money on war, biased laws and systems, and fences or other immigration reform policies. The entire world can become stronger and wealthier if countries respected and worked together for the general interest of world citizens. If the educational system was teaching such a theory, millions of innocent lives would be saved and the world would be a better place to live in. Countries and people do not grow by just imitating and admiring others, and their products will never be influential on the market by supporting only others. Each citizen will be recognized in the development of their continent and the world, if these school officials at least try to educate and enlighten the world citizens properly instead of copying and following the dead ones—who created the mess in the first place. The present world citizens have no choice but to go down a blind alley, and to remain in these difficulties because the education that they received was not created for them to exercise foresight rather than hindsight. By defending it, the world citizens will never find their way out of their present difficulties, but rather drive themselves deeper into the nasty hole. If the future educated people and world citizens develop an educational system to nurture the world as a whole, a utopian life will be possible for future generations to live. The present world experts and leaders must understand that a modern and liberal contemplation will create new social, technological, and economic programs for the future. The opportunities of future generations lie in the hands of current presidents, experts, and leaders of world universities. With a better educational program, future generations will be able to see and live the dreams that are worth sacrificing and dying for, instead of dying to imitate or kill one another for a lost cause, like we do in the modern world.

The continents' main universities have to create new modern schools of law and politics to teach each country's school officials the right way to teach their students how to create political and legal systems to serve and protect their citizens, country, and continent socially and economically. They also have to create new world leadership programs for future leaders to study the proper way to pass a new-world civil and business foreign policy so future generations can learn how to respect each other socially and economically. They have to teach all children from infancy to adulthood to respect each other, regardless of their skin color, sexual orientation, social class, culture, custom, and religion, no matter what. Each country's law and political school officials and teachers will have to teach their future students to respect each other's land from infancy to adulthood, and also teach their citizens that they have a natural right to protect their home from government officials and overseas citizens as well. People will have to learn that they have a natural right to demand that others who exploit and oppress them leave their country or continent so they can grow economically and socially. However, if they refuse, they will have to ask their countries' leaders to ask the world leader to help them remove the oppressors from their lands as soon as possible, and by any means necessary. Each country's law school officials will have to know that they should be free from peonage, and they should not let their economic and social freedom and rights be determined by people who do nothing about their pains and status, and couldn't care less. Each country's future leaders will have to learn how to join to create a new fair and unbiased foreign policy rather than one made by people who only want to keep them in the dark. All future leaders of the world will have to learn that there are no special solutions to their ordeal except to put their differences aside peacefully, and think, respect, and work with each other as a team. It would not do any of them any good to harm, despise, oppress, and fight one another. Great leaders are people who find themselves in an awful situation and work their way out of it, rather than getting deeper in it or accepting it as final. By dealing with their conditions wisely, instead of following the dead ones, they will elevate and take better care of themselves. Each country's leader will have to learn to guide the citizens to think, plan, and act for themselves and their lands rather than taking an abundance of old theories that the ancient ones developed to oppress and exploit others. By bettering, serving, and leading their country and continent socially and economically, future generations will develop into worthy citizens. They as leaders will have to listen and pay attention to the people and the social and economic problems that they have on their land. They have to be great leaders for the people rather than taking orders from the corporations and other leaders who have led their country and the rest of the world where it is today.

Future school officials and leaders will have to teach that the previous and present system failed socially and economically mainly because they were trying to measure up to the demand of self-preservation. Each country's future law school officials will have to learn and drill into their citizens' minds that countries never grow if they do not create general law and foreign policy for all people to respect each other socially and economically. If they create a one-sided system, like the previous and present system and foreign policy, then racism, sexism, tension, war, terrorism, high cost of living, immigration, and other social and economic problems will always exist. They will never stop fighting, hating, despising, and exterminating each other until they get an unbiased and equal system. Therefore, social and economic problems will get worse generation after generation, century after century. The result will be that no country or continent will ever grow and be able to go forward until they learn how to appreciate, respect, and work together for their general welfare.

Each country's law and politics school officials will have to teach their students to modernize national and foreign policies and laws so the wiseacres can be prevented from exploiting, controlling, and destroying everything. The continents' main universities will have to teach each country's law and politics school officials that the increasing vigor of the world is purely based on the laws and foreign policies that they will vote to pass. Therefore, the politicians or leaders should not be allowed to get money from the businessmen because they will always serve them more sufficiently than the people and their lands. Furthermore, once a person decides to run for public office, nearly everything about that person's life has to be publicly checked by the media or others before getting elected. The people and media have a right to speak and ask any questions about them, as long as it relates to the country's and continent's interest. In other words, any country should have freedom of speech to say or write anything they want to, as along as it will not harm or damage the youth of the country and the world. Every country's people will have to learn that the power of any government derives from them because they are the people and the voters. Moreover, the people will have the power and freedom to request a new leader when necessary. The future world leader will have to study and drill into their minds that the power of the world leader derives from the citizens of the entire world. Therefore, when the majority of the people in the world vote against a certain foreign policy, it has to change as soon as possible. Trying to keep it would cause more harm in the long run. Each future leader will have to learn to respect the people's whishes and needs. For instance, if the majority of the people vote for a leader to resign peacefully, that wish has to be followed through. Refusing to resign will cause more innocent people to be injured and killed. In the end, the country will be dying. Such fateful leadership needs to be refined for the future because the people's welfare and wishes should come above everything. Again, politicians and leaders with such an attitude and behavior have to be imprisoned and have their properties taken away from them because they are not bringing the light of salvation into the people and their lands; they are losing them in the darkness. Future leaders will have to learn to be docile and tractable with the people, instead of harsh and brutal like the modern ones.

The main continents' schools of law/politics will have to teach each country's school officials to teach their citizens not to get into national politics for selfish political purposes. They should get into national and international politics to serve, lead, protect, and enrich their citizens, country, continent, and the rest of the world. Also, each continent's main university will have to establish a sort of negotiator or mediator program to teach the future citizens and leaders the proper way to put their differences aside and settle their disunion and conflicts in a peaceful manner before the disagreement and conflict escalates to a higher level. And they need to study the proper way to change and better the old and modern laws for future citizens, and change any law as long as the majority of the people vote against it or suffer from it. They need to study to see whether the laws bless and enrich the people, or if the laws empower and bless the oppressors. Furthermore, future leaders should not endeavor to protect their party's interest, oppress other citizens and countries, or raise taxes for the people. And the future citizens must be taught to elect the best and most qualified candidate among them. However, if the person becomes a public official, and they do not get a good result or see any salvation, they must not vote for or support that person again. If they do vote for such a candidate two or more times, they deserve to be ignored, suffer, and be disenfranchised. The main continents' universities have to train each country's officials to teach their citizens to get into national politics if they see they can serve and lead their people and their country into the light of salvation, regardless of their gender, creed, sexual orientation, and other silly things. They must be educated to not give their votes away to people who have been isolated from them, want to remain conservative, and only come to them and their communities when they need their votes. In fact, they should give their votes to people who only have a genuine heart and love, and are looking for peace and to better the world, not those who have an interest in their pockets, social class, or political party or want to agitate the ill situations and hold them and their country where they are. Teach citizens to hold onto their vote, rather than giving them away to people who have no interest in bettering their situation or the constitution when it needs to be, and couldn't care less about their conditions.

Future generations will have to learn that a country and the world need a leader to show the people the right path that has the bright light. Therefore, if a leader cannot lead the people into a light that shines brighter and brighter, that leader is worthless. How can a leader be excellent, if she or he cannot lead the people to find a bright light and salvation? For example, why would we need parents, and what good would they be to us if they could not show us the right direction to flourish and grow. Everything is there for a reason. Therefore, each continent's main university will have to teach the future leaders to work together to make the world desirable where it is undesirable. Otherwise, if their insight cannot show how to solve these real problems, they should not even endeavor to be a figure in national and international politics or any other type of leader. Each continent's citizens will have to learn and study from nursery school to higher education to not contribute to and support a politician's campaign merely because they are a certain race, sexual orientation, gender, religion, or came from a certain social class. They have to learn to support and contribute to leaders who have accomplished something extraordinary before deciding to run for or become their leaders. Do not vote for politicians or leaders who do not know that the real purpose of government is to serve and lead the citizens to accomplish something great and to enrich their land. Leaders who cannot ask other leaders to behave or resign when they disrespect and demean a certain group and do not vote for world citizens' civil rights movements must not be elected to serve the public and the country. Leaders who cannot set a great example for future citizens will not be willing to modernize the biased system so the future school tuition, high cost of living, medical costs, crime, welfare, immigration, war, racism, sexism, and prejudice problems can diminish drastically, rather than accepting them as an end. Those people should not endeavor to run for public office. Leaders who will not help their fellow citizens and instead treat them as criminals, or allow people to exploit them for cheap labor and torture them to a point that they will have to confess to terrorism or other criminal acts which they did not commit must be properly awakened because our troops and citizens will suffer for such acts. Leaders who will not be willing to be great neighbors with all the citizens and leaders around the world, to respect and to treat them fairly and equally, should not be running to govern any lands; lack of harmony and respect leads to more lynching of their people for amusement. The future leaders will have to be taught and trained to help and to assist their neighbors' leaders who have social and economic problems, rather than trying to make profit off their fellow brothers' and sisters' ordeals by charging them higher interest because exploiters and oppressors always collapse in the end.

The continents' main universities have to teach each country's law and political science school officials to teach their students to be great humanitarians before getting involved in national or international politics. They have to try to give the world something new, such as creating world development and civil rights movement so all people around the world will respect each other's customs, languages, heritage, manners, cultures, and religions, no matter what. Each country's leaders will have to be taught and trained to give the world something new rather than allowing wiseacres to exploit, enslave, and oppress their citizens for cheap labor. The future leaders must not learn to control and extract something from the weak ones, or think other countries and continents owe them something. And they should spend most of their time doing something valuable with the citizens because it will lead them to the development of things of enduring value for future generations. By teaching and preparing the future world leaders in such a way, all citizens will be comfortable and respect each other's territory and citizens. And they will work together to become a constructive force in the development of the world for the next generation. All leaders will have to learn to work together to overcome things that cripple their countries, continents, and the rest of the world socially and economically such as immigration, poverty, war, terrorism, high cost of living, disease, hatred, racism, exploitation, oppression, prejudice, illiteracy, high tuition costs, and others. Also, they have to study and learn to offer modern bills, laws, and foreign policies to overcome these torments. The future leaders will have to study and train to liberate the world from these awful conditions, instead of restricting them. They must be trained to see the future of the whole social and economic order of each country in their continent and the rest of the world as the world's upward movement. Each leader will have to learn and study in order for the entire world to be liberated from this upheaval. They will have to change their conservative minds into liberal ones. They will have to learn from the errors of those dead and living to improve. Also, they must learn to let the dead past remain dead. They will have to learn not to hate each other for what the ancient ones did and caused them to do in the modern world, but to learn from them; then, to bring their mind and elements together for the common good. With such a new method and way of training, nearly all the future world citizens will be able to find the sweetness in each other, life and humanity.

This first edition of "Loss of Vision of the Modern World" was produced by CBH Books in Lawrence, Massachusetts and printed in Quebec, Canada in 2007.

For comments about this publication or permission requests, please write to:
CBH Books
A division of Cambridge BrickHouse, Inc.
60 Island Street
Lawrence, MA 01840 U.S.A.